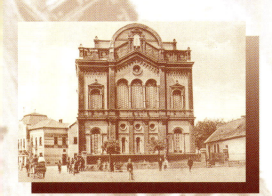

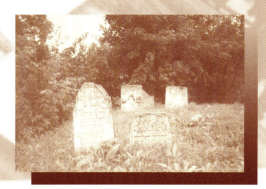

Лубны. Хорольскій спускъ.

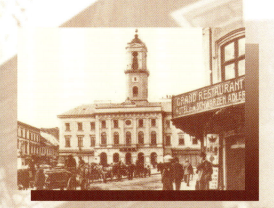

JEWISH ROOTS IN UKRAINE AND MOLDOVA

PAGES FROM THE PAST AND ARCHIVAL INVENTORIES

The publication of this book was made possible through a major contribution from

The Joseph S. and Diane H. Steinberg Family Fund
at the Jewish Communal Fund of New York

in memory of

Paul S. Steinberg, Sylvia Neikrug Steinberg, Max Steinberg,
Rachela Weinberg Steinberg and Sonia Steinberg

and through the generosity of

Harvey M. and Constance Krueger

AND

The Seevak Family Foundation
in memory of our family in Ukraine who perished in the Holocaust in June 1941
in Novograd Volinskiy, Ester-Ruchel Seevak (age 32), Musya Seevak (age 12), Eva Seevak (age 4), and Infant Boy Seevak
in Rovno, Tanya Seevak (age 35), Tanya Seevak (age 10), and Eva Seevak (age 3)

Alan Fortunoff
in honor and memory of my father, Max Fortunoff, and my grandparents, Louis Fortunoff and Rachel Cohen Fortunoff,
and all our Fortunoff and Cohen relatives who remained in Nemirov, Ukraine, and who perished during the Holocaust

Mitchell Goldhar, Stephen Goldhar and Karen Goldhar White
in memory of our maternal grandparents, Israel and Feiga Armel, from Stryj and Wyzlow, Ukraine
and in honor of our parents, Sala Armel Goldhar and Leo Goldhar, Toronto
and our mother's adoptive parents, Ike and Terry Greenberg, Toronto
Dr. and Mrs. Israel Schorr, Chortkov, Ukraine; and Israel

AND

Conference on Material Claims Against Germany
David and Rhoda Chase

The Estate of Herta Lande Seidman (1939–1997)
born in Czernowitz, Bukovina (now Chernivtsy, Ukraine)

The Eleanor, Adam and Mel Dubin Foundation
Alan and Marjorie Goldberg
Keren Ruth Foundation, Inc.
Neil D. Levin
Bruce Slovin
Lawrence G. Tesler
Walter H. Weiner

Joseph A. Bonamarte, Jewish Community Center of Houston, Leonard and Judy Polisar
Jonathan L. Rosner, Jill Sagarin, Alan Steinfeld and Aaron Ziegelman

Melvyn and Dorothye Abels, Brock D. Bierman, Selma W. Black, Sam and Lilly Bloch, Hal M. Bookbinder, Nancy Felson Brant, Debra Braverman and David Rosensaft, Sidney Braverman, Michael and Marilyn Brenner, Matthew Bucksbaum, Jeffrey K. Cymbler, Linda and Ronald F. Daitz, Doma International, Marc Erlitz, William H. Fern, Karen S. Franklin, Abraham P. Gannes, Paul Gass, Barbara B. Gellman, Lucille Gudis, Estelle Guzik, Elmer and Dede Hertzmark, Iscol Family Foundation, Mike and Ginger Jacobs, Jewish Community Foundation of MetroWest, Jewish Genealogical Society of Michigan, Jack and Irma Katz, Roman Kent, Florence Krauss, Sanford and Joan Krotenberg, Jay S. Kwawer, Mark and Anita Lester, Michael Maidenberg, Leonard Markowitz, Helen N. May, Max Mermelstein, Lisa Clyde Nielsen, Kenneth M. Packouz, Paul Rosenbaum, Sylvia and Bill Rosenberg, Robert M. Rosier, Stephen M. Rosman, Harry J. Saal, Michael D. Salzberg, Alan M. Wagshul, Sheldon E. Waxenberg, Sandy Weber, Becky and Joe Williams, Simon Ziff

JEWISH ROOTS IN UKRAINE AND MOLDOVA

PAGES FROM THE PAST AND ARCHIVAL INVENTORIES

by

MIRIAM WEINER

in cooperation with the

UKRAINIAN STATE ARCHIVES

and the

MOLDOVAN NATIONAL ARCHIVES

YIVO Institute for Jewish Research
ייִדישער װיסנשאַפֿטלעכער אינסטיטוט – ייִװאָ

New York, New York

Secaucus, New Jersey

Editorial board:	Jeffrey K. Cymbler, Professor Gregory Freeze and Professor Zvi Gitelman
Maps courtesy of:	*Atlas of the Holocaust*, rev. ed., by Sir Martin Gilbert (New York: William Morrow, 1993). *Atlas of Russian History*, by Sir Martin Gilbert (New York: Oxford University Press, 1993). *Encyclopaedia Judaica*, Cecil Roth, ed. (Jerusalem: Keter Publishing House Ltd., 1971–1972). *Genealogical Gazetteer of Galicia*, 3rd ed., by Brian J. Lenius (Anola, Manitoba, Canada: B. Lenius, 1998). Historical *Atlas of the Holocaust* by the United States Holocaust Memorial Museum. Copyright 1996 by Yechiam Halevy (New York: Macmillan Publishing USA, a Simon & Schuster Company). *Pinkas Hakehillot, Rumania, Vol. 1, Encyclopedia of Jewish Communities* (Jerusalem: Yad Vashem, 1969). *Ukraine Map #6827*, Havenstein Verlag Company, 1995.
Map adaptations:	Stephen Freeman and Dorcas Gelabert
Design director:	Dorcas Gelabert
Design implementation:	Stephen Freeman

Published jointly by

The Miriam Weiner Routes to Roots Foundation, Inc.
P.O. Box 1376
Secaucus, NJ 07096-1376
<http://www.rtrfoundation.org>

YIVO Institute for Jewish Research
15 West 16th Street
New York, NY 10011
<http://www.baruch.cuny.edu/yivo>

Printed by Parker Communications Group, Lawrenceville, New Jersey

Printing Number
1 2 3 4 5 6 7 8 9 10

Publisher's Cataloging-in-Publication
(*Provided by Quality Books, Inc.*)

Weiner, Miriam.
 Jewish roots in Ukraine and Moldova: pages from the past and archival inventories / by Miriam Weiner; in cooperation with the Ukrainian State Archives and the Moldovan National Archives. -- 1st ed.
 p. cm. -- (Jewish genealogy series)
 Includes bibliographical references and index.
 LCCN: 99-70974
 ISBN: 0-9656508-1-2

 1. Jews--Ukraine--Genealogy--Archival resources--Catalogs. 2. Jews--Moldova--Genealogy--Archival resources--Catalogs. 3. Jews--Ukraine--History--Archival resources--Catalogs. 4. Jews--Moldova--History--Archival resources--Catalogs. 5. Holocaust, Jewish (1939–1945)--Ukraine--Archival resources. 6. Holocaust, Jewish (1939–1945)--Moldova--Archival resources. 7. Archival resources--Ukraine--Catalogs. 8. Archival resources--Moldova--Catalogs. I. Title.

DS135.U4W37 1999
929/.3477/088296   QBI99-338

FOREWORD

DEDICATION

ACKNOWLEDGMENTS

Jewish cemetery near
Zhmerinka, Ukraine, 1992

INTRODUCTION

INTRODUCTION

Trostyanets, Ukraine, 1998

ONE

THE JEWS OF UKRAINE AND MOLDOVA

Konotop, Ukraine, c. 1917

UKRAINE

TWO

GENEALOGICAL RESOURCES
OUTSIDE OF THE STATE ARCHIVES

Kremenchug, Ukraine,
c. 1917

CITIES AND TOWNS IN UKRAINE: *Pages from the Past and Present*

Drohobych, Ukraine
c. 1917

TOWN ENTRIES

SOURCES FOR JEWISH GENEALOGY IN THE UKRAINIAN STATE ARCHIVES

Ukrainian State Archives, 1996

FIVE

THE JEWISH COMMUNITY OF UKRAINE: ITS STATUS AND PERSPECTIVES

Podol District of Kiev along the Dnieper River, c. 1918

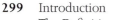
THE JEWISH EXPERIENCE IN UKRAINE & MOLDOVA

SIX

THE PEOPLE AND THE PLACES

Smozhe, Ukraine, 1998

SEVEN

THE HOLOCAUST

Babi Yar Memorial in Kiev, Ukraine, 1998

MOLDOVA

CITIES AND TOWNS IN MOLDOVA: *Pages from the Past and Present*

Khotin, Bessarabia, 1909
(now in Ukraine)

JEWISH GENEALOGICAL RESEARCH IN THE MOLDOVAN NATIONAL ARCHIVES

The Moldovan National
Archives, 1992

THE JEWS OF MOLDOVA

Devastation of Torahs
during the Kishinev
Pogrom, 1903

ELEVEN

TOWN CLIPS

This section both expands upon and supplements Chapter 3 and Chapter 8 by providing a further glimpse of what was and what is, through a collection of striking photographs in towns throughout Ukraine and Moldova.

Market square in Lvov, 1920

TWELVE

ARCHIVAL INVENTORIES

Birth records, 1830

TABLE OF CONTENTS

LIST OF MAPS

APPENDICES

Rabbi Yakov Dov Bleich (chief rabbi of Kiev and Ukraine) in the Kiev Synagogue, 1993   1

American Jews have long struggled with their European roots. In their new homes, the immigrants from the shtetls tried, often with success, to preserve something of the past in a world that was strange to them. They gathered in *landsmanshaftn* with fellow immigrants from their native towns to be with someone who remembered their villages, someone who could sing a familiar song or pray with the proper intonation, someone for whom the sights and the sounds of the Old World could evoke a sense of nostalgia.

In truth, those immigrants had broken with their European roots. They had left behind parents and siblings, even spouses and children, to journey forth to an unknown land. Often when they parted with their family, they knew that this was their last meeting, their final goodbye. They would not return for illnesses or funerals; they would not be there when needed. Separation by an ocean so large was somewhat final. Communication was confined to letters. The break was not without guilt.

Their children were first-generation Americans, embracing all that was American. Even if they arrived in school speaking only Yiddish, they soon spoke an unaccented English fluently and absorbed American culture. Bernard Malamud wrote *The Natural*, still today one of the great baseball stories. Chaim Potok began *The Chosen* with a confrontation between Hasidim and more worldly Orthodox Jews on the baseball field—not quite a diamond, but a concrete schoolyard. These first-generation children of immigrants entered the American mainstream. They moved from the Lower East Side and other Jewish enclaves to less intense neighborhoods— more Americanized, less ethnic. They regarded everything American as progressive and their European roots as backward, something to throw off, to abandon and leave behind. Only the future was of interest. The past did not beckon.

The second generation, however, and later the third and the fourth, sought to remember what their parents had chosen to forget. They turned back to Europe in search of something. But it was a different Europe at which they looked back. The fires of the Holocaust had consumed the world that was. Only the ashes remained, of abandoned graves, destroyed synagogues and memories. Ukraine and Moldova were the home of dead Jews or of oppressed Jews, of victims of nazism and communism, of graveyards and killing fields, often unmarked, often without any recognition of the Jews— who died there as Jews because they were Jews.

The Holocaust, the systematic, state-sponsored annihilation of the European Jews, destroyed the world that would have permitted American Jews access to a living past. The Holocaust looms large in American

Dr. Michael Berenbaum, president and CEO of the Survivors of the Shoah Visual History Foundation, Los Angeles; former director of the Research Institute at the United States Holocaust Memorial Museum, Washington, D.C.

2

Jewish consciousness, larger in the past decade than when I was growing up in the 1950s and '60s, larger still than in the decades of the '70s and the '80s. Thus, interest in the European roots of American Jews grows as the links that bind us with our European roots become ever more attenuated.

In recent years, a new ritual has arisen. Or, more precisely, an ancient ritual has been renewed. Pilgrimage. It is among the most ancient religious acts. One journeys to and one journeys from. A part of all religions, it is an essential part of Judaism.

The first call to the first Jew, God's summons to Abraham, was *Lech lecha*—Journey forth from your land, your birthplace, from your father's house to the land that I will show you. Hasidic sages offer a different reading: *Lech lecha*—Go unto yourself. We leave everything behind in search of the unknown, yet it is the great unknown, ourselves, that we take along.

Our ancestors journeyed from Egypt to the Sinai Desert to the Promised Land. Save for two, Caleb and Joshua, those who began the journey did not enter the land. Even Moses could bring them but to the edge. He then had to cede his position to Joshua, his disciple.

In our generation, pilgrimage has returned as an essential religious act, but along a new path. If our ancestors went from Egypt to the Promised Land, if our parents, grandparents or great-grandparents went from Europe to America, we, their descendants, follow the tortured path of modern Jewish history from Auschwitz to Jerusalem.

We go as pilgrims back to Europe. For many of us, planes, trains and buses provide the means of return. For those who cannot make the pilgrimage physically, it is the access to documents that allows for the return, for the encounter with the past, for the sense of self-discovery.

Thus Miriam Weiner's painstaking work *Jewish Roots in Ukraine and Moldova*, like her earlier work *Jewish Roots in Poland*, is most valuable. She has initiated and made available to the public for the first time, in a concise and readable form, the inventories of records relating to the Jewish experience in these countries that are held in their archives. She has taken us through these archives and offered us a peek at their treasures. She has empowered fellow pilgrims—scholars and novices alike—to begin their own search, to commence their own journey.

We travel with Miriam on the path that she has taken. We traverse the cities of Ukraine and Moldova with their once vibrant Jewish populations, and we explore their remnants—physical buildings and documents—in a way that may permit those of us who trace our roots there to rediscover our past, to touch the generations that preceded those who came to America.

These efforts must be celebrated. Miriam was brave and bold, persistent, disciplined and demanding. She has opened to us an entire world for exploration and has saved all of us, even the most informed, months of effort and false starts. She has made a daunting task appear ever more possible, even more beckoning.

This book is not Miriam's first contribution to memory, but it must surely rank among her finest. I first met Miriam when she worked with the American Gathering of Jewish Holocaust Survivors as it was beginning to gather what is now known as the Benjamin and Vladka Meed Registry of Jewish Holocaust Survivors, located today in the United States Holocaust Memorial Museum. She worked with skill and dedication. She created order and empowered the survivors, especially Benjamin Meed, the indefatigable president of the American Gathering, to do so much. I admired Miriam then, and that was just the beginning. I am honored to have written the *Foreword* to this book as well as for her earlier work on Poland.

She then wrote on the issue of genealogy. She became a guide, a mentor and a leading authority. Still later, she helped people to find their past, and in turn she discovered her mandate, perhaps even her destiny.

Both *Jewish Roots in Ukraine and Moldova* and *Jewish Roots in Poland* are Miriam Weiner's singular achievements. Yet she did not work alone and did not write the books on her own. She asked for and received the assistance of the state archives in Ukraine and Moldova and of individual archivists throughout both countries. From archives large and small, from scholars of distinction and ordinary paper pushers, she received splendid cooperation. Only one who has worked in these archives and with these people can understand the magnitude of her achievement. She must have been cajoling and persistent. She must have persuaded by force of reason and of personality.

As a rule, archivists belong to one of two schools. They are hoarders or sharers. The hoarders gather treasures that they deem all the more valuable because they are unknown and unexamined. They know the true mystery of what they have, and they have a sense of power in knowing its importance and how only a handful of people know the true value of what they possess. From these archivists, Miriam demanded the ultimate sacrifice: to reveal the concealed, to make known their treasures, to share what they have.

For the sharers, she became the midwife, the vehicle by which their treasures could become known, their documents explored. Reading page after page, I could sense the depth of their gratitude as well as the anguish of those archivists for whom sharing is so difficult.

Miriam Weiner's book is a gift to all of us would-be pilgrims. The true measure of its value is to be found in the journeys we undertake, the secrets we uncover. These acts of pilgrimage return us far beyond the world of the Holocaust, to the moments when Berdichev, the ancestral home of my father-in-law, was synonymous with its Hasidic rebbe, Reb Levi Yitzhak, whose very breath echoed a love of Israel, when Kiev was a town of so many Jews and Uman was the site of pilgrimage for the disciples of Rabbi Nachman of Bratlav, when Hasidim and Misnagdim, secularists, Zionists and Bundists walked the streets of these towns and cities and the alleyways of the hundreds of Jewish villages and hamlets. We return with Miriam's aid not to the world of destruction, but to a time when the world was whole. We can taste its spiritual richness and be charged by its vibrancy.

Such a journey can change our sense of who we are, of where we have come from, and, above all, of what we must become.

Dr. Michael Berenbaum
Survivors of the Shoah Visual History Foundation
Los Angeles, California

Bayla Rovinskiy Ochs (1865-1940)

Malka/Molly Ochs Winikur (Weiner) (1883-1955)

Helen Rabkin Weiner (1913-1992)

Miriam Odnopozov Rabkin (1875-1924)

Sister of Alexander Rabkin (author's maternal grandfather) First name unknown

Molly Weiner and her granddaughter, Miriam Weiner

This book is dedicated in honor and memory of the mothers, grandmothers and great-grandmothers in our Jewish family trees. These grandmothers from the "Old Country" often worked long hours in homes without electricity, running water, kitchen appliances and all the other conveniences we take for granted in the world we live in today. Often, these women married very young and had many children. In addition to taking care of home and family, these women frequently worked alongside their husbands in the family business or were the sole provider for the family if their husbands were religious scholars.

In gratitude and appreciation for all they gave to their families and the inspiration they have been to me, I dedicate this book in loving memory of my mother, Helen Rabkin Weiner and my two grandmothers: Miriam Odnopozov Rabkin, born in Priluki, Ukraine; and Malka Ochs Winikur, born in Sudilkov, Ukraine. The examples they set as women and mothers continue to influence the next generations.

Ukrainian State Archives

The Main Archival Administration under the Cabinet of Ministers of Ukraine is the central body of administrative power that executes the state policies in the archival field. It provides the management of the archival field, takes responsibility for its condition and future development, and coordinates the activities of archival institutions.

Within the Ukrainian State Archives we have numerous documentary sources on the history of the Jewish people who have lived on the territory of the present-day Ukraine for many centuries. These documents tell complicated and sometimes dramatic stories about the lives of Jews in Ukraine. Many of these archival sources contain very valuable documents that will be helpful to Jewish genealogists, such as metrical books of synagogues and fonds of administrative, legal, fiscal and census institutions, educational institutions and religious societies.

Documents of modern Ukraine also reflect many elements of interest to the family historian, but with less detail. These documents describe the participation of Jews in revolutionary movements; their suffering and sacrifices during pogroms, repressions, and the Holocaust of World War II; and their lives during the Soviet period.

Without any doubt, research of this data is still a very complicated matter. It was not until 1988 that genealogy research was officially permitted throughout the archival system of the former Soviet Union. In modern Ukraine, genealogical research is not well established for that reason but also due to the lack of computer systems and other technological advances throughout the archival system.

In 1991, Miriam Weiner met with Boris V. Ivanenko, then director of the Main Archival Administration, who agreed to cooperate with Ms. Weiner in the gathering of archival data in order to compile a town-by-town inventory of archival documents. When Mr. Ivanenko retired five years later, his replacement, Nina V. Kistruska, also enthusiastically supported this project. I became director in early 1998, and after meeting with Ms. Weiner and learning about this ongoing work, I too have endorsed this important book.

We thank Ms. Weiner for her outstanding work in publishing (in English) the first guide to archival inventories in Ukraine to be officially sanctioned by the Ukrainian State Archives. After compiling this material, Ms. Weiner submitted the draft archival inventories, which were then sent out to our archivists for review. They have done so to the best of their abilities. We consider the verification process by our archivists essential to the validity of any publication about our holdings.

Taking into consideration the often difficult working conditions and lack of Western-style facilities and technology in Ukraine today, the enthusiastic efforts of

Dr. Ruslan Y. Pirig, director of the Main Archival Administration under the Cabinet of Ministers of Ukraine

3

Ms. Weiner deserve our full support. This book depicts the many different types of documents within our archives and, together with the hundreds of poignant and historic photographs, is a remarkable resource for those who wish to know more about their family history in Ukraine.

Readers of this book will be able to find information about Ukrainian towns that had Jewish communities, the availability of metrical books and other documents, and for what years the books exist and where they are stored. The administrative subordination of Ukraine's territory changed so many times, especially during the twentieth century, that archival documents about residents of the same town could be stored in several different archives (and in more than one country).

We are very grateful to Miriam Weiner for the huge amount of work performed in cooperation with more than 100 Ukrainian archivists, which has included the analysis and publication of undoubtedly unique materials and about places of storage of not only the Jewish records but other documents of interest to Jewish genealogists. We are sure that the publication of this book will help further the development of genealogical research not only in the United States but also in Ukraine.

Dr. Ruslan Y. Pirig, Director
Main Archival Administration
Kyiv, Ukraine
May 1999

Український державний архів

Головне архівне управління при Кабінеті Міністрів України є центральним органом виконавчої влади, що реалізує державну політику в галузі архівної справи. Воно здійснює керівництво архівною галуззю, несе відповідальність за її стан і подальший розвиток, координує діяльність архівних установ.

Національний архівний фонд містить численні документальні джерела з історії єврейського народу, який упродовж багатьох століть жив і живе на території сучасної України. Ці документи відбивають складні, а часом й драматичні сторінки буття єврейства на українських теренах.. Чимало з цих архівних джерел містять цінні документи, які будуть корисними для дослідників єврейської генеалогії, насамперед, це метричні книги синагог, фонди адміністративних, юридичних, фінансових і статистичних установ, учбових закладів та релігійних громад.

Документи сучасної України відображають також чимало елементів, які зацікавлять того, хто вивчає сімейну генеалогію, але менш докладно. Ці документи свідчать про участь євреїв у революційному русі, державному та господарському житті радянського періоду, як і про їхні страждання і жертви під час погромів, репресій та Холокосту в роки Другої світової війни.

Безперечно дослідження в цій галузі є досить складною справою. До 1988 року ці роботи могли здійснюватись лише офіційно через архівну систему колишнього СРСР. Тому в сучасній Україні генеалогічні дослідження ще не набули достатнього розвитку через брак комп'ютерної мережі в архівній системі та інших сучасних технологій.

В 1991 році Міріам Вайнер зустрілась з Борисом Васильовичем Іваненком, тодішнім начальником Головного архівного управління, який погодився співпрацювати з нею у збиранні архівних даних з метою упорядкування та інвентаризації архівних документів у кожному місті. Після того, як через п'ять років Борис Іваненко залишив свою посаду в зв'язку з виходом на пенсію, його наступниця Ніна В.Кіструська, також з ентузіазмом підтримала цей проект. Я став керівником архівного управління лише на початку 1998 року і після зустрічі з М.Вайнер та ознайомлення з тим, що вона вже зробила, я також підтримав ідею написання цієї важливої книги.

Ми вдячні Міріам Вайнер за її видатну працю з метою публікації (англійською мовою) першого бібліографічного путивника до архівних описів в Україні, яку офіційно підтримало Головне архівне управління України. Після упорядкування цих матеріалів М.Вайнер подала їх інвентаризаційний проект на розгляд нашим архівістам і останні зробили свою справу на високому професійному рівні. Ми вважаємо, що процес перевірки нашими архівістами є суттєво важливим для встановлення відповідності будь-якої публікації нашим архівним фондам.

Беручи до уваги часом нелегкі умови праці та відсутність західного устаткування та технологічних можливостей, ентузіазм Міріам Вайнер заслуговує на нашу всіляку підтримку. Ця книга містить опис багатьох типів документів, які є в наших архівах, і разом із сотнями вражаючих до болю та історичних фотографій стане незвичайним джерелом для всіх, хто бажає більше дізнатися про свою родинну історію в Україні, що, на мою думку, є нескінченною історичною темою.

Читачі цієї книги зможуть віднайти інформацію про українські міста, в яких мешкали єврейські громади, про наявність метричних книг та інших документів, про те, коли ці книги велися та де вони зберігаються. Адміністративне підпорядкування територій України змінювалося багато разів, особливо протягом XX століття, тому архівні документи про місце проживання мешканців одного й того ж міста можуть знаходитись і зберігатись в різних архівах (і не тільки однієї країни).

Ми вдячні Міріам Вайнер за ту велику працю, яку вона здійснила в співпраці з українськими фахівцями-архівістами, яких було більше ста, працю, зміст якої полягає в аналізі та публікації незаперечно унікальних записів про місце зберігання не лише матеріалів про життя єврейства, а також інших документів цікавих для дослідників єврейської генеалогії. Ми впевнені, що публікація цієї книги допоможе подальшому розвиткові генеалогічних досліджень не лише в Сполучених Штатах Америки, але й в Україні.

Руслан Я. Пиріг, начальник
Головного архівного управління,
Київ, Україна
Травень 1999 року

Moldovan National Archives

In 1989, the National Archives received a letter from Miriam Weiner. That was unusual at the time, because letters from foreign countries generally went directly to the Ministry of Justice. In the letter, Ms. Weiner inquired about documents related to people with her family name, Rovner, in Faleshty, Moldova. When the letter arrived, I was the chief of the Research Department, and it was my responsibility to respond to this inquiry. Thus, we began that research, which was both difficult and very challenging. We found many interesting documents about Ms. Weiner's family.

In 1991, Ms. Weiner first visited our archive. We were able to discuss the results of our research with her and to assist her with another research project about the Bronfman family of Ataki, Moldova. Our relationship and friendship began then, and they continue to this day. We both share the belief that people must know about the past in order to understand the future.

It is a difficult and complicated process to work in the National Archives; our archivists need both patience and intuition. Many files were closed previously and their contents were unknown, even to our archivists. We do not have an alphabetical index to our material or inventory lists by town name. It is necessary first to locate the correct fond, then the correct files, and after that, it is sometimes necessary to search through literally thousands of pages, name by name. Also, we do not have specifically "Jewish fonds" because Jewish names appear in almost every file.

Over the last ten years, as a result of Ms. Weiner's frequent inquiries, questions and actual research, she has developed an inventory of many interesting documents in our archives. Our archivists have also been working to develop inventories, since our system of cataloging documents is different from Ms. Weiner's and is based upon our particular needs. We have cooperated with her and verified the information for this book, and we have provided new data as well. In the course of compiling these inventories, our archivists have seen and worked with many documents and books that had been closed (in some cases for more than fifty years). Most of the documents in our archives are in either Romanian or Russian. Also, documents for some towns in Moldova can be found in archives in Ukraine and Romania. This book will enable researchers to locate the material for their ancestral towns in Moldova (including areas of the former province of Bessarabia).

Antonina A. Berzoy, director, Moldovan National Archives   4

Ms. Weiner has worked in our country during difficult times, and we have seen her adaptation to and acceptance of our situation, even to the point of her buying an apartment within a three-hour drive of our archive in Kishinev. She has shared the stressful working conditions we sometimes endure, and we have come to count her as a friend as well as a colleague.

We are grateful to Ms. Weiner for her dedication and perseverance in compiling this material and presenting it in such an attractive way. Since this book will be published in English, many more people will be able to learn about the thousands of documents and photographs in our archives.

Antonina A. Berzoy, Director
Moldovan National Archives
Kishinev, Moldova
December 1998

Arhiva Națională
a Republicii Moldovei

În anul 1989, Arhiva Națională a primit o scrisoare de la Miriam Weiner. Fapt neobișnuit pentru acea perioada de timp, deoarece în general corespondența externă era trimisă direct Ministerului de Externe. În această scrisoare, d-na Weiner solicita arhivei date despre familia ei, familia Rovner, din Fălești - Moldova. La momentul primirii scrisorii eu eram șefa secției Valorificare și intra în functiile mele să fac cercetările necesare. Am început depistarea care era, în același timp și dificilă și interesantă. Ca rezultat am găsit multe documente interesante despre familia d-nei Weiner.

În 1991, d-na Weiner a vizitat pentru prima oară arhiva noastră, am purtat o discuție privind rezultatele cercetării noastre la acel moment, și am ajutat-o în demararea unui nou proiect, privind familia Bronfman din Ataki - Moldova. Colaborarea și prietenia noastră a început atunci și continuă și în prezent. Noi avem convingeră că, oamenii trebuie sa-și cunoască trecutul pentru o mai bună înțelegere a viitorului.

Este un proces dificil și complicat să lucrezi în arhivele noastre și arhiviștii au nevoie, în aceeași măsură, de răbdare și intuiție. Multe dosare nu erau cercetate înainte, conținutul acestora era necunoscut chiar și arhivarilor noștrii. Noi nu avem un indice alfabetic pentru materialul existent, sau liste de inventariere ordonate după denumirea orașelor. Astfel, pentru început, trebuie să localizezi exact domeniul, apoi fondurile archivistice și după aceea este necesar să cauți, nume după nume, câteodată de-a lungul a mii de pagini. De asemenea, documentele evreești nu au o evidență separată, întrucât numele evreești apar aproape în fiecare dosar.

În ultimii zece ani, ca rezultat al multiplelor studii efectuate, al investigațiilor și cercetării actuale, d-na Weiner a realizat și dezvoltat un inventar conținând multe documente interesante din arhiva noastră. Arhiviștii noștri lucrează, de asemenea, pentru desăvîrșirea inventarelor deși sistemul nostru de catalogare a documentelor este diferit de al d-nei Weiner, bazat în special pe utilități de păstrare. Am colaborat, de asemenea, la verificarea materialului care intră în componența acestei cărți, adunînd date noi. În perioada realizării acestor inventare, arhiviștii noștri au catalogat și inventariat multe documente și cărți neatinse de mai mult de 50 de ani. Majoritatea documentelor din arhivă noastră sunt în limba română și rusă. La Arhivele Naționale ale Ucrainei pot fi găsite documente aparținând unor vechi orașe din Moldova. Aceasta carte va permite cercetătorilor sâ se orienteze în materiale pâstratea în Arhiva din Moldova (Basarabia).

D-na Weiner a lucrat în țara noastră într-o perioadă grea de timp caracterizată de profunde schimbări economico-sociale și noi am văzut cu cât entuziasm a acceptat și s-a adaptat situației noastre, chiar și asupra faptului că a trebuit sâ-și cumpere și să locuiască într-un apartament aflat la trei ore distanță de arhivele din Chișinău. Ea a suportat alături de noi condițiile stresante de lucru, cu care ne întîlnim adesea, și o considerăm în aceeași măsură prieten și coleg.

Suntem recunoscători d-nei Weiner pentru dedicația și perseverența dovedită în realizarea acestui material și prezentarea într-un mod atât de atractiv. Publicarea în limba engleză a acestei cărți va permite, începînd cu data apariției, informarea unui public tot mai larg despre miile de documente și fotografii din arhiva noastră.

Antonina A. Berzoy, Direktor
Arhiva Națională a Republicii Moldovei
Chișinău, Moldova
Decembrie 1998

AUTHOR'S ACKNOWLEDGMENTS

Virtually all research projects involve many people who, while not necessarily linked to one another, are linked to the project coordinator (in this case, the author), and ultimately a team is formed. This book is the result of the concentrated efforts of a dedicated team consisting of numerous colleagues and many friends throughout the world who have shared their knowledge in their various fields of expertise and cooperated in helping me to produce this book. I am indebted to all of them and thank them for their quick responses, thorough research, and dedication to this project.

In 1989, a landmark book was published: *Archives and Manuscript Repositories in the USSR: Ukraine and Moldavia* (Princeton, NJ: Princeton University Press, 1988) by Patricia Kennedy Grimsted, a well-known and much-respected author in this field. As a result of a one-page entry in her book about a regional museum in Priluki, Ukraine, the birthplace of my maternal grandmother, I wrote a letter to the museum director asking about the availability of any Jewish documents there. The letter reached Natalia B. Elkin, a Jewish woman working in the museum, who had the letter translated and then went to the local town hall, where she found many documents for my family, including the birth certificate for Miriam Odnopozov, my maternal grandmother. At that time, access to this sort of material was more wishful thinking than reality, and seeing my grandmother's name in Natalia's letter brought me to tears. Ultimately, I visited Priluki and with Natalia's help, located more than 50 documents about my family. I, therefore, thank Professor Grimsted for being the first one to open a door that ultimately led me on a quest and adventure that continues to this day. I hope it never ends.

MY PARTNER IN UKRAINE AND MOLDOVA

In 1991, I went to visit Ataki, a small town in northern Moldova. There, I met the mayor, Vitaly Chumak, who was very helpful during that first visit and even more so during the next two visits later that year. Subsequently, my translator emigrated to Israel (as had the previous one), and I was faced with finding someone who could not only translate for me but who would understand my work well enough to represent me in the archives and at various other official meetings when I couldn't be there. I could see that Vitaly was the right person, if only he spoke English. It didn't take long for him to learn, and since 1992, Vitaly has worked with me in dozens of archives in three countries and has conducted many meetings on my behalf. He knows what I want to say probably better than I do.

He has met with mayors, local historians, rabbis and representatives of the Jewish community, and has done a myriad of other jobs I have asked him to do. He provides security for me during my trips, which eases the concerns of family members here at home. Vitaly has visited more than 100 Jewish cemeteries and synagogues in Ukraine, Moldova, Lithuania and Belarus, with me or on my behalf. He has taken thousands of photographs of Jewish sites, some of which can be seen in this book. He has done everything I have asked him to do and then gone the extra mile. My quest has become his quest. There are not enough words in my vocabulary to acknowledge my admiration for him and his contribution to this book, except to say that it would not have happened without him.

▌ *Miriam Weiner, author*   5

UKRAINE

In 1990, I received a letter from the Main Archival Administration in Ukraine, inviting me to visit the archives, which I did the following year. I met with the vice-director, Dr. Volodymyr S. Lozytskyi, who promised to help me not only in my own research in Priluki but also in organizing tours for others who wanted to visit their ancestral towns and look for archival documents. I also met and worked closely with the director, Boris V. Ivanenko, who responded enthusiastically when I proposed the idea of publishing a town-by-town inventory of archival documents throughout Ukraine. I had begun a similar project in Poland the previous year, and we decided to follow the same format as agreed upon with the Polish State Archives.

Later, Mr. Ivanenko retired, and I continued to work with the current director, Dr. Ruslan Y. Pirig, who shared the same enthusiasm for this project. This book would not have been possible without the support and cooperation of Messrs. Lozytskyi, Ivanenko and Pirig. Over the years, I have come to know these gentlemen, and they are truly dedicated archivists.

Although I met many of the hundreds of archivists in the Ukrainian State Archives, there are also those I have not met in person but who were helpful in verifying and supplementing the archival inventories. Space considerations prohibit me from naming them all here, but my gratitude to them is no less deep. In particular, I want to acknowledge several people at the Central State Historical Archive in Kiev who were helpful and kind to me in those early years: Irina Antonenko, Ludmila I. Lozenko, Valentina Kaplun and Olga V. Marushak.

In Lvov, I worked with many archivists at the Central State Historical Archive. I particularly want to thank the archive's director, Dr. Orest Y. Matsuk, who gave me complete access to archival holdings and always found the right person to help me with the task of the moment. Also at this archive, I want to thank Diana I. Peltz, vice-director; and archivists Elizabeta M. Stetsev, Galina I. Svarnik, Maria E. Murin and Nina Shestakova. I am especially grateful to Mark Shraberman, a former archivist who now lives in Israel and who compiled many of the archival inventories for this book; and to Natalia N. Tsariova, chief of the Department of Ancient Acts.

In Ukraine, the ZAGS offices (local vital-record registrations) are under the jurisdiction of the Ministry of Justice. In 1991, I met with Emilia M. Sych, then director of all ZAGS offices in Ukraine. She has now retired, but our friendship and cooperation for more than five years were critical to this project. Ms. Sych provided me with a town-by-town listing of the Jewish metrical books in ZAGS offices throughout Ukraine. In addition, I want to thank Vasyli V. Onopenko, former Minister of Justice, and Volodymyr M. Chernysh, Deputy Minister of Justice, for their cooperation. Also in this office was Evgeni Kornichuk, who was helpful there and in his subsequent position with the Ukrainian Consulate in New York.

Several years ago, I met Igor Skochilas, a historian and researcher in Western Ukraine. He has compiled inventories for me in several archives, and I want to thank him for his professional and thorough work.

I also want to thank Felix Pechersky for hosting me during my many trips to Kiev. To me, "Hotel Felix" is a five-star hotel. I also want to thank the staff at the Grand Hotel in Lvov, and in particular Natalia Semenova, for making me feel at home.

Hundreds of people in Ukraine have been helpful to me, including in *Belaya Tserkov*: Semyon I. Zlobinskiy; *Kiev*: Rabbi Yakov Dov Bleich (chief rabbi of Kiev and Ukraine); Vadim Feldman (director, Holocaust Memorial Commission in Ukraine); Dr. Irena Sergeyeva (Vernadskiy Library); Klara Vinokur (now living in Philadelphia); Rabbi David Hillel Wilfond; Josef Zissels (Vaad of Ukraine); *Khmelnitskiy*: Pavel A. Linik; *Luboml*: Mikola Dzei; *Lvov*: Ludmila Beregovaya; Josef Gelston; Professor Rudolf Mirsky; Igor M. Portnov; Meylach Sheychet; *Mogilev Podolskiy*: Nikolai D. Maluta (former mayor); Boris Shlayfer; *Ostrog*: Larisa S. Mazurenko (director, Regional Museum); and *Stryy*: Josef I. Foyer.

MOLDOVA

In 1992, I visited Moldova for the first time and was warmly welcomed at the Moldovan National Archives. While they have moved on to other jobs, I am very grateful to both Mitru Gitsiu, former chief of the Department of State Archival Services in Moldova, and Aleksander Roman, former director of the Moldovan National Archives, both of whom were instrumental in the initial stages of researching this book. Other staff members and archivists who helped me were Ada Panchuk, Alla Bubulich and Eugene D. Maximenko. Antonina A. Berzoy, the current director, deserves bouquets of thanks and my eternal gratitude for her caring and her willingness to answer an endless stream of inquiries during the last stages of preparing this book. She is truly a professional, and I am so pleased to have her as the author of Chapter 9.

Special thanks are due to Dmitri Antonovich, former director of the ZAGS offices at the Ministry of Justice, Moldova; and to Sara Shpitalnik at the I. Manger Jewish Library in Kishinev.

I traveled to Soroki in northern Moldova often, where I was welcomed by Sylvia Kotich, director of the local ZAGS office. She hosted me in her home and also helped me with research.

I now own an apartment in Mogilev Podolskiy, Ukraine, directly across the river from the town of Ataki in Moldova. I spend weeks at a time there, and I am deeply grateful to Ludmila Chumak for the many dinner invitations to her home in Ataki, for the loan of her washing machine, and for inviting me to share holidays and other celebrations with her family.

POLAND

Since areas of Western Ukraine were formerly within Polish borders, many documents for towns in Western Ukraine can be found in Poland. I am grateful to Grzegorz Mucha, archivist, and Urszula Oszewska, director, of the Urząd Stanu Cywilnego, Warszawa Śródmieście office in Warsaw, for updating their inventories for this book.

I also want to thank Professor Feliks Tych, director of the Jewish Historical Institute, for his continuing support, friendship and cooperation. Also at the Institute, I owe so much to Jan Jagielski and Eleonora Bergman, both of whom were indispensable in verifying data, checking translations, providing photographs and the unselfish giving of their time whenever I asked. They began years ago as colleagues, and I am now proud to count them among my friends.

Special kudos go to Mariola Jeziak, my translator, assistant and friend, who spent countless hours verifying material for me and accompanying me during the research process throughout archives in Poland. Mariola is dedicated, thorough and dependable. I couldn't ask for more.

UNITED STATES

From the beginning, my friend Jill Sagarin, who coincidentally shares my ancestral roots in Priluki, has been a researcher, a proofreader and a good listener. I want to warmly thank and hug Jill for her constant support and helpfulness, and especially for taking care of literally everything for me while I am away, sometimes for months at a time, in Ukraine.

The book was designed by Dorcas Gelabert, who did the same magnificent job as she did on *Jewish Roots in Poland*. She always has a solution to whatever design questions I pose, and her presence on this team is vital. Her "feel" for this project is a testimony to her artistic creativity.

The page layout of the book fell once again to Stephen Freeman. His monumental job included implementing the page-by-page layout of the book; the scanning and retouching of more than 1,200 photographs and documents; the adaptation of the typeface to include Polish, Russian, Ukrainian and Romanian characters; and the design of several maps. His artistic eye and attention to detail are reflected throughout the book and particularly in the maps. He continually made suggestions and improvements, which resulted in a much better book. Most important, he really cared and understood the importance of what we were doing. The challenges posed by this book were more than most people could manage, but Steve met them all, and I am deeply grateful to him.

The computer database program for the archival inventories was developed and refined by David Kleiman for *Jewish Roots in Poland*. He is a fellow genealogist as well as a computer specialist. This book presented new challenges and made many demands upon David. He was always there with a solution, often late at night, but always there.

Many people wrote introductory letters on my behalf, including Oleh H. Bilorus (former ambassador of Ukraine to the United States), Ralph Goldman (Joint Distribution Committee), and Patricia Eames (National Archives). All these letters were helpful. I want to thank Max Mermelstein for his careful review of the town entry on Skala Podolskaya and for his photographs for this section. I am grateful to Samuel J. Gruber, president of the Jewish Heritage Research Center, for his support and advice. I wish to thank Avotaynu, Inc. for permission to reproduce updated and revised versions of the articles by Dr. Volodymyr S. Lozytskyi and Professor ChaeRan Y. Freeze that appeared previously in *Avotaynu*.

One of the most important resources in the world for the research of Jewish genealogy is the JewishGen Web site on the Internet, under the masterful guidance of Susan King, president of JewishGen, Inc. I want to thank Susan and also Martin Kessel, project manager of the Yizkor Book Project, for giving us permission to include the JewishGen *yizkor* book list in Appendix 1. I also want to thank Zachary M. Baker, the original compiler of the list; and the Jewish Genealogical Society, Inc. in New York, which first published the data, for its permission to use the list.

The intricacies of foreign-language translation for this book were guided by Zachary M. Baker and Jeffrey Salant (YIVO Institute for Jewish Research); Eleonora Bergman and Jan Jagielski (Jewish Historical Institute in Warsaw, Poland); Vitaly Chumak (Moldova and Ukraine); Radu Dmitru (Romanian Mission to the United Nations); Professor Gregory Freeze (Brandeis University); William F. Hoffman; and Professor Jonathan D. Shea (Central Connecticut State University).

A couple of years ago, I met with Yuriy Bohaievsky, then deputy permanent representative of Ukraine to the United Nations. Since then, he has assumed a new post, as Consul General of Ukraine in New York. His interest in this project was heightened by his background in the publishing business, and he volunteered to help with the Ukrainian translations in various sections of the book. It was obvious from his comments that he really knew the publishing field. His input was very valuable.

To publish this book, it was necessary to continually verify information that would intimidate most researchers by its sheer volume. I am grateful to Roberta Saltzman (The New York Public Library) for her meticulous and prompt attention to my never-ending requests. I am also indebted to Marshall Winokur, who years ago answered endless questions and researched places that at the time I could barely pronounce.

Many colleagues and friends helped with translations, photographs, document examples, computer expertise, archival holdings and their encouragement. For all of this I thank Rabbi Chaskel O. Besser, Brock Bierman, Warren Blatt, Harry Boonin, Debra Braverman, Sidney Braverman, Leon Brown, Rita Chernyak, Maurice R. Commanday, Gennikh Deich, Stephen J. Dubner, Craig Ellison, Pipo Engel (deceased), Alex Friedlander, David Goberman, Lucille Gudis, Carolyn Starman Hessel, Leonid Kogan, Herbert I. Lazerow, Joseph G. Maciora, Leonard Markowitz, Sanford S. Masovitz, Stephen Mednick, Stefan Pankevicz, Leonard and Judy Polisar, Ruth Rosenbloom, David Rosensaft, Robert M. Rosier, Watson Sagarin, Michael D. Salzberg, Jacquelyn Sanders, Zinaida Sandler, Dr. William L. Shulman, Steven W. Siegel, Carol Skydell, Benjamin Solomowitz, Jon Stein, and Tomas Wiśniewski.

At the new Center for Jewish History in New York, I want to thank Joyce C. Kitey, senior vice-president, for her unfailing interest and support of my work.

The Conference on Jewish Material Claims Against Germany was very supportive of my work, and I am grateful to Saul Kagan, executive vice-president, retired; Greg Schneider, director of Institutional Allocations; and board member Roman Kent.

For his interest, involvement and continuing support in all ways, I want to thank Walter H. Weiner, chairman of the board, Republic National Bank of New York.

My dozens of trips to Ukraine since 1991 (and Poland since 1989) have all been on LOT Polish Airlines, and I am very grateful to LOT for getting me to my destination safely, on time and with all my baggage. Krzysztof Ziębiński, Ewa Czarnecka-Kortylewicz, Paweł J. Łodziński, Joram Kagan and the LOT staff at Newark Airport have been especially helpful.

My assistant, Regina Germinario, helped with a myriad of details to produce this book. Her unfailingly sunny disposition and enthusiastic approach to her work made my job much easier.

I am grateful to Jon G. Parker of Parker Communications Group, printers of the book, and Rush H. Housel, Jr., of Integrated Imaging Systems for their special expertise.

WORLDWIDE

Many others provided invaluable assistance to me. I want to thank Galina Tikhonovska, my first translator in Moldova, who ultimately traveled with me throughout Ukraine and Moldova until she emigrated to Israel and then to Canada. Vassili Schedrin of the Jewish Heritage Society in Moscow also helped by providing a list of libraries in Ukraine and Moldova. I benefited from the advice and counsel of Brian J. Lenius in Canada, a recognized specialist in Galicia, who graciously allowed me to reproduce one of his maps in this book.

I am very appreciative that Sir Martin Gilbert in London kindly permitted me to reproduce several of his maps in this book, along with the identifying text. In Israel, special thanks are due to Dr. Sergei Kravtsov (formerly of Lvov), a researcher in the Architecture Section of the Center of Jewish Art, Hebrew University of Jerusalem; and Benjamin Lukin at the Central Archives for the History of the Jewish People. I also want to thank Dr. Gyemant Ladislau, director of the Dr. Moshe Carmilly Institute for Hebrew and Jewish History at Cluj University in Romania, for his valuable assistance.

ILLUSTRATIONS

Choosing the photographs, document examples and maps for this book was perhaps the most enjoyable part of the project for me. While text for the chapters was provided by the various named authors, the illustrations were wholly my choice.

Many friends permitted their photographs to be reproduced in this book, as listed in Appendix 7. I want to particularly thank Dmitry Peysakhov, formerly of Kiev and now living in Philadelphia, for sharing his extraordinary collection of black-and-white photographs, some of which can be found in this book and also in his book, *Jewish Life in Kiev* (Konstanz, Germany: Hartung-Gorre, 1992). Dmitry and his family befriended me during my early years in Kiev. The vivid images captured by Dmitry and his camera add a dimension to this book that enhances it beyond all expectations.

I am grateful to the following for permission to reproduce some of the pre–World War I photographs in this book: the Jewish Historical Institute and the Instytut Sztuki Polskiej Akademii Nauk in Warsaw; Nina N. Slonchak, director of the Central State Cinephotofono Archive of Ukraine, Kiev; and YIVO Institute for Jewish Research, New York.

YIVO INSTITUTE FOR JEWISH RESEARCH

YIVO Institute for Jewish Research is co-publisher of this book and the two others in *The Jewish Genealogy Series*. I would like to thank Tom Freudenheim (former executive director of YIVO), who warmly embraced this project from the beginning; and YIVO staff members Dina Abramowicz, Assaf Astrinsky, Zachary M. Baker, Stanley Bergman, Dr. Lisa Epstein, Krysia Fisher, Leo Greenbaum, Ella Levine, Jeffrey Salant and Marek Web. I am particularly indebted to Bruce Slovin, chairman of the board of YIVO, for his unfailing support in so many ways. His active involvement in this project made an immeasurable impact.

CHAPTER AUTHORS AND CONTRIBUTORS

Although I have acknowledged them elsewhere, I want to thank the following people, who made major contributions to this book, including Professor ChaeRan Y. Freeze (Introduction); Professor Zvi Gitelman and Hal Bookbinder (Chapter 1); Rabbi Moishe Leib Kolesnik (Chapter 2); Dr. Volodymyr S. Lozytsky, Dr. Ruslan Y. Pirig, Olga Marushak, Dr. Orest Y. Matsuk, Zinaida M. Klimishina, Sergei A. Borisevich, Faina A. Vinokurova and Oleksander S. Petrenko (Chapter 4); Josef Zissels (Chapter 5); Antonina A. Berzoy (Chapter 9); Dr. Clara Jignea, Professor Yakov Kopansky and Semion Shoikhet (Chapter 10); and William F. Hoffman (Appendix 4).

REVIEWERS AND EDITORS

I want to thank the book's editorial board: Jeffrey K. Cymbler, Professor Zvi Gitelman and Professor Gregory Freeze, who reviewed the book and provided important and insightful comments. I also wish to thank William F. Hoffman for preparing the alphabets in Appendix 4 and for his multiple reviews of other segments of the book.

Several sections were reviewed by Joshua Safran, with his usual meticulous notes in red pen.

New additions to the production team are Professor Gregory Freeze and his wife, ChaeRan. Their many years of hands-on experience in the archives of the former Soviet Union were a resource that was really a blessing for me. They never lost patience with my endless questions.

Professor Zvi Gitelman has long been recognized as an expert on the Jews of Russia, and it was because of his book *A Century of Ambivalence: The Jews of Russia and the Soviet Union, 1881 to the Present* (New York: YIVO Institute for Jewish Research, 1988) that I asked him to write an article for Chapter 1. I am delighted to have him as part of the team.

Much of the team remained intact from those who worked on *Jewish Roots in Poland*, and I was again privileged to work with

Lisa Clyde Nielsen, who served as the editor for this book. This project challenged both of us and pushed us past limits we didn't think possible. Her careful multiple readings of this manuscript, wise counsel and professional guidance are reflected in the final product. I was buoyed by her encouragement as we neared the final stages of the project and am deeply touched by her commitment.

FAMILY MEMBERS

During the last few years, my preoccupation with getting this book published has necessitated my absence at family gatherings. Relatives have been patient and understanding. I want to tell them how much I appreciate this and that I love them very much, including my dear sister, Karen Weiner, and her daughter and my precious niece, Molly Troy; my cousins Dorothye and Melvyn Abels, Barbara Gellman, Dede and Elmer Hertzmark, and David and Toby Weiner (and dozens of others); and my aunts and uncles, including Paul and Bernice Wyner, Ruth and Louis Olsman, and Ethel Davidson.

THE OTHERS

This book would not have been published without extensive financial support, all acknowledged on a separate page in the book. Here I wish to add my special thanks to Joseph S. Steinberg; Harvey M. and Constance Krueger; Sheldon Seevak; Alan Fortunoff; Mitchell Goldhar, Stephen Goldhar and Karen Goldhar White; Conference on Material Claims Against Germany; David and Rhoda Chase; The Estate of Herta Lande Seidman; Keren Ruth Foundation; Alan and Marjorie Goldberg; Neil D. Levin; The Eleanor, Adam and Mel Dubin Foundation; Bruce Slovin; Walter H. Weiner; and Lawrence G. Tesler.

I am deeply indebted to Dr. Michael Berenbaum for writing the *Foreword* to this book, as he did for *Jewish Roots in Poland*. His eloquent and moving words reflect his deep understanding about the importance of knowing one's roots. Only someone who has worked in the archives of Eastern Europe can understand the challenges and difficulties of working there. His *Foreword* sets the tone for this book.

The board members of the Routes to Roots Foundation were asked to serve because of their interest in "roots" and their commitment to *The Jewish Genealogy Series*, which includes *Jewish Roots in Poland*, *Jewish Roots in Ukraine and Moldova*, and *Jewish Roots in Belarus and Lithuania* (forthcoming). They attended board meetings, made important suggestions, and have guided the first two books to publication. They have supported this project in every sense of the word. My deep appreciation goes to my friends and fellow board members, Michael Brenner, Marjorie Goldberg, Alan Fortunoff, Harvey M. Krueger, Ernest W. Michel and Leonard M. Polisar. Each of them contributed something unique from their wealth of experience and expertise.

Finally, I want to thank my parents, Edward Weiner and Helen Rabkin Weiner, both of whom were involved in the early planning and preliminary research for *The Jewish Genealogy Series*, and both of whom passed away before they could hold the first book in their hands. Their guidance, financial support, love and faith gave me the strength to finish what I began.

Miriam Weiner
Secaucus, New Jersey
June 1999

Jewish Eastern Europe, 1830–1914

Legend:
- Jewish Eastern Europe 1830–1914
- Provincial capital
- Major city
- See Map 19, Appendix 3

Map 1

INTRODUCTION

by
Miriam Weiner

Until recently, there was a strong perception in Jewish communities worldwide that virtually all documents pertaining to Jews in Eastern Europe were destroyed by the Nazis during World War II.

While it is certainly true that many documents were lost, a significant number survived and can be found in archives throughout the former Soviet Union and Eastern Europe.

The interest in family history is very strong among Jews around the world. It is estimated that more than 75 percent of American Jews can trace at least one grandparent to towns within the Soviet borders as defined in 1945. The number of Jews visiting ancestral towns in the former Soviet Union is growing rapidly, and the interest in surviving archival materials has brought family historians in pursuit of genealogy into the fold of scholarly research.

With the political changes in Eastern Europe during the past few years, it has become possible to visit places and work in archives that one could only dream of a decade ago. With this access, it has become clear that there is a need to identify resources for people who wish to know more about their family history—specifically, what documents have survived, for what time periods, and in which archival repositories the documents can be found.

I visited Ukraine for the first time in 1991 and have returned several times each year since then, working in various levels of archives throughout the country. During my first visit, I met with Boris V. Ivanenko, then director of the Main Archival Administration under the Cabinet of Ministers of Ukraine, with a

proposal to compile and publish an inventory of the documents in Ukrainian State Archives, accessible by town name and with a focus on the Jewish material. He was enthusiastic and expressed his willingness to cooperate. For the purposes of genealogical research, it is essential to be able to identify documents by the geographical location in which they were created—that is, either by town or district. The following methodology for gathering the material was discussed and agreed upon with Mr. Ivanenko, based upon the same format utilized in my previous book, *Jewish Roots in*

▌ *Sevastopol, Ukraine, 1911*

6

1

Poland: Pages from the Past and Archival Inventories. Mr. Ivanenko and his staff, as well as subsequent directors appointed upon his retirement, have cooperated with and assisted me throughout the project.

My first visit to Moldova was in 1992 and included lengthy meetings with the director of the Moldovan National Archives. In Moldova, I worked primarily with Antonina A. Berzoy, vice-director of the Moldovan National Archives since 1992 and director since 1995. Ms. Berzoy also agreed that the archival inventory format established for *Jewish Roots in Poland* would be followed in gathering material for this book.

METHODOLOGY OF ARCHIVAL SURVEY

Data for the archival inventories came from many sources, including, but not limited to, archival inventories published by various archives in the former Soviet Union and elsewhere; published lists of Jewish records microfilmed by the Family History Library (FHL) in Salt Lake City, Utah; inventories prepared by the author and contracted researchers; district archivists in Ukraine and Moldova who reviewed the compiled inventories; and revised and updated inventories from the Urząd Stanu Cywilnego, Warsaw Śródmieście (the repository housing twentieth-century vital records for localities formerly in Eastern Poland and within the current borders of Western Ukraine).

The information gathered from the above sources was translated and then analyzed by the author prior to coding. This was a lengthy process that led to coding by document type, which was subsequently entered into the database developed for the first volume in this series.

A computerized listing by repository, based upon the above research, was provided to the director of the Ukrainian State Archives, who then had the data sent to each oblast (district) archive and the branch or subarchive of the district archive, with the request that the material be corrected and supplemented where possible. The applicable inventory data were also sent to the director of the Moldovan National Archives for verification and supplementation. The revisions were then incorporated into the database.

It was clear from comments received from archivists that, while the bulk of the data was correct, there were entries that had been accurate at one time but no longer were since documents are transferred periodically from the ZAGS archives to the Ukrainian State Archives. Every effort has been made to update and include the most current information.

Most archives were responsive to requests for review of inventory lists and provided helpful additions and clarifications. However, some archives in Ukraine stated that the sheer size of the project was more than they could accommodate and thus did not provide the requested archival file numbers or expand the inventory lists we provided. This was particularly true in Beregovo as of December 1998, as the archive and the documents contained therein were badly damaged by heavy rains and flooding. In these cases, inventory data came primarily from published archival inventories.

FOCUS OF THE BOOK

One of the most difficult decisions in producing this book was what had to be omitted. The focus of the book prohibits an exhaustive study of all repositories in Ukraine and Moldova. Those associated with this project agreed that the primary purpose was to concentrate on archival holdings in the state and branch archives along with documents in the ZAGS (local government offices where vital records are registered). The reader should also be aware that there is material of interest to Jewish researchers in virtually all the archives in Ukraine and Moldova (see Chapters 4 and 9). Also, there are extensive document collections relating to the Jews of Ukraine and Moldova throughout the archives in Moscow and St. Petersburg, Russia, which have not been inventoried for this book.

Of necessity, we have also made reference to some significant collections in local museums and in the homes of local citizens because of the uniqueness of the material.

Important Note to Remember

The inventory lists provided by the Ukrainian State Archives and the Moldovan National Archives often list only the year-span of documents, followed by the archives' file numbers. For example:

Years: 1842–1844;1857;1859–1861;1873
Archive file numbers: 270/2/4,7,9,12;273/1/3–4

As a result, it is not always possible to identify which archive number corresponds to a particular year or year-span. Therefore, the archival inventories in this book should be used **in conjunction with** the *fond/opis/delo* (name/number) descriptions held in the Ukrainian State Archives and the Moldovan National Archives.

YIZKOR BOOKS (MEMORIAL BOOKS)

Yizkor books were published after World War II by groups of *landsmanshaftn* societies (Jews from the same town or region) to commemorate the history and destruction of their towns. These books, hundreds of which have been published, are generally in Hebrew and Yiddish. They contain many photos, maps, memoirs, testimonies, town histories and lists of Jews who perished in the Holocaust. Many of these books are indexed. Often a *yizkor* book for one town will include information about smaller nearby towns and villages.

The largest collection of *yizkor* books can be found in the Yad Vashem Library in Jerusalem. In the United States, the Library of Congress; the New York Public Library; the Holocaust Memorial Center in West Bloomfield, Michigan; the YIVO Institute for Jewish Research; and the United States Holocaust Memorial Museum have the largest collections of *yizkor* books.

On the Internet, a current listing of *yizkor* books (together with other books about specific localities) can be found at <http://www.jewishgen.org/yizkor/database.html>.

DOCUMENTS INCLUDED IN ARCHIVAL INVENTORIES

Documents included in the archival inventories can be divided into two groupings:

- Documents created by the Jewish community, including metrical books; Jewish school records and Jewish hospital records; *kahal* (Jewish community council) documents (including Jewish community and organization records); *pinkassim* (Jewish register books); and other documents relating to the Jewish community.

- Documents created by local and district government offices, institutions and organizations that include birth, death, marriage and divorce records; family lists and books of residents; lists of males created for conscription lists; election and voter lists; documents created during the Holocaust period, including transport lists, property records, lists of people confined in ghettos and concentration camps, and confiscated property lists; emigration records; property records; police files; public-school records; name changes; tax lists; bank records; applications for business licenses and occupational lists; notary records; local government records, including wills and transfer of property to and from the Jewish community; and many other related documents.

LANGUAGE: TOWN–NAME SPELLINGS AND ALPHABET

A major consideration in preparing this book for publication was the issue of language and how it related to the spelling of town names. Due to border changes during various wars and the recent emergence of the independent countries of Ukraine and Moldova, documents within the archives of these countries are written in Polish, German, Russian, Hungarian, Ukrainian, Moldovan (the same language as Romanian) and Yiddish. The Ukrainian language came into official use when Ukraine declared its independence in 1991. For example, pre–World War II documents in Ukrainian archives are usually in the Russian language, while documents in the archives in Western Ukraine in Ivano-Frankovsk, Lvov and Ternopol (pre–World War II) are written in Polish or German, and documents in Southwestern Ukraine are in Hungarian. The finding-aids and indices are generally in Russian throughout Ukraine. In the Moldovan National Archives, documents written prior to 1917 are in the Russian language, while those documents written from 1917 to 1945 are in Moldovan.

This book deals with both documents and localities. Towns in Ukraine are now known under their Ukrainian names, but at the time many of the photographs in this book were taken (particularly town signs), the Russian names were still on the signs, or in some cases, the town signs reflected a combination of both Russian and Ukrainian letters.

The language spoken by the general populace in Ukraine varies. In Western Ukraine, one is more likely to hear Ukrainian or Polish and in Southwestern Ukraine, people speak Hungarian. Throughout the rest of Ukraine, Russian is the primary language. In Moldova, it is common to hear both Moldovan and Russian spoken among the populace.

The dilemma of how to accommodate both the current national language (town names) and Russian spellings (archival documents) was a major issue in the layout of this book.

This typical home in Russia brings to mind stories told by many immigrants of sleeping on shelves above the fireplace in order to keep warm, c. 1905.

7

Contributing authors and archivists tend to use either the Ukrainian or Moldovan language. Yet those people reading this book will remember their ancestral roots in Lvov (or Lemberg or Lwów), but not present-day Lviv. This is especially true in Western Ukraine, where the pronunciation changed, as in the city of Rovno (Russian), now known as Rivne (Ukrainian). In Western Ukraine, town names changed significantly, both in spelling and pronunciation, and the reader is referred to Appendix 3, *Place-Name Variants in Eastern Galicia*. In all other areas of Ukraine, the difference between Russian and Ukrainian place names is less marked. If spelled differently, it is also pronounced differently, if only slightly.

While it would have been preferable to be consistent throughout this book in the transliterated language of the town names, due to the foregoing factors and the ultimate goal of wanting this book to be consistent with ancestral town names as we knew them (as well as the language of the documents), town names in this book are transliterated from the Russian language in the archival inventories and in the pictorial sections of towns (Chapters 3, 8 and 11; and Appendix 1, *Selected Bibliography* [localities]). The transliterated spelling (from Russian) of town names is based upon the entries in *Where Once We Walked: A Guide to the Jewish Communities Destroyed in the Holocaust*, by Gary Mokotoff and Sallyann Amdur Sack (Teaneck, NJ: Avotaynu, 1991) and as defined by the U.S. Board on Geographic Names.

Therefore, the Ukrainian transliteration and spelling of town names are used in addresses only. For transliteration purposes and style consistency, the apostrophe found in current Ukrainian spellings was omitted.

In Appendix 3, *Place-Name Variants in Eastern Galicia*, the town names are listed in Polish first, but are alphabetized according to the Roman alphabet, since it is anticipated that the primary readership of this book will be an English-speaking audience.

Town names ending in -skiy (including Khmelnitskiy, Kamenets Podolskiy, Novograd Volynskiy, Vladimir Volynskiy, and others) are spelled in a modified version of the Library of Congress System (which would normally be transliterated from Ukrainian with the ending -skii or -sky) in order to be consistent with the locality spellings in the *Selected Bibliography* and archival inventories.

ADDITIONS TO THE ARCHIVAL DATABASE

In a project of this magnitude, it is inevitable that errors and omissions will occur. The database is being maintained on an ongoing basis and updated upon receipt and verification of new information. Therefore, readers are invited to submit any additions or corrections to the publishers' attention, and new data will be included in any future editions of the book.

TOWNS IN WESTERN UKRAINE (GALICIA)

It is important to know the names of the district and sub-district for towns located in Western Ukraine (Eastern Galicia) in order to determine where documents might have been registered. See the extensive listing in *Finding Your Jewish Roots in Galicia: A Resource Guide*, by Suzan F. Wynne (Teaneck, NJ: Avotaynu, Inc., 1998).

NOTES ON THE TRANSLITERATION OF HEBREW AND YIDDISH

Hebrew

A slightly modified version of the American Library Association/Library of Congress (ALA/LC) Hebrew romanization table is used for the transliteration of Hebrew bibliographical information. The ALA/LC Hebrew romanization table uses ḥ for the Hebrew letter *het*, kh for *khaf*, ' (apostrophe) for *'ayiin*, and ts for *tsade* (with the exception of ḥ [*het*], diacritical marks appearing in the ALA/LC Hebrew table have been omitted). In other respects, Hebrew transliterations should be straightforward.

Proper names (including place names) are transliterated according to the ALA/LC Hebrew table when they appear within the bodies of bibliographical entries (*e.g.*, titles, names of publishers). *Author headings* appearing at the beginning of entries usually employ either Roman-alphabet forms that appear within the works or forms that are found in standard reference sources (encyclopedias, bibliographies and library catalogues). In cases where this information is not available within the works, names are systematically transliterated according to the ALA/LC Hebrew romanization table.

Yiddish

The YIVO Yiddish romanization table, found in Uriel Weinreich's *Modern English-Yiddish, Yiddish-English Dictionary* (New York: YIVO Institute for Jewish Research, 1968), is used for the transliteration of Yiddish bibliographical information. The YIVO table uses kh for the letters *khof* (Hebrew *khaf*) and *khes* (Hebrew *het*). Yiddish words of Hebrew or Aramaic derivation (*e.g.*, *matsev*) use transliterations found within entries appearing in the Weinreich dictionary. In other respects, Yiddish transliterations should be straightforward.

Proper names (including place names) are transliterated according to the YIVO Yiddish table when they appear within the bodies of bibliographical entries (*e.g.*, titles, names of publishers). Author headings appearing at the beginning of entries usually employ Roman-alphabet forms that either appear within the works or are found in standard reference sources (encyclopedias, bibliographies and library catalogues). In cases where this information is not available within the works, names are systematically transliterated according to the YIVO Yiddish romanization table.

Important Note to Remember

It is anticipated that the primary readership of this book will be an English-speaking audience. Accordingly, town names in the archival inventories in Chapter 12 are alphabetized in the alphabetical order of the English language, based upon transliterated Russian names of localities.

JEWISH HISTORICAL INSTITUTE

The Jewish Historical Institute (JHI) in Warsaw, Poland, is the central repository in Eastern Europe for Jewish documents relating to localities in Poland as defined by the pre-1939 borders. Therefore, holdings at the JHI include documents for towns located in the former Polish provinces of Stanisławów (now Ivano-Frankivsk), Tarnopol (now Ternopil) and Lwów (now Lviv). These provinces (formerly known as Eastern Galicia) are within the current borders of Ukraine. The JHI archival holdings include many unique and interesting documents.

OTHER REPOSITORIES IN POLAND

The Urząd Stanu Cywilnego (USC) offices throughout Poland are the repository for civil vital-record registrations. In Warsaw, the Urząd Stanu Cywilnego, Warszawa-Śródmieście office's unique collection of Jewish vital records from Eastern Galicia is subject by law to access restrictions, but research requests for specific records are permitted, and certified copies of records are provided when located. Documents older than 100 years are transferred to the Polish State Archives, Archiwum Główne Aakt Dawnych (AGAD), located in Warsaw.

LDS COLLECTION OF VITAL RECORDS

The Family History Library of the Church of Jesus Christ of Latter-Day Saints (LDS Library) has microfilmed civil transcripts of church records and Jewish records worldwide, including those from some towns in Ukraine and Moldova. Consult a local Family History Center's Locality Catalogue to determine whether vital records for a specific town have been filmed.

Microfilming in Ukraine and Moldova is an ongoing project, and to date, only a very small part of the Jewish records (metrical books) has been filmed.

THE INTERNET

Until recently, genealogists were limited in their research by having to spend countless hours in libraries and dusty archives—many of which were hundreds, if not thousands of miles away from home, had limited hours and contained books or documents in foreign languages. With the advent of the Internet, there is now a wealth of information available that can be accessed from the comfort of one's home by computer through the World Wide Web, mailing lists, USENET newsgroups, e-mail and a rapidly expanding list of other resources.

For example, rather than consulting a gazetteer, anyone with Internet access can utilize the JewishGen ShtetlSeeker and locate an ancestral town's latitude and longitude and a list of towns within a certain distance of such a town.

JewishGen is the official home of Jewish genealogy in cyberspace, hosting a mailing list and Web site. Additional projects of JewishGen include the ShtetLinks project, which allows people with an interest in a particular shtetl or larger locality to share information; and the JewishGen Family Finder (JGFF), which is a computer-indexed compilation of surnames and towns currently being researched by almost 20,000 genealogists worldwide. It contains entries for most towns in Eastern Europe where Jews once lived.

The advent of the Internet has provided a major tool whereby genealogists can tap into a wealth of resources and databases to share information around the globe. Ten years ago, it was difficult to fathom a communications explosion that would provide access to such extensive resources. Today the ease and speed of e-mail communication and Internet access has motivated people in even the most obscure and small towns to participate equally in the search for their roots in archival and library databases.

JEWISH GENEALOGICAL SOCIETIES AND SPECIAL INTEREST GROUPS

There are more than 70 Jewish genealogical societies (JGSs) worldwide, with the number increasing steadily. For a complete and current list, contact:

INTERNATIONAL ASSOCIATION OF JEWISH GENEALOGICAL SOCIETIES, 104 Franklin Avenue, Yonkers, NY 10705 <http://www.jewishgen.org/iajgs>

In addition to the JGSs, the following Special Interest Groups (SIGs) are composed of genealogists interested in a specific geographic region of Ukraine and Moldova:

GALICIA	<http://www.jewishgen.org/galicia>
ODESSA	<http://www.jewishgen.org/listserv/sigs.html>
VOLHYNIA	<http://shangrila.cs.ucdavis.edu:1234/heckman/volhynia>

JewishGen Internet URLs:

JEWISHGEN	<http://www.jewishgen.org>
JRI-PL	<http://www.jewishgen.org/jri-pl>
SHTETLINKS	<http://www.jewishgen.org/ShtetLinks>
SHTETLSEEKER	<http://www.jewishgen.org/ShtetlSeeker>
SHTETLSCHLEPPERS	<http://www.jewishgen.org/ShtetlSchleppers>
JGFF	<http://www.jewishgen.org/jgff>

Eastern European genealogical societies in North America:

EAST EUROPEAN GENEALOGICAL SOCIETY, INC., P.O. Box 2536, Winnipeg, Manitoba, Canada R3C 4A7 <http://www.eegsociety.org>
FEDERATION OF EAST EUROPEAN FAMILY HISTORY SOCIETIES, P.O. Box 510898, Salt Lake City, UT 84151 <http://feefhs.org>

PHOTOGRAPHS AND DOCUMENTS

Photographs and documents are numbered sequentially within the book. The source of each graphic is listed in Appendix 7, *Photo and Document Credits*.

SELECTED BIBLIOGRAPHY (APPENDIX 1)

The *Selected Bibliography* (Appendix 1) is divided into segments based upon subject. The language of publication is indicated at the end of the bibliographic entry, with abbreviations as follows:

(F)	French	(HN)	Hungarian	(R)	Russian
(G)	German	(P)	Polish	(U)	Ukrainian
(H)	Hebrew	(RM)	Romanian	(Y)	Yiddish

All books with no such language designation are in English. If a book is in both English and another language, a bibliographic entry of (E) is added to show that the book has an English section.

The *Selected Bibliography* focuses on publications about localities within the current borders of Ukraine and Moldova. The *Selected Bibliography* is divided into several sections:

- Publications by category: General, Pre–1900, 1900–1939, Holocaust, Post–World War II, Bibliographies, Periodicals, Genealogy, Collected Biographies, Synagogues, Cemeteries, Films, Gazetteers and Atlases, and Travel Guides
- Publications by localities: includes *yizkor* books (memorial books) and books about specific towns
- Selected articles from *Avotaynu: The International Review of Jewish Genealogy*
- Bibliography of published archival inventories in Ukraine and Moldova
- Selected bibliography in Russian, Ukrainian and Romanian

AUTHOR'S NOTES

There are several instances where material overlaps with similar material in another chapter or is actually duplicated. Explanatory information that is pertinent to more than one chapter is repeated in the appropriate place. This is intentional and done to assist the reader so that there will be a minimum of cross-referencing between chapters.

The term *metrika* in various Slavic (and other) languages refers to, among other things, registers of vital statistics. However, in many transliterated English-language versions of material referring to these registers, the registers are commonly referred to as *metrical books*. That terminology is used in this book.

Some segments of the foregoing material in this *Introduction* are excerpted from the *Introduction* and *Chapter 1* of Miriam Weiner's *Jewish Roots in Poland: Pages from the Past and Archival Inventories* (Secaucus, NJ/New York: The Miriam Weiner Routes to Roots Foundation/YIVO Institute for Jewish Research, 1997).

References to localities in this book are primarily for towns in Ukraine and Moldova. When the town is located in a country outside of Ukraine, the town name is followed by the country where it is located, *e.g.*, Teleneshty, Moldova or Warsaw, Poland. **When the town is located in Ukraine, the name of the country is generally not given.**

USEFUL ADDRESSES

BETH HATEFUTSOTH MUSEUM OF THE DIASPORA, Klausner Street, Ramat Aviv, P.O.B. 39359, 61932 Tel Aviv, Israel
   <http://www.bh.org.il/>
CENTER FOR JEWISH HISTORY, 17 WEST 16TH STREET, NEW YORK, NY 10011 <http://www.cjh.org>
CENTRAL ARCHIVES FOR THE HISTORY OF THE JEWISH PEOPLE, P.O. Box 1149, Jerusalem 91010, Israel
FAMILY HISTORY LIBRARY, 35 North West Temple Street, Salt Lake City, Utah 84150 <http://www.lds.org>
JEWISH HISTORICAL INSTITUTE, 3/5 Tłomackie Street, 00-090 Warsaw, Poland
JEWISH NATIONAL AND UNIVERSITY LIBRARY, Hebrew University, Givat Ram Campus, P.O. Box 503, Jerusalem 91004, Israel
JEWISH THEOLOGICAL SEMINARY, 3080 Broadway, New York, NY 10027
NEW YORK PUBLIC LIBRARY, 42nd Street & Fifth Avenue, New York, NY 10018 <http://catnyp.nypl.org>
POLISH STATE ARCHIVES, Archiwum Główne Akt Dawnych (AGAD), 7 Długa Street, 00-263 Warsaw, Poland
   <http://ciuw.warman.net.pl/alf/archiwa/index.eng.html>
U.S. COMMISSION FOR PRESERVATION OF AMERICA'S HERITAGE ABROAD, 1101 15th Street NW #1040, Washington, D.C. 20005
UNITED STATES HOLOCAUST MEMORIAL MUSEUM, 100 Raoul Wallenberg Place SW, Washington, D.C. 20024
   <http://www.ushmm.org>
UNITED STATES NATIONAL ARCHIVES, Cartographic & Architectural Branch, 8601 Adelphi Road, College Park, MD 20740-6001
   <http://www.nara.gov>
URZĄD STANU CYWILNEGO, Warsaw Śródmieście, skr. poczt. 18, 1/3 Jeziuka Street, 00-950 Warsaw, Poland
YAD VASHEM, P.O. Box 3477, Jerusalem 91034, Israel <http://www.yad-vashem.org.il>
YIVO INSTITUTE FOR JEWISH RESEARCH, 17 West 16th Street, New York, NY 10011 <http://www.baruch.cuny.edu/yivo>

FOLLOWING THE PAPER TRAIL
GENEALOGICAL RESOURCES
IN THE UKRAINIAN AND MOLDOVAN ARCHIVES

by Professor ChaeRan Y. Freeze

The collapse of the Soviet Union in late 1991 unleashed an archival revolution that inaugurated an unprecedented phase in Jewish genealogical research. Prior to its collapse, Communist rule meant that documents pertaining to national minorities such as the Jews were virtually inaccessible and, indeed, segregated in special storage (*spetskhran*) to avert use by nationalists and "ethnic conflicts." Moreover, access to archival materials was almost exclusively restricted to participants in official exchanges, chiefly from the United States and Great Britain. Private citizens, whether Soviet or foreign, had virtually no right to use archival materials, even for private matters like family history.

Independence brought profound changes to the republics of the former Soviet Union, including the declassification of hitherto secret collections. That process encompassed not only classified repositories (such as the Ukrainian Communist Party Archive) but also materials pertaining to Jews, which were gradually transferred from special storage to the main collections. Moreover, many archivists who had once denigrated genealogical research as a "decadent bourgeois pursuit" now take an active interest in assisting individuals to locate family records. This shift in access and attitude has been extended not only to citizens but also to foreigners, including those without formal academic credentials and support. Although conditions and access vary kaleidoscopically (among archives and from time to time), what was once unthinkable is now truly feasible.

To be sure, researchers still face important challenges, especially in Ukraine. The hardships caused by Ukraine's transition to a market economy have taken a significant toll on the archives and their capacity to service researchers. As Patricia Grimsted warns:

"[With the] shortages of staff, lack of technical facilities, storage space limitations, and deteriorating physical condition of many archival repositories…worries abound regarding the adequate preservation of the Ukrainian archival heritage for future generations."[1] At a rudimentary practical level, the state's fiscal crisis has meant drastic reductions in archival staff, working hours and duplication facilities—even the occasional unpredictable suspension of operations altogether. If political repression was the main obstacle to research in the past, the severe economic crisis poses the primary threat today.

Although Ukrainian archives are officially open to the public, researchers should anticipate various problems and take a few preparatory measures prior to a trip to Ukraine. First, it is essential to obtain an updated schedule of closings and holidays, especially for those taking short trips. For example, Ukrainian archives often reduce hours or close for staff vacations in the summer; in addition, reading rooms are closed at least once a month for *sanitarnyi den'* (cleaning day). More recently, some archives have limited their hours in response to budget cuts and inability to pay staff salaries. Ideally, a local contact should call the pertinent archive for details; in some cases, a fax, e-mail or telephone call might be available to clarify these matters.

Second, it is recommended that one obtain an official letter of introduction, preferably from a Ukrainian institution or at least a sponsoring organization in the United States. Genealogists have found that letters from their mayor or congressperson (with an official stamp or seal) usually satisfy archival directors. Such letters, which should describe your background and the purpose of your visit, should be translated into Ukrainian (as required by the Central

Entrance to the State Archive of Chernovtsy Oblast (formerly a church), 1993

8

State Historical Archive in Kiev), or at least into Russian. It is also customary for archive officials to register a researcher's passport and to ask the researcher to fill out an *anketa* (information sheet). Third, if one cannot read Russian or has only limited time to spend in the archive, it may be most productive to request the archive to conduct a genealogical search *prior* to your visit. Cooperation, costs and results will vary according to the archive. It is also wise to have a firm agreement (in writing) regarding the price of photocopies and labor to avoid any misunderstandings. For those who plan to conduct their own research, it is helpful to consult published finding-aids (*putevoditeli*) for references to collections (*fondy*) to make a short visit more productive.

In Moldova, historical documents are located in the Moldovan National Archives in Kishinev. The archivists here are very receptive to visiting researchers. While it is also helpful to notify the archives prior to arrival so that some books could be prepared for the visitor's arrival, it is not mandatory and the staff is ready to assist anyone who wishes to work there.

Finally, oblast (provincial or district) archives often lack the facilities to photocopy or microfilm documents. In that event, be prepared to improvise by using a 35-mm camera or hiring a local photographer (with the permission of the archive, of course). If the archive does have its own equipment, expect high and even exorbitant rates, sometimes as much as several dollars per page. (For bankrupt and underfunded institutions, foreign researchers represent a unique opportunity to raise funds.)

SIX COMMON TYPES OF REGISTRATION RECORDS

The Ukrainian and Moldovan archives hold six major types of registration records that constitute an excellent starting place for genealogical research. While this article will focus on documents from Ukraine, similar materials can be found in Moldova. These include: (1) *kahal* records; (2) poll-tax records; (3) metrical books; (4) social estate registration records; (5) family registers; and (6) recruitment lists. While the adage "God is in the heavens and the Tsar is far away" may have held true in Jewish daily life, it hardly corresponded to the intrusiveness of the state when it concerned registration. Behind this energetic interest was the state's overriding concern to ensure the regular collection of taxes and, after 1827, the military conscription of Jews.

Archival records reveal that enforcement of these laws was very vigorous in the Ukrainian provinces; authorities there were exceptionally vigilant in their prosecution of Jews (especially men) who failed to register. Ironically, what Ukrainian Jews of the nineteenth century viewed as "a bad plague" (especially those without registration papers) has proven highly advantageous for descendants searching for their roots.

Kahal records: list of contributors to the Jewish Community Chest in Skala Podolskaya, including #133, Dawid Elo Seidenfeld, 1935

Kahal Records

Following the partitions of Poland, Empress Catherine II was confronted with the daunting task of extracting taxes from her new subjects. Rather than assign this complicated task to Russian bureaucrats, she elected to utilize the existing Jewish regional council (*kahal*), which had performed similar functions under Polish–Lithuanian rule. She, therefore, ordered that Jews enroll in their local *kahal* and that these records be used to assess and collect the poll tax. The *kahal* was also responsible for issuing passports for internal travel and thus regulating the geographic mobility of the Jewish population.

Kahal records that can be found in Ukrainian archives (dating back to the late eighteenth century) reveal several important details about family members. Whenever Jews were expelled or left a town, they not only had to apply for a passport but also for registration in another *kahal*. For example, a thick file about the expulsion of Jews from Kiev in 1828 included individual requests for inclusion in the Vasilkov *kahal*; however, the latter agreed to accept only those who could afford to pay the poll tax or who volunteered their sons for the conscription quota. Given the parental fears about forced conversion in the army and the

25-year term of military service, it is hardly surprising to find bitter complaints about these harsh prerequisites. Although these documents do not always indicate if an individual was accepted into a given *kahal*, they offer valuable clues for tracking down relatives who migrated to other towns.

In addition to registration lists, Ukrainian archives contain more substantive petitions to the Kiev general-governor about unfair treatment at the hands of the *kahal*. One common complaint concerned "dead souls": that is, the refusal of the *kahal* to remove a deceased relative from the poll-tax registers, thereby forcing the family to pay taxes on them. To be sure, the *kahal* was merely following Russian law (which fixed taxes according to the revision lists compiled every two decades) and refused in the interim to complicate the task by deleting the dead or adding newborns; however, this did not lessen the burden for families visited by untimely disease and death. More tragic were the denunciations from impoverished Jews that the *kahal* had hired *khappers* to abduct their young sons (often under the age of 13) as military recruits in the place of wealthy co-religionists. Many complaints came from Jewish women who protested that their sons had been brutally snatched from their arms and who often signed their own petitions in Yiddish.

Poll-Tax Census (Reviziya)

The second type of registration was the poll-tax census (*reviziya*), based on documents called the *revizskie skazki*. Tsar Peter the Great first ordered a systemic head count of the male population in 1718; his purpose was to establish a direct capitation tax and put his government on a more secure, predictable financial footing. This system divided Russian society into two basic categories: the great mass of unprivileged "poll-tax population" (which later came to include the Jews) and the "non-poll-tax population," exempt from the capitation tax. Inclusion in the poll-tax category also entailed various other disabilities—conscription, liability to corporal punishment, restrictions on geographic mobility and travel, and exposure to other forms of discrimination. Thus, in contrast to the privileged groups (clergy, nobility, and civil and military servitors) exempt from this onerous duty, the poll-tax population had to bear this "stigma, conferred by birth" until it was finally abolished in 1883. Although the poll tax receded in relative importance as the state came to rely more on indirect taxes, it nevertheless remained a heavy burden. That was especially true for impoverished Jews who struggled to pay the double poll tax (imposed on Jews and various other groups). Significantly, the government used this tax to induce desired behavior—for example, by granting a tax exemption to persuade Jews to join agricultural colonies and serve as state rabbis.

Of the 10 poll-tax revisions, the fifth revision census (1794–1796) was the first to include the territories of partitioned Poland, and hence of interest to Jewish genealogists (subsequent revision lists were compiled in 1811, 1816, 1834, 1850 and 1858). The poll-tax record followed a standard form, with the male members of the household listed on the left-hand side and females on the right-hand side of the two-page census (see page 18). The left-hand section inquired about the ages of male family members at the last revision census and their current age, the absence of any individual from his primary residence and sometimes the current occupations. Female subjects also provided names, current ages and any "temporary absences" from their residence. Since dates of birth were not recorded, the reported ages must be treated with caution, particularly for records prior to 1835, when the Russian government began to enforce the registration of births more stringently. Until then, oral declarations served as the primary verification of age.

List of inhabitants in Krivoye Ozero in 1875, including documents #292–#294, listing Aron Polisar (born 1833, son of Yankel) and his sons Maiorko (born 1861) and Leizer (born 1874). Document #295 lists Mordko Polisar (born 1848, son of Yankel). All of the Polisars were official residents of Bendery, Moldova, but they were registered in Krivoye Ozero, Ukraine.

However, knowledge of one's age was at best an approximation; as one townsman confessed, "I have lived many years [but] how many years, I do not know."[2]

The revision record was compiled in two copies: one for the district treasury office, the other for the Provincial Office of the Treasury (*Gubernskaia kazennaia palata*), which, in turn, sent a summary of the data to the Senate and the Ministry of Finance in St. Petersburg. In most cases, the best-preserved and most easily accessible copy is found in the fond of the Provincial Office of the Treasury. For example, the revision censuses of the Zhitomir Jewish community are located in this collection (State Archive of Zhitomir Oblast, fond 118). For the towns and villages in Kiev Province, numerous records are also found in the State Archive of Kiev Oblast (fond 280). Some *revizskie skazki* include not only Jewish families but also co-residents from groups such as townspeople and peasants. As a result, one must often search general revision files to locate Jews included with other social groups. To be sure, some files contain only Jewish families—for example, the revision censuses of the Jewish communities of Vasilkov, Belaya Tserkov and Berdichev in Kiev Province. Such records are easier to locate because they included "*evreiskii*" ("Jewish") in the title of the file. Revision records are also found under the rubric of *podatnye spiski* (poll-tax lists), organized by towns; the State Archive of Kiev Oblast, for example, contains 10 census files for the town of Fastov (fond 344).

In general, the revision censuses are valuable not only because they provide data on the structure of the household (*e.g.*, the number of children and, sometimes, the occupation of individuals), but also because they indicate if an individual left the town. Hence, these files can also provide critical clues to help locate those who left their permanent place of residence. Finally, one must keep in mind that not all revision census records are entirely accurate and may include Jewish males from other families. As archival records indicate, it was not uncommon for the *kahal* to recruit a poor boy as a substitute for a wealthier family; thus the former's name would appear with a different family, not with his own.

Metrical Books (Metricheskie Knigi)

In 1826, the Russian state extended the system of metrical books (the communal records of births, deaths, marriages, and divorces) to the Jews and made the state rabbi (better known as the *rabbiner*, in Yiddish) responsible for recordkeeping. The state or crown rabbis were not regarded by their communities as authentic rabbis but as mere official registrars. As Sholom Aleichem once wrote, "To old-country Jews I don't have to explain what a rabbi of the crown is. They know the breed.... He fills out birth certificates, officiates at circumcisions.... To take it for granted that among our people a rabbiner is well-loved—let's not say any more."[3] The testimony of Yitzhak Baer Levinson is also telling: "Some of the small towns have elected, quite cleverly, people who can just about write and sign their names in Russian and are ostensibly called rabbis, while the real rabbi, an expert solely of the Torah, remains in his place—the two of them [being]

Marriage record of Berko Odnopozov, widower, age 26, and Brocha Avroskin (divorcée), daughter of Avrum, age 26, married in Priluki, Ukraine, in 1891

grafted together like the lame and the blind."[4] Given the dearth of qualified Jewish "rabbis" for the task of recordkeeping in the early nineteenth century and the disincentives to register (taxation and conscription), it is hardly surprising that the early records were incomplete and unreliable. Such evasion and error, predictably, caught the attention of the government and impelled it to adopt a new strategy to ensure registration.

The government took the first step in 1835 when it issued published bound volumes with individual entry numbers to standardize recordkeeping and prevent *ex post facto* tampering. The new standard format made it all but impossible to "doctor" the records by ripping out (numbered!) pages or inserting retroactive entries. Moreover, each year the rabbi was required to deposit one copy of the metrical book with the provincial board (*gubernskaia uprava*), thereby making it possible to detect retroactive alterations and prevent future additions. To be sure, the inefficient and venal Russian administration admitted some errors. Thus, some Jews still neglected—or dared to ignore—the legal obligation to register; eventually, some requested their state rabbi to insert the information under a later date. Although most state rabbis were reluctant to accommodate such requests (the harsh penalties included fines, imprisonment and conscription), some—either out of compassion or greed—acquiesced. For example, five years after his daughter was born, a certain Gurvich in Odessa realized that he must register her birth. His local rabbi declined to amend the oversight but advised him to visit a so-called Rabbi Kagan, who had a reputation for "fixing" such problems. Much to the father's surprise, the state rabbi recorded the birth in the metrical books of Varvarova (Kherson Province) without any hesitation. For genealogists, the lesson is clear: Given such opportunities, especially in the new areas of settlement like Odessa, Kherson and Ekaterinoslav, relatives (in particular, females) may have registered in a different town under a wrong date—if they bothered to registered at all.

To ensure the accurate identification of subjects, the tsarist state insisted on the consistent spelling and transliteration of names. Inconsistencies and errors such as the omission of letters were cause for punishment. That included a strict ban—an extension of the general policy to prevent fraud and deception—on "any corrections in Jewish metrical books, with the exception of errors made by the clerk [the state rabbi]."[5] But the burden of demonstrating that "exception" rested on the victim, and the resolution of such cases was subject to the caprice of local officials. For example, when the provincial board of Kiev fined Sheina Beila Zatulovskaya 300 rubles in 1912 because her son failed to report for military service, she could hardly have been more astonished: her son had died almost 10 years earlier. A brief inquiry revealed the cause of the misunderstanding; the state rabbi had recorded the death of "Moise Khazan" instead of "Moishe Khazan." And once made, the mistake proved impossible to rectify. Despite the

mother's repeated attempts to confirm his death (e.g., pictures of his tombstone and family poll-tax records), the provincial board stubbornly refused to rescind the fine, evidently convinced that Moishe was not dead or, at least, determined to punish his kin and community for failing to keep proper records.

As this case indicates, the government used the metrical books to compile essential information for taxation and recruitment. For researchers, however, this impulse meant that the data invited verification and included valuable personal data. As Peter Czap, Jr., once observed about analogous records for the Russian Orthodox Church, they "reflect identifiable individuals whose lives can be traced from beginning to end."[6] The standard form for the registration of birth, for example, included details about the child's sex, the mohel who performed the circumcision, the date and place of birth, and the names and social status of the parents and the infant. Marital registers recorded the ages and names of the bride and groom, the name of the rabbi who performed the ceremony, the date of marriage, obligations of the marital contract (usually the amount of the ketubah) and the signatures of two witnesses. The entries for divorce included the names and ages of the spouses, the name of the rabbi who supervised the divorce or halitsah (levirate divorce), the "reason" for the dissolution of the marriage and the date of the final divorce. The form for deaths provided the name and age of the deceased, burial site (e.g., the town and sometimes the cemetery), and the date and presumed cause of death. For genealogists, details about the place of burial can be very valuable, especially if the cemetery is still intact.

Most state rabbis provided only the required information and, often, resorted to stereotypical phrases. Perhaps the best examples are descriptions such as "mutual hatred" or "mutual agreement" as grounds for divorce, or "illness" as the cause of death in every single record. There were exceptions, however. For example, in the 1870s, the state rabbi of Kharkov conscientiously recorded more specific causes for marital dissolution (e.g., infidelity, childlessness, conversion or "extreme poverty"). He even noted when the wife received the get (bill of divorce) through an official courier, not the husband.

How reliable are these sources? For the earlier period at least, the "forgeable" forms and disincentives unquestionably encouraged distortion and evasion. Those who married off their children prior to the minimum age (set by the state in 1830 as 16 for girls and 18 for boys) entered an older age to avoid punishment. To all this must be added the sheer cost of registration (one to five rubles). Increasingly, however, Jews had strong incentives to comply and file accurate data, precisely because the metrical books could prove social origins, marital status and the identity of legal heirs. For example, Russian gymnasiums (high schools) required students to present a copy of a birth certificate (e.g., a copy from the metrical book) in order to receive a diploma, state courts demanded written documentation of death before executing a will and the military required a marriage certificate for Jewish widows to claim the army pensions of their deceased husbands. In one

Birth record of Leya Rozenberg, born July 15, 1890, in Odessa, daughter of Sender Rozenberg (son of Yudko) and Khaya Sura

poignant case involving Lipa Froima Goldberg, a widow, the state denied her application for a military pension on the grounds that the couple had failed to register their marriage in a metrical book.

Various recently published guides provide a list of metrical books in the archives of the former Soviet Union. To be sure, they do not always include the phrase *metricheskie knigi* (metrical books) in the descriptions. In Dmitrii A. Elyashevich's guide, for example, archival collections include metrical books when they refer to: (1) the name of a Jewish *ravvinat* (rabbinate), such as the *Korostyshevskii ravvinat* in the Central State Historical Archive of Ukraine, Kiev (fond 663 with 203 files dating from 1840 to 1916); (2) a Jewish *obshchestvo* (society or community); and (3) an *obshchina* (commune). Some fondy described as synagogue or *kahal* records may also include metrical books.

For researchers whose families lived in very small shtetlach, records were usually kept by the state rabbi of the closest town. Throughout the nineteenth century, there were bitter debates among Jews in small towns whether to maintain their own state rabbi, whose salary was paid from the tax on kosher meat (known as the *korobochnyi sbor*), or to unite into a single rabbinical district (*ravvinskii uchastok*) with a neighboring town, thereby sharing the cost of supporting the unpopular registrar. But the latter option could be highly inconvenient. The Jews of Bukov (Kiev Province), for instance, requested permission to elect their own official because it was very difficult to persuade the state rabbi—who lived more than 20 miles away—to perform the duties of registration. Hence, archive guides sometimes overlook small towns; that is especially likely if the town was combined with another for registration. Thus, it is sometimes worthwhile to locate the closest town with extant metrical books.

Social Estate Registration Records

According to the Statute of 1804, the Jews were to register under one of four social categories: (1) "agriculturalists" (*zemledeltsy*); (2) manufacturers and artisans; (3) merchants (*kuptsy*); and (4) petty townspeople (*meshchane*). The latter was a catch-all term to encompass those outside the three more specific status categories. After 1832, Jews (like other subjects) who had rendered exceptional service could be inscribed in the privileged status group of "honorary citizen" (*pochetnyi grazhdanin*), who enjoyed a host of special rights, including exemption from the poll tax and conscription.

Registration served both to identify taxpayers and to assign them to a specific town and administrative jurisdiction. Given the critical importance of registration, the state imposed severe consequences for evasion or deception. In the words of the law: "Jews who cannot present a written document in standard legal form, certifying their membership in a class, will be regarded as vagrants and will be treated according to the full severity of the law."[7] In the case of a Jewish woman, the law automatically assigned her to the social status of her father and, after marriage, to that of her husband. In the event of divorce, she retained the status of her former husband. When

a Jew planned to move to another town, his local town council had to confirm that he had paid all outstanding taxes and dues. Only then was the district police administration able to authorize his departure and make the necessary insertions into his internal passport.

Although the law did not specify precisely how one was to register in a social estate, such registration was based in principle on the poll-tax revisions. More difficult was the problem of those who had changed their status. For example, one case in the Kiev State-City Archive, which dragged on for two years (1875–1877), involved a certain "A. Berenshtain" who sought to register as a new "honorary citizen" in Kiev, but he encountered long delays as state bureaucrats sought to verify his new status and wealth. It is also worthwhile to look at files in the *meshchanskaiya uprava* (townsmen's administrative board) collections, which have lists of registered townspeople. For instance, the State Archive of Kiev Oblast holds 46 such fondy, which cover many of the major towns in Kiev Province, such as Belaya Tserkov (fond 948) and Fastov (fond 344).

List of taxpayers in Samgorodok, Ukraine, in 1911, including four members of the Fortunov family: Govshei, Itsko, Mordko and Usher

Family Registers (Posemeinyi Spisok)

The fifth category of registration documents was the family register (*posemeinyi spisok*). State laws required that the male head of each household enter the same name that he used in the poll-tax census for the family register and supplementary "alphabetical register." Each record included the individual's social status (*e.g.*, merchant or townsperson), name, age, poll-tax registration number, place of permanent residence, primary occupation, current locus of residence, and finally a notation about his military draft status. This registration did not include females (*e.g.*, records of Radomysl, district of Kiev), but that is not surprising, given the tax and military function of such documentation. These records were to be deposited with the city duma and updated every two years or whenever an individual changed his social status or residence.

Recruitment Lists

The final type of registration record was the recruitment list for each town. Like the family register, this record usually excluded women (although there were a few exceptions) and drew upon the previous poll-tax census. From left to right, the standard form included: (1) the registration numbers of each household for the current list, the last poll-tax census and previous recruitment list; (2) the names of male members of the household, including sons and brothers; and, finally, (3) the ages at the last poll-tax census, as well as the current ages.

CREATIVE SOURCES FOR JEWISH GENEALOGY

Unlike registration records, which provide minimal biographical data, invaluable information can be gleaned from archival materials such as court, educational and administrative records, which offer rich detail about the daily lives of family members and their communities. However, this type of advanced research requires intensive preliminary study of family recollections and oral histories. Thus, prior to my research trip to Ukraine in 1994, Professor Marvin Fox of blessed memory asked me to be alert for materials about his family in Korostyshev. Without his "map" of family stories, the search would have been fruitless. He had told me, for instance, about the election of the state rabbi (a dentist by the name of Aron Ratner) in his parents' hometown. My search led to a file on the "election of the

Recruitment list, 1846, from Balta Uezd (district), including #34 entry for Ios Myaskovsky (born 1802, son of Abram); Ios' sons Itsko (born 1827) and Danel (born 1833); and Ios' brother Borukh (born 1803). Note: The year of birth was calculated from the age at time of the census.

Korostyshev state rabbi" (located in the State Archive of Kiev Oblast), which included signatures of his grandfather and uncle, who had participated in this contentious election, as well as the names of other members of their *bet midrash* (house of study). Extraordinary material about his family emerged from these files—from their role in town politics to their position on the kosher-meat tax that paid the state rabbi's salary.

Court Records

Court records are an important, if difficult, source for learning about Jewish life in Ukraine and finding relatives who failed to register. Following the judicial reforms of 1864, Jews turned increasingly to the secular state courts rather than the traditional *beit din* (rabbinical court) to resolve their disputes, especially over financial matters. The latter gradually lost the capacity to enforce its rulings, forcing litigants to appeal to state courts for justice. As a result, state authorities came to prevail, even on private, family matters: traditional use of the *herem* (excommunication) or flogging to force Jews to comply with rabbinical injunctions gave way to fines, imprisonment or military conscription. In the end, the rabbis had but one means at their disposal—namely, "persuasion and exhortation." The erosion of the *beit din's* authority also stemmed from the decline in popular veneration of rabbinic authority and the fear of communal ostracism among some Jews. Moreover, the judicial reforms of 1864 made state courts not only accessible but affordable even for ordinary Jews. To be sure, the penchant for litigation did not guarantee justice. Indeed, as the courts complained, the profusion of litigation encouraged widespread corruption; despite attempts to combat this, bribery was still rampant and successful.

What types of issues brought Jews into the state courts? First, in some matters, only state courts had jurisdiction. That was most notable in the difficult question of registration. Some Jews—despite all the government's injunctions on registration—nevertheless sought to procrastinate or to evade this obligation altogether. That noncompliance was particularly true of Jewish girls, whose parents had little incentive to pay for the registration of births, especially in view of the high rates of infant and child mortality. However, parents soon discovered that the state treated unregistered offspring as "illegitimate children"—a status fraught with severe restrictions and discrimination. In response, some parents attempted to undo the damage caused by their negligence, whether intentional or accidental. The problem was that the state rabbi could not amend the metrical books from previous years, since the originals were preserved by local civil authorities. Nor was "adoption" an easy alternative: legal adoption required the personal consent of the tsar himself. A Senate ruling in 1900 sought to facilitate the correction of records by permitting Jews to file suit in district court to alter their status, but this procedure was neither cheap nor guaranteed.

The profusion of Jewish names (*e.g.*, Finkelshtein, Zilberman, Groisman, Shpilberg) in the archival registers demonstrates how widespread the problem had become. In the State Archive of Zhitomir Oblast, a typical petition to legitimize a birth reads as follows: "On June 10, 1886, I was born in Zhitomir to my parents Shamai Froimovich and Rukhel Iosevna Libavich, who were legally married in August 1874 in the same town, but my parents completely forgot to record my birth in the metrical book . . . and without a copy of the metrical registration of my birth, I cannot receive a certificate that I have completed [my studies] at the Kopropovich gymnasium in Berdichev." The costs for such an oversight could be astronomical, especially in contested cases where the litigant required a lawyer, the compilation of numerous documents, and—as so often was reported—a generous flow of bribes. In 1908, for example, Khava Abramovna Drakh discovered that her name had not been recorded in the metrical book of births for 1862. To correct the error, she hired a lawyer to demonstrate that her birth was indeed legitimate. She later claimed that the total legal costs amounted to 500 rubles—

Court record with terms of parole from prison for Itsko Grinshtein (son of Leib), who was released from prison after one year (as a thief), 1897. This document enabled Itsko to register with the local police department in Balta and then become an official resident of that city.

15

several times the average annual income of the lower social classes. These files often include the marriage certificate of parents or oral depositions (transcribed by the court investigator into Russian) to support the case.

Second, Jews turned to the state civil courts with suits to confirm or contest last wills and testaments of deceased family members. Not even the fear of interacting with the state could intimidate an individual who was intent on claiming a bequest. However, such litigation could sometimes boomerang, especially in the case of plaintiffs who proved to be unregistered and could not produce valid documentation of their identity. Such suits typically involved widows seeking legal recognition of their claims to control their husbands' estates. These cases include a copy of the last testament (usually translated into Russian), which stipulated how the assets must be divided. Interestingly, many if not most records provided for a monetary bequest to a local synagogue, prayer house or charitable institution. Other family members also filed suits to legalize their claim to inheritance, as in the case involving Saul-Aron and Duvid Gershkovich Radinov, who claimed that their grandfather had left them 10 percent of his immovable property (viz., a plot of land in Zhitomir). This file included a copy of the grandfather's will, the marriage certificate of their parents (Gersh Moshkovich and Rakhelia Khelimer) and their birth certificates—all to prove their claim and identity. In other cases, family members waged legal battles to contest the validity of a will or to ask the court to adjudicate the distribution of assets. Such legal challenges sometimes prevailed; thus, in a lawsuit involving Abus Bronshtein and his relatives, the state court referred the case back to the local beit din with an order that it review the inheritance and order a division of property.

The third type of civil suits—accusations of misdemeanors—contains fascinating detail about the lives of ordinary Jews who struggled to eke out a living in small towns. Another example from the State Archive of Zhitomir Oblast is a complaint from a domestic servant against an employer who failed to pay the promised wages. Brukha Gintsbuerg, who lived on Malaya Berdichevskaya Ulitsa (Little Berdichev Street) in Zhitomir, informed the court: "I worked for 10 months as a cook for Dveira Model at 50 rubles per year according to our contract. On June 6, Dveira Model dismissed me from work and did not pay my salary for half a year [25 rubles]; thus I am bringing this suit against her." The cook cited the names of witnesses to support her but apparently did not prevail—the file breaks off without a resolution. Some suits describe the daily routines and tasks of an ordinary domestic servant. In the case of Khaya Sura Shtatland, resident of Khlebnaya Ulitsa (Bread Street), the plaintiff argued that her 13-year-old daughter had worked for the Maizlish family, sewing linens, and that her contract stipulated a wage of 20 rubles per year. The plaintiff claimed that the Maizlishes still owed her daughter 7.50 rubles for work she performed during the winter months. Her employers denied these allegations, claiming that they had paid the girl early so that she could buy a pair of shoes. They also accused her of failing to perform her duties during the second half of the year.

The garment industry seemed especially prone to litigation in state courts. Some consumers lodged suits against tailors for failing to complete the work on time or for ruining their

Passport issued in 1910 to Zanvel Mednik (son of Moishe-Itsko), of the village of Kalyus in Novaya Ushitsa District, age 32, a tailor, married. Mednik completed his military service in 1897 and, with this passport, could travel anyplace where Jews were permitted to live.

the draft. His neighbors sought to rebut that accusation and testified that, in fact, his eye had been deformed since birth. One witness, Moshko Dubov, claimed that as long as he remembered, the accused did not have a healthy right eye. Notwithstanding such depositions, Iosi Bronshtein was found guilty and sentenced to prison.

Educational Records

During the reign of Tsar Nicholas I, the government and *maskilim* (enlightened Jews) sought to propagate secular education among the Jewish population. Initially, these plans met with strong resistance. As one observer put it, "The greatest indignation against the proposed reforms of the schools was unanimously manifested. The leading members of the *beit ha-midrash* threatened with banishment and excommunication anyone who dared support such a frivolous scheme...."[8] Gradually, however, the state schools gained "acceptance" both among poor families (seeking to shield their sons from conscription) and enlightened families (desiring to broaden economic and social opportunities for their children). The Universal Military Conscription Act (1874) provided a significant additional incentive by reducing the term of military service in direct proportion to one's education. Institutions for women's secondary education also expanded dramatically beginning in the second half of the nineteenth century; by 1914, the women's gymnasiums had approximately 40,805 Jewish students. Moreover, trade and artisan schools for both men and women gained popularity among the Jews and showed a similar pattern of geometric growth.

The records of educational institutions preserve valuable information about family members who attended a state or private school. The richness of such files is evident from the records of Jewish students in the Moscow and Odessa women's gymnasiums: (1) applications from prospective students, providing basic biographical data—name, place and date of birth, and names and social status of parents; (2) a short essay of the student's intentions and plans; and (3) a small photograph (not present in all files). Most archival collections also include the by-laws of the school and information about the curriculum, which can shed light on the goals of the instructors. If the school records are well-preserved, the collection may also contain student grades, disciplinary files, and the service records of faculty (including Jewish teachers). A sample report card of Leya Fuksman from Korostyshev lists the courses she took (such as history, science, calligraphy, drawing and other classes) as well as her final marks.

Where can one find these records? First see Chapter 12 of this book. Also, some of the private Jewish schools are listed

clothing. Conflicts between competitors also ended up in court. For instance, Hersh Mermilshtein, a tailor, lodged a complaint against Khaya Laiman, a seamstress, on the grounds that she had opened her own store without first obtaining permission from the state artisan board.

Minor civil cases involving Jewish traders and small business owners revolved around such matters as fraudulent promissory notes, unpaid debts, improper sales, and property claims (*e.g.*, the case of Tykman vs. Gersheingorn over the use of a forest under lesseeship). The oblast archives hold thousands upon thousands of such cases, especially in towns with a large Jewish population, such as Zhitomir and Odessa. These records—although serendipitous and difficult to search—can contain a gold mine of documents and data.

Finally, the criminal courts prosecuted Jews for a variety of offenses ranging from petty crime (*e.g.*, theft, false scales and the production and sale of moonshine) to more serious crimes like homicide and rape. Some of these "crimes" would hardly fit in any modern classification but were specific to the Russian Empire—such as vagrancy or lack of valid documents, an offense regarded as important and treated severely by the tsarist government. Another offense was alleged self-mutilation (*chlenovreditelstvo*), prosecuted by the state as an attempt to avoid military conscription. This desperate act was not uncommon among religious Jews, who lived in dread of forced conversion in the tsarist military. If the long list of files in the Zhitomir criminal court is any indicator, such cases were anything but rare. In 1880, for example, the state brought a case against Iosi Gershkovich Bronshtein from the village of Kodin (Volynhia Province), alleging that he had willfully injured his eye to escape

16

in Dmitrii Elyashevich's guide (see p. 561), but by no means is his list complete. One must also look in the collection of each educational district or the Chancellery of the Administrator of . . . School District (*Kantseliariya popechiteliia… uchebnogo okruga*). In principle, one should search for educational records in the oblast archive closest to the town where the family members resided.

Administrative Records

Administrative records relevant to Jewish genealogical research consist—first and foremost—of documents filed by Jews at various government offices. These consist of petitions to the general-governor about matters that could not be satisfactorily resolved by a local institution and records of the state rabbinate elections.

The general-governor received letters from Jews petitioning for a revision of metrical books. These letters address mistakes made by the state rabbi in the spelling of names, birth dates and the omission of entries. Unfortunately, such Jewish files are scattered throughout various administrative fondy and may take time to find; still, they can be valuable for locating "missing relatives." For instance,

the State Archive of Kiev Oblast holds numerous revision letters, including a 72-page file about the mistakes made by the state rabbi of Kiev in 1899, along with petitions from Jews demanding corrections in their registrations.

The archival collections of the general-governor also contain important files on personal matters that the *beit din*, state courts, or police authorities had been unable to resolve. An example from the State Archive of Kiev Oblast concerns Vera Portugalov of Poltava Province, who appealed to the general-governor of Kiev for assistance in locating her husband: "Four months ago, my husband, Avraham Portugalov, deserted me and my children in the town of Lubny, and we have not received any word of his location or money to support myself and my children." She had heard rumors that her husband was living on a street in Kiev called Malaya Vasilkovskaya, without a passport, and asked that the police assist in locating him and bring him to accountability. Other Jewish women petitioned the general-governor of Kiev for assistance and intercession in a broad variety of cases involving kidnapped sons in the tsarist army, innocent husbands incarcerated in prison, abuse by police and a plethora of other personal matters.

Finally, the records of the state rabbinate also provide useful information about religious organizations and politics in Ukrainian towns. As a rule, the male members of each prayer house and synagogue (the franchise normally being restricted to males over age 25) elected 10 delegates, who in turn cast votes to choose the state rabbi. Sholom Aleichem, who once served as the state rabbi of Kiev, described the procedures as follows: "Every three years, a proclamation is sent to us: 'Na osnovanii predpisaniya…' ['On the basis of the order…']. Or, as we would say: Your Lord, the Governor, orders you to come together in the synagogue, poor little Jews, and pick out a rabbiner for yourself…. Then the campaign begins. Candidates, hot discussions, brandy, maybe even a bribe or two…. That was life!"[9]

Researchers who are fortunate enough to find their relatives on these lists will not only learn what prayer house they belonged to (*i.e.*, prayer houses of the butchers, tailors, shoemakers or the Hasidic *kloiz* of a certain rebbe), but also the names of other families with whom they may have been closely associated. Moreover, these records indicate the prices for registration reached after extensive negotiations between the new state rabbi and town residents.

As this overview of archival materials suggests, the opportunities for genealogical research in Ukraine are immense and exciting. Numerous registration records, even for small towns, have remained intact despite the destructive legacy of war on Ukrainian soil. In addition, researchers should not overlook the rich store of materials in collections bequeathed by the state courts, schools and various administrative institutions. The latter files, moreover, are not mere lists of names but contain a wealth of detail that can greatly complement family memories and help reconstruct life and relations in the Ukrainian shtetl.

Diploma from a school in Rovno, dated 1933, issued to Chaja-Frejda Finkielsztejn, born in 1914

Key Russian Terms for Genealogical Research

archival notations:

fond, fondy or **fonds** (collection, collections; record group[s])

opis, opisi (inventory, inventories, subdivisions of the collection)

delo, dela (file, files)

list, listy (folio, folios)

administrative or geographic divisions in Imperial Russia:

guberniya (province); **uezd** (district); **volost** (township) or **gorod** (town)

administrative or geographic divisions in the Soviet Union and in Russia:

oblast (province or district); **raion** (region); **gorod** (town)

duma (a representative council in Russia; Russian legislature)

Evrei (Jew)

evreiskaya sinagoga (Jewish synagogue)

gubernskaya kazennaya palata (provincial or guberniya Office of the Treasury)

metricheskie knigi (metrical books/registers of births, deaths, marriages and divorces)

molitvennaya doma (prayer house)

podatnye spiski (poll-tax lists)

posemeinyi spisok (family register)

putevoditeli (published archival guides to fonds and collections)

revizskie skazki (poll-tax census)

soslovie (social estate)

meshchanstvo (petty townspeople)

kupechnestvo (merchant)

remeslennik (artisan, often included with the **meshchanstvo**)

pochetnoe grazhanstvo (honorary citizen)

zemledelets (agriculturalist)

ZAGS Archive or Department of ZAGS (Otdel Zapisi Aktov Grazhdanskogo Sostoyaniya): where vital records are registered, usually located in the local town hall or mayor's office

Notes

[1] Patricia Kennedy Grimsted, "Archives in Ukraine," on the Archeo Bibliobase Web site: <http://www.sabre.org/huri/abbukr/>. See also Patricia K. Grimsted, *Archives and Manuscript Repositories in the USSR* (Princeton, NJ: Princeton University Press, 1988).

[2] Jacob Goldberg, "Die Ehe bei den Juden Polens im 18 Jahrhundert," *Jahrbücher für Geschichte Osteuropas*, 31 (1983): pp. 483–515.

[3] Sholom Aleichem, "Tit for Tat," in *The Old Country*, trans. by Julius and Frances Butwin (New York: Crown Publishers, 1946), p. 200.

[4] Azriel Shochat, *Mosad 'ha rabanut mi-ta'am' be-Rusyah* (Haifa: University of Haifa, 1975), p. 9.

[5] L.M. Aizenberg, "Ob ispravlenii dopushchennykh v evreiskikh metricheskikh knigakh oshibok," *Evreiskii mir* 14–15 (1911): pp. 42–43.

[6] Peter Czap, Jr., "Marriage and the Peasant Joint Family in the Era of Serfdom," in David Ransel, ed., *The Family in Imperial Russia: New Lines of Historical Research* (Urbana: University of Illinois Press, 1978), p. 121.

[7] Paul R. Mendes-Flohr and Jehuda Reinharz, *The Jew in the Modern World* (Oxford: Oxford University Press, 1980), p. 304.

[8] Michael Stanislawski, *Tsar Nicholas and the Jews. The Transformation of Jewish Society in Russia* (Philadelphia: Jewish Publication Society, 1983), p. 74.

[9] Sholom Aleichem, "Tit for Tat," in *The Old Country*, p. 200.

ChaeRan Y. Freeze is an assistant professor of East European Jewish History at Brandeis University and an associate at the International Research Institute on Jewish Women. Since 1993, she has worked in the central, provincial and city archives in Moscow, St. Petersburg, Kiev, Kharkov, Odessa, Zhitomir, Lvov, Vilnius and Kaunas. Professor Freeze is currently preparing for publication a book on the history of Jewish marriages and divorces in Tsarist Russia.

Editor's Note: This article is revised and adapted from an article that appeared in *Avotaynu*, vol. 13, no. 1 (Spring 1997): pp. 6–11.

▌ Remains of devastated Jewish cemetery in Zborov, 1998

18

Editor's Note: The following words appear on the subscription form of the *Kyiv Post*: "Those interested may well ask: how do you spell the name of this city? Kiev or Kyiv? The issue of how to spell the name of this city is not fully resolved, with linguists, historians, traditionalists, Ukrainian nationalists, Russophiles, the Ukrainian Diaspora, legalists and many other parties weighing in. At present in Ukraine, both spellings are in use; however, the national government has stated, in legislation, its preference for Kyiv."

РЕВИЗСКАЯ СКАЗКА

РЕВИЗСКАЯ СКАЗКА

(Handwritten Russian census table, 1859 — Revizskaya Skazka)

Итого мужескаго пола на лицо 19

Итого женскаго пола на лицо

❚ Revizskaya Skazka (list of inhabitants), 1859, living in Khotin. No. 45/33 is the family of Duvid Shteinberg, with five generations and 22 names.　　19

Editor's Note: *Below is a translation of a portion of the original document (highlighted above). It has been reformatted for clarification; years of birth were determined by subtracting the age listed above (in the right column on both pages) from the year of census, 1859.*

MALES	FEMALES
Duvid Shteinberg (son of Leib), born 1795–died 1853	
his wife:	**Dvoira** (daughter of Ios), born 1802
his sons: #1 **Mekhel**, born 1818	
his wife:	Genya, born 1821
his sons: Volko, born 1835	
his wife:	Khaya, born 1832
his daughter:	Tsirlya, born 1857
his son: Yankel, born 1858	
Itsko, born 1840	
Shlioma, born 1846	
Ios, born 1855	
his daughters:	Tsirlya, married
	Leya, married
	Merka, born 1849
#2 **Shaya**, born 1826	
his daughter (from first wife):	Khaya, born 1855
his wife #2:	Basya, born 1819
#3 **Moshko**, born 1843	
his daughters:	**Golda**, married
	Chantsya, married

18

הועד הפועל של ההסתדרות הציונית הארצית בלבוב.
Egzekutywa Krajowej Organizacji Sjonistycznej we Lwowie.

Lwów, dnia 15. października 1934.

Kwestjonarjusz — שאלון

Miejscowość *Skała 72br* powiat *Borszczów* wojew. *Tarnopolskie*
Ilość mieszkańców ogółem *5200* ilość mieszkańców żyd. *1700*
Dzień targowy *środa każdego tyg.* Odległość stacji kolejowej od miasta *½ km*
Czy ktoś z towarzyszy kierujących posiada telefon i jaki numer *członek Kom. lok.*
lov. B. Frieder Tel. № 12.

I. Sprawy organizacyjne

Czy istnieje u Was komitet lokalny *tak*

Kiedy było ostatnie Walne Zgromadzenie Towarzyszy na którem wybrano komitet lokalny

Wyliczyć imiennie członków Komitetu lokalnego, zapodać jaki referat prowadzi i przy zastępcach młodzieży dodać do jakiej organizacji młodzieżowej należy

Czy istnieje u Was ugrupowanie młodzieży ogólno sjonist. zapodać ilość członków każdego ugrupowania):
Achwa *2.-* Hanoar Hazioni *48.-* H. A. Z.

Czy istnieją w Waszem mieście inne ugrupowania młodzieży (zapodać jakie i ewent ilość członków)

Ile kart rejestracyjnych wykupiła każda z istniejących u Was organizacji młodzieży ogólno sjonistycznej):
Achwa *2.-* Hanoar Hazioni *11.-* H. A. Z.

II. Praca palestyńska

Czy istnieje u Was komisja K. K. L. *tak* i ilu członków *12.-*
Jaki jest udział ogólnych sjonistów w składzie komisji *5 os.*

Jaki jest ogólny kontyngent miasta na rzecz K. K. L. za rok 5694 i ile z tego zebrali ogólni sjoniści

Jaki jest skład prezydjum komisji K. K. L. wyliczyć imiennie i podać przynależność partyjną

Czy istnieje u Was komitet Keren Hajesod
Jak pracuje komitet Keren Hajesod
Kto kieruje pracą K. H. (wyliczyć imiennie, zapodać przynależność partyjną)

Czy istnieje u Was komitet Ezry *mąż zaufania*
Kto kieruje komitetem Ezry (wyliczyć imiennie, zapodać przynależność partyjną)

Ile zebrano w r. 5694 na Ezrę wogóle i ile z tego zebrali ogólni sjoniści *40.-*

Co uczyniono z zebranemi pieniędzmi Ezry *odesłano do centrali.*

III. Praca kulturalna

Czy istnieje w Waszem mieście szkoła hebr. *tak*
Pod czyją egidą jest ta szkoła *og. sjon.*
Ile jest kursów (klas, oddziałów) *5* ile uczniów razem *78.-*
Ile nauczycieli udziela nauki *1.-*
Zapodać nazwiska nauczycieli i ich przynależność partyjną

Jakie są dochody szkoły (miesięcznie) *275 zł.-*
Czy szkoła korzysta z subwencji od kogo i w jakiej wysokości

Jeśli niema szkoły hebr. podać dlaczego

Czy istnieje u Was bibljoteka *tak* w czyim zarządzie
Ile tomów liczy ogółem *1812* ile hebr. *452* ile żyd. *733* ile innych

IV. Praca organizacji kobiet żyd.

Czy istnieje w Waszem mieście organizacja sjonistyczna kobiet żyd. (Koło Kobiet Żydowskich. WIZO lub tp.)

Ile członkiń liczy każda z tych organizacji

Czy dana organizacja kobiet posiada kierunek partyjny jeśli tak zapodać jaki

Kto kieruje organizacjami kobiet (wyliczyć imiennie i zapodać ewent. przynależność partyjną

Na czyj adres należy się zwracać w sprawach organizacji kobiet

V. Cionim Baalej Mikcoa

Czy istnieje w Waszej miejscowości grupa C. B. M.
Ilu liczy członków Kto kieruje grupą prezes
sekretarz
Czy istnieje jako stowarzyszenie odrębne, czy jako sekcja przy organizacji sjonistycznej

Jaką pracę kulturalną prowadzi grupa C. B. M.

VI. Sprawy polityczne

Czy istnieje u Was zarząd Gminy Żyd. wybrany (czy komisarjat) *wybrany*

Kiedy odbyły się wybory *w 1932 r.* Ogólna ilość radnych *Osk. Feuerach*
Czy sjoniści zasiadają w Radzie względnie Zarządzie gminy żyd. *tak*
Ilu jest sjonistów *wszyscy* Ilu z tego ogólnych sjonistów
wyliczyć imiennie ogólno sjonistycznych radnych

Czy istnieje u Was wybrana rada miejska (czy komisarjat) *wybrana*
Kiedy odbyły się wybory *w grudniu 1933 r.* Ilość radnych miejsk. ogółem *16.-*
Ilu Żydów *3.-* Ilu Polaków *9.-* Ilu Ukraińców *4.-*
Z żyd. radnych ilu jest sjonistów i do jakiej frakcji należą *2 og. sjon.*
Wymienić imiennie radnych miejskich ogólnych sjonistów

VII. Sprawy gospodarcze.

Czy istnieje u Was Stowarzyszenie Kupców Żyd. *nie.-*
Ilu liczy członków Ilu w tem sjonistów
Ilu sympatyków Ilu przeciwników Ilu ogóln. sjon.
Kto kieruje Stow. kupców (zapod. imiennie i przynależność partyjną)

Czy istnieje u Was „Jad Charuzim" wzgl. podobna organizacja rzemieślników żyd.

Ilu liczy członków Ilu w tem naszych towarzyszy i sympatyków

Kto kieruje Stow. „Jad Charuzim"
(imiennie i przynależność part.)

Czy istnieje u Was spółdzielnia kredytowa społeczna *tak*
Do jakiego Związku Rewizyjnego należy
Pod czyim zarządem pozostaje (zapodać imiennie i przynależn. part.)

Czy istnieje u Was Kasa „Gmiluth Chesed" *tak*
Kto kieruje kasą imiennie i przynależność. part.

VIII. Ogólne

Ogólne uwagi o stanie organizacji ogólno sjonist. w Waszem mieście:

Four-page questionnaire, dated 1934, submitted by the National Executive Committee of the General Zionist Organization in Lvov to its branch office in Skala. The response contains important data about the Jewish community, including population figures (5,200, total; 1,700 Jews); names and functions of the 12 members of the branch leadership; and data on schools, the library (1,812 books), city council (16 members, three of them Jews), and the Hebrew school (78 children).

Rabbi Moishe Leib Kolesnik of Ivano-Frankovsk, at home with his library, 1998

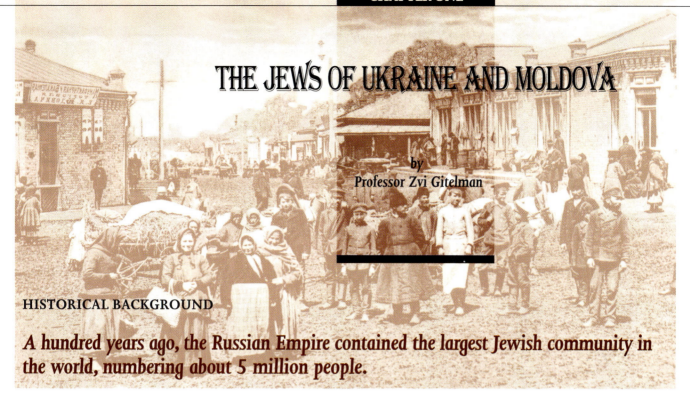

THE JEWS OF UKRAINE AND MOLDOVA

by
Professor Zvi Gitelman

HISTORICAL BACKGROUND

A hundred years ago, the Russian Empire contained the largest Jewish community in the world, numbering about 5 million people.

More than 40 percent—2 million of them—lived in Ukraine and Bessarabia (the latter territory was subsequently divided between the present-day Ukraine and Moldova; here, for ease of discussion, we use the terms "Bessarabia" and "Moldova" interchangeably). Some 1.8 million lived in Ukraine (west of the Dniepr River) and in Bessarabia, and 387,000 made their homes in Ukraine (east of the Dniepr), including Crimea. Thousands of others lived in what was called Eastern Galicia—now Western Ukraine.

Today the Jewish population of those areas is much reduced, due to the cumulative and devastating impacts of World War I, the 1917 Russian Revolution, World War II and the Holocaust, massive emigration since the 1970s, and a natural decrease resulting from a very low birth rate and a high mortality rate.

When World War II began, there were about 1.5 million Jews in Ukraine—which had been made a constituent republic of the Soviet Union in 1922. In 1970, the Soviet census counted about 777,000 Jews in Ukraine and 98,000 in Moldavia (now independent Moldova, but then also a part of the Soviet Union). By January 1989, when the Soviet Union conducted its last census, Ukraine was home to only about 486,000 Jews (constituting 35 percent of Soviet Jewry), and Moldavia had 65,800 (4.5 percent of Soviet Jewry).

In 1989, a new wave of massive Jewish emigration began. From 1989 to 1998, more than 222,000 Ukrainian Jews went to Israel, and about 96,700 to the United States. Some 44,000 Jews left Moldavia for Israel during that period, while a far smaller number went to the United States. According to some demographers, today about 200,000 Jews reside in Ukraine and 35,000 to 40,000 in Moldova. (Estimates vary considerably, however, depending upon the definition of the word *Jew*.)

SHIFTING SOVEREIGNTIES

Nearly a thousand years ago, Moldova was populated by a Romanian-speaking people, descended from Romans, who intermarried with the indigenous Dacians. A principality was established in the territory in the fourteenth century, but it did not last long. Moldova then became a tributary state of the Ottoman Empire, which lost parts of it to the Russian Empire in the eighteenth and nineteenth centuries.

After the 1917 Russian Revolution, part of Moldova lay within the borders of Romania. Eventually part of it became the Autonomous Soviet Socialist Republic (SSR) of Moldavia, a unit within the larger Ukrainian Soviet Socialist Republic. In August 1940, as Eastern Europe was being carved up between the Germans and the Soviets, Bessarabia—the historic designation of the region between the Prut and Dniester Rivers—was seized by the Soviet Union and was joined with the Autonomous SSR of Moldavia to form the Soviet Socialist Republic of Moldavia. That republic, occupied by Nazi Germany and its allies from July 1941 until August 1944, was one of the smallest republics in the Soviet Union. When the latter collapsed in late 1991, the Soviet Moldavia became independent Moldova.

JEWS IN BESSARABIA/MOLDOVA

Jews have been living in Bessarabia/Moldova since the end of the fourteenth century. Sephardi merchants traded there in the fifteenth century, and later, Polish-Jewish merchants were also active in the region. About 20,000 Jews lived in Moldova by 1812, many engaged in commerce and liquor distilling. By 1897, the Jewish population had expanded to 228,620, constituting about one-third of the urban population. Yet, unlike in other regions of the Russian Empire, thousands of Jews in Bessarabia were engaged in agriculture.

Bessarabian Jews were subjected to pogroms in 1870, in 1903 and again in 1905–1906, but they nevertheless were culturally and religiously active. The major religious, intellectual and political movements of modern Jewry made their mark in Bessarabia, as they did in Ukraine. Among the Hasidic groups in Bessarabia were the Ruzhin dynasty and various branches of the Twersky Hasidic family, which originated in Ukraine. The Hovevei Zion ("Lovers of Zion") were active in Bessarabia in the latter part of the nineteenth century, as were Hebrew and Yiddish poets and playwrights. By 1920, when the area was under Romanian rule, it was estimated that there were 267,000 Jews in Bessarabia. In the mid-1930s, about 3,000 Jewish families were still farming, although they were hard hit by droughts, the European (and worldwide) economic depression and separation from Russian markets.

Thus, at various times the Jews of Bessarabia have been Moldavian, Ottoman, Russian, Romanian, Soviet, and Moldovan subjects. Yet, since the Jews mostly have conceived of themselves as ethnically neither Russian, Romanian nor Moldavian—and non-Jews have shared this perception—they have at all times been outsiders in some sense.

Bessarabia in 1897, Showing Total Jewish Population According to Districts　　**Map 2**

Bessarabia has at times been ethnically very mixed. Its inhabitants have included Russians, Romanians, Turks, Roma (Gypsies), Ukrainians, Jews, Greeks, Bulgarians and others. Most Jews have been loyal to the state in which they lived, whatever its name and character, but they have been acutely aware of the ethnic diversity surrounding them and of competing claims to the region.

JEWS IN MULTIETHNIC UKRAINE

As in Bessarabia/Moldova, Jews in Ukraine have been citizens of different states over the centuries. A Jew born in Lemberg in 1915 would have been a citizen of Austro-Hungary. However, he or she would have been a Polish citizen in Lwów after 1918, a Soviet citizen in Lvov after 1939, and a resident of Lviv and a citizen of Ukraine after 1991.

While most of Ukraine historically was not as ethnically complicated as Bessarabia, the territory itself was divided between Tsarist Russia and the Austro-Hungarian Empire, and later between Poland and the Soviet Union. Ukrainians and Russians were the major ethnic groups, but there were also substantial numbers of Poles, Germans, Magyars, Greeks, Armenians, Romanians and others. While in Bessarabia conflicts among states were compounded by overt social, cultural and political tensions among Romanians, Russians, Ukrainians and others, in Ukraine the political struggle was mainly among Russians, Poles and Ukrainians. There were other ethnic tensions in the region as well. Some of these crystallized into well-organized political movements and parties. Jews thus found themselves in a familiar situation, tugged in different directions by contending nationalities— each competing for Jewish support but also suspecting that the Jews' allegiance lay with its competitors. As in the Czech lands (Bohemia and Moravia), Transylvania, and the Baltic region, Jews in Ukraine have historically tended to identify more with the ruling power and the culturally dominant nation.

THE JEWISH POPULATION IN UKRAINE

Jews have lived in the territory of Ukraine probably since around the tenth century, long before a Ukrainian nation emerged. By the end of the 1500s, there were about 45,000 Jews in the regions now constituting Ukraine. Despite pogroms such as the massacres of 1648 (discussed below), the Jewish population grew rapidly. By the mid-1800s, there were almost 600,000 Jews in the parts of Ukraine under Russian rule.

At the turn of the twentieth century, more than one-third of the Jews in western and central Ukraine lived in towns and shtetlach where they formed an absolute majority. Another fifth or so lived in places where they comprised nearly half of the population. Jews constituted nearly one-third of Ukraine's urban population, putting them in close contact with the largely Russian city dwellers but also, as traders and merchants, with the overwhelmingly Ukrainian peasantry. Though Jews were generally barred from owning land in Ukraine, there were Jewish farmers in some areas, as from time to time the tsars would give Jews lands in territories they wanted to colonize.

In the aftermath of World War I and the Russian Revolution, Ukraine was divided between independent Poland and the emerging Soviet Union. A substantial number of Ukrainian Jews came under Polish rule in 1918, but a far larger group, more than 1.5 million, lived in what would become the Ukrainian Soviet Socialist Republic. The Soviet government encouraged Jewish agricultural settlement in the 1920s. Some Jewish collective farms survived in Ukraine and Crimea, as well as in Belorussia (now the Republic of Belarus), until the German invasion of the Soviet Union in 1941.

ECONOMICS AND ETHNICITY

Beginning in the sixteenth century, Jews managed estates worked by Ukrainian peasants for Polish landowners. Jews were also heavily involved in producing and selling alcoholic beverages, small-scale manufacturing, the sugar-beet industry, crafts and commerce. As managers of estates, Jews became the immediate objects of peasant resentment of landowners. When peasants rose against the often-absentee landowners, Jews were massacred, as in 1648–1649, when perhaps 100,000 were killed, and in the eighteenth century, during the Haidamak uprisings. The 1648 rebellion against the Polish landlords set a pattern to be repeated over the course of the following centuries: Ukrainians rebelled against their non-Ukrainian oppressors and attacked the Jews as well, because they saw Jews as allies of their oppressors.

The statue of Bohdan Khmelnitsky (the leader of the 1648 uprising) in one of Kiev's main squares represents to Ukrainians national pride and the struggle for independence. To Jews, it stands for Ukrainian anti-Semitism and the massacre of perhaps as many as 100,000 of their brethren. To the Soviets, it symbolized the rising of exploited masses against their class enemies.

THE FLOURISHING OF JEWISH CULTURE

Despite—or perhaps because of—these travails, Jews in Ukraine were remarkably creative. Hasidism first appeared in the eighteenth century in the Podolia Province of Ukraine. Several cities in Ukraine—Slavuta, Zhitomir and, later, Kiev—became important centers of Jewish publishing. The Hibat Zion ("Lovers of Zion") movement and the Bilu group (the first to emigrate to Palestine for Zionist political reasons), emerged in Ukraine. Odessa, a Black Sea port city that developed rapidly and attracted people of many nationalities, became a center of Haskalah ("Enlightenment"), Zionism, Hebrew and Yiddish literature, and traditional Jewish learning, as well as Jewish commerce and industry. Yiddish theater and modernist Yiddish literature flourished in Ukraine well into the Soviet period, and many early Israeli writers in Hebrew were born and educated in Ukraine.

POGROMS

The pogroms of 1881–1882 were carried out mainly in Ukraine. In 1903, there was an infamous pogrom in Kishinev, the capital of contemporary Moldova, and there were more pogroms in 1905–1906, during the Russo–Japanese War and an abortive Russian revolution. However, it was in 1918–1921, during the Civil War between the Bolsheviks and their opponents, that the most massive pogroms since the seventeenth century were perpetrated. Conservative estimates are that 35,000 Jews were killed and 100,000 left homeless when the White (anti-Bolshevik) and Ukrainian nationalist armies, as well as local bands, attacked Jews, whom they saw as favoring the Bolsheviks or the Poles and Russians over the Ukrainians. Though the short-lived Ukrainian government (Central Rada) granted Jews national autonomy and a ministry for Jewish affairs, the pogroms put an end to Ukrainian–Jewish political cooperation and reinforced the

Postcard view of a Jewish cemetery in Russia following a pogrom where tombstones were toppled and destroyed, c. 1917   22

image of Ukrainians as anti-Semitic. The pattern of the 1648 uprising was repeated as Jews were caught among the Whites, Reds, Ukrainian nationalists, anarchists and roving bands (whose ideology was largely to plunder).

Though Jews were accused of being Bolshevik sympathizers, hostile to Ukrainian independence, it was precisely the pogroms that drove them into the Red Army in self-defense, and then into Soviet posts and the Communist Party. Contrary to popular belief, Bolshevism was unpopular among Jews until the pogroms began—there were fewer than 1,000 Jewish Bolsheviks at the time of the 1917 Russian Revolution. The pogroms left the Jews with no alternative but the Soviet government, because most of its opponents attacked them.

Tragically, within 20 years, the pattern was repeated. The myth of "Judaeo-Communism" was widely believed in Poland, which ruled Western Ukraine until 1939. When some Western Ukrainians perceived Jews as welcoming the Soviet takeover from Poland in 1939, they took murderous revenge in Lwów (later Lvov and now Lviv) and other places when Soviet forces retreated in 1941. The extent and nature of collaboration by some Ukrainians with the Nazis in the mass murder of Jews is

still a contentious and highly sensitive issue, and only in recent years has it begun to be aired, though mostly outside Ukraine.

THE EMERGENCE OF A UKRAINIAN-JEWISH IDENTITY

Most Jews seem not to have been highly conscious of Ukraine as a distinct political entity and of Ukrainians as a distinct people. The Jews' tendency to identify with rulers and upper classes more than with the peasantry may explain why Ukraine is absent from Yiddish rhetoric and "Jewish geography" until after the 1917 Russian Revolution. Sholom Aleichem, the great Yiddish writer born in Ukraine in 1859, uses a good deal of Ukrainian in his works and portrays clearly Ukrainian characters, but my impression is that he does not refer explicitly to "Ukraine" or "Ukrainians." Ukrainians themselves did not generally refer to themselves as such—they used the term "Ruthenians"—and Russians referred to them contemptuously or patronizingly as "Little Russians" until well into the nineteenth century. So it is not surprising that the "Jewish map" of Eastern Europe includes Poland, "Liteh" (roughly, present-day Lithuania, northeastern Poland and Belarus) and

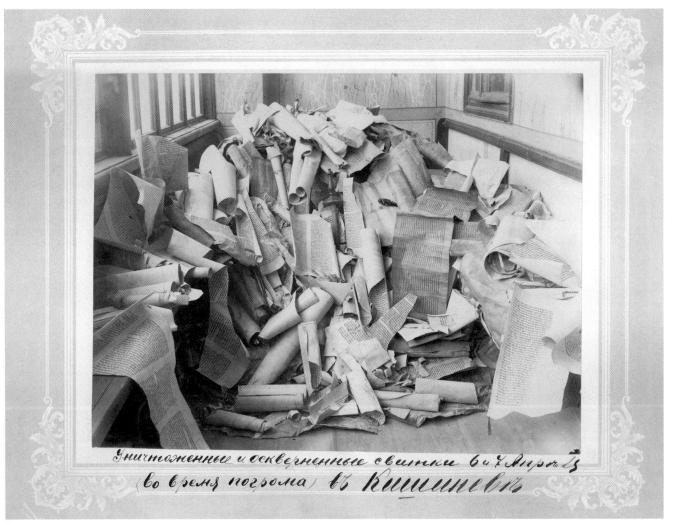

Уничтоженные и оскверненные свитки 6 и 7 Апрѣ (во время погрома) въ Кишиневѣ

▌ *Torahs defiled and destroyed in the Kishinev Pogrom, April 6–7, 1903*

23

Galicia, but not "Ukraine." Prayer books describe their contents as being "according to the rituals of Polin, Liteh, Reisin [roughly, parts of Belarus and Western Ukraine] and Zamut [an area in Lithuania]." But no prayer book or other religious text mentions the "rituals of Ukraine."

Even "Ukrainian Jewish history" as such began to be written only recently. Since Ukraine was independent only very briefly and was for most of its history part of Polish-Lithuanian, Austro-Hungarian, Russian, Polish or Soviet states, Jews treated Ukraine as a vague entity with no defining characteristics. The history of Jews in Ukraine was generally treated as part of the history of Russian or Polish Jewry. Jews who lived in Ukraine were regarded as *Rusishe Yidn*, not as *Ukrainishe Yidn*, and they so regarded themselves. When Jews emigrated to the United States from Ukraine before 1918, they were classified as "Russian."

A second reason why a Ukrainian-Jewish identity did not emerge until recently is that Jews felt no strong affinity to Ukrainians, a people who defined themselves rather late in history in any case. What exactly constituted Ukraine was by no means clear even to Ukrainians. Novorossiya (south-central/southeastern Ukraine) was not included in their mental map until quite late. Russians and Poles, though largely peasants like Ukrainians, had urban populations and high, literary cultures. Ukrainians were seen as exclusively peasants, quite an accurate perception until after World War I. Of course, most Jews were not concerned with whether Ukrainians had their Tolstoys and Pushkins, Mickiewiczes and Slowackis, though this might have been important to the *maskilim* ("enlightened" Jews), but all could appreciate the fact that Russians and Poles owned the land and wielded political power, whereas Ukrainians did not.

The Ukrainian language was generally referred to by Jews as *goyish* (Gentile), as were languages like Lithuanian and Belorussian. Dominant languages such as Polish, German and Russian were called by their proper names, but languages spoken by peasants were almost never systematically studied by Jews (and until relatively recently not even by their native speakers). Jews picked up these languages in the marketplace or on the street and thought of them simply as *goyish*, or "peasant talk." (It might also be noted that until little over a century ago, Jews commonly referred to their own language not as Yiddish but as *zhargon*.)

THE JEWS OF UKRAINE TODAY

Today, Jews in Ukraine still identify more with Russians and Russian culture than with Ukrainians and their culture. In the 1989 Soviet census, only 2 percent of Jews living in Ukraine named Ukrainian as their mother tongue, whereas 91 percent named Russian, and the rest, Yiddish. (Many Jews understand and speak Ukrainian but consider Russian their mother tongue.) Emigration from Ukraine has been proportionally greater than from Russia, but this may be primarily because the economic situation in Ukraine has been perceived as worse—at least until the collapse of the Russian economy in 1998.

Ukrainian Jews do not perceive themselves to be in a dangerous, hostile environment, but Russian Jews are far more closely tied to Russians and their culture than Ukrainian Jews are to Ukrainians and their culture. In a survey of 3,300 Jews taken in 1997, whereas 41 percent of Russian Jews said that the culture of "another" (not Jewish) people was closest to them—they presumably meant Russian culture for the most part—only 27 percent of Ukrainian Jews said so, and they seemed to have in mind Russian rather than Ukrainian culture. Ukrainian Jews see themselves as part of the Russian cultural community in Ukraine and seem to have weaker attachments to a Ukrainian state, though many profess to love the land and its peoples. They have been more willing to leave than their compatriots in Russia, who have actually viewed their situation more pessimistically but have found it more difficult to tear themselves away from a people and a culture to which they are closely tied.

Emigration from Ukraine is being driven not by anti-Semitism but by strong family ties with a substantial Ukrainian-Jewish emigrant community and by an economic situation that, at least until 1998, has been perceived as worse than that in Russia, where more people saw positive future prospects. In a 1993 survey, nearly twice as many Ukrainian as Russian respondents said that "we live from payday to payday, often have to borrow in order to buy essential goods, and can save nothing." In 1997, only 19 percent of Russian respondents placed themselves in this category, whereas 44 percent of Ukrainians did. Future emigration will be determined, in part, by economic developments in Russia and Ukraine as well as by the situations in the potential host countries.

JEWISH CULTURE AND INSTITUTIONS IN UKRAINE AND MOLDOVA TODAY

At the end of the twentieth century in both Moldova and Ukraine, Jewish institutions have been re-created and Jewish communal life has been revived. Synagogue buildings have been returned to Jewish communities by governments; Jewish schools—full day, supplementary and Sunday—have been opened; Jewish newspapers and magazines are being published; and there are Jewish Studies programs in universities in Kiev, Lvov, Donetsk and other places in Ukraine and Moldova. Thousands of Jewish youngsters attend camps sponsored by local Jewish communities and by the Jewish Agency, foreign religious organizations and others. None of this activity was possible before 1989.

Yet while this re-creation of Jewish public life and renaissance of Jewish activities go on, thousands "vote with their feet" and leave Ukraine and Moldova, thereby weakening the revival of Jewish communities. Those who are most committed to some form of Jewish expression, and the youngest and perhaps most energetic people, are most heavily represented in the ongoing emigration. They take enormous talents as well as educational, vocational and demographic assets to Israel, the United States, Germany and other host countries, but in so doing they deprive their native lands of those very same assets. Reasonable people can differ over whether the paradox of Jewish revival coexisting with massive Jewish emigration is "good for the Jews" or not, but clearly the emigration has a direct and profound impact on prospects for the future of Jewish life in Ukraine and Moldova.

OPTIONS FOR JEWS WHO CHOOSE TO REMAIN

Four options seem to be available to those who will stay in Ukraine and Moldova. They can remain as permanent sojourners—that is, residents with a mixed, ill-defined Russian/Jewish/Ukrainian or Moldovan identity, however contradictory and uncomfortable that status might be. Or they can build on their acculturation into Russian culture and become part of the russophone, and perhaps even Russian, communities, themselves marginalized in some of the successor states to the Soviet Union. (Russians and russophones, the ruling class in the Soviet Union, now see themselves as second-class citizens in the successor states.) Third, Jews can acculturate again, but this time to Ukrainian or Moldovan culture. Finally, they can preserve what was a state-imposed Jewish identity but fill that empty form with positive cultural and/or religious content and "integrate" as a national minority into a multiethnic, "civic" Ukrainian or Moldovan state. Jews' choices will be influenced by geography (in which part of the country they live), age, friendships, attitudes regarding members of other nationalities and their cultures, the attitudes of others toward Jews and other variables.

The Jews of Ukraine and Moldova, along with others in the successor states to the old Russian Empire, have been at the center of some of the most dramatic events of modern history: two world wars, the Holocaust, revolutions, pogroms, political liberation, repression, the breakup of the Soviet Union and the establishment of independent states. Jews in these countries have gone through dizzyingly rapid changes in economic and social mobility. In just one century, Russian, Soviet and post-Soviet Jews have expanded the literature of Hebrew and Yiddish and made major contributions to Russian, Ukrainian, and Belorussian literature as well as to some of the other cultures of the area. When given the chance, they have contributed greatly to science and technology, scholarship and arts, industry, commerce, politics and popular culture.

For these achievements, they have been applauded and cursed, praised and envied. Jews themselves have disagreed profoundly about where and how to make their contributions.

Throughout most of the period, Jews have felt that their situation was abnormal, in need of improvement. While some have believed that this condition could not be changed, others have been determined to find ways of improving their situation, whether by finding a comprehensive solution to the problems of their countries or by devising a particular one for the problems of the Jews. Throughout the twentieth century, some Jews have sought to merge themselves into the larger society completely, either because they have seen little value in Jewish culture or because they have concluded that Jewishness is mostly a burden and the only way to escape from it is to cease being Jewish. Others have taken the opposite tack, affirming their Jewishness and rejecting societies and states that, in their view, have rejected them. Some have dedicated their lives to the countries of their birth, while others have rejected them and sought to build up other lands or simply to build better lives there. Whether in their native lands or in those to which they have emigrated, Jews have made enormous contributions to the economies, cultures and politics of many countries. Yet Jews and the peoples among whom they have lived have been locked into a tempestuous, intense relationship from which none of the parties has been able to free itself completely, nor, in many cases, resolve their differences. Thus the modern history of the Jews in Ukraine, Moldova and the other successor states to the Soviet Union is streaked with light and shadow. It is a story still unfolding, one likely to continue to evolve from multiple ambiguities and complex ambivalences on the part of everyone involved.

Zvi Gitelman is professor of political science, Tisch professor of Judaic Studies and director of the Frankel Center for Judaic Studies, all at the University of Michigan, Ann Arbor. He is author, editor or co-author of nine books on politics in the former Soviet Union and Eastern Europe and has published more than 80 articles in scholarly journals. Professor Gitelman's most recent book is *Bitter Legacy: Confronting the Holocaust in the Soviet Union* (Bloomington: Indiana University Press, 1997). He is currently working on Jewish identities in Russia and Ukraine and on oral histories of Soviet Jewish veterans of World War II.

Editor's Note: Parts of the foregoing article were adapted from the Introduction that originally appeared in Zvi Gitelman's *A Century of Ambivalence: The Jews of Russia and the Soviet Union, 1881 to the Present* (New York: Yivo Institute for Jewish Research, 1985) and are reproduced here with the permission of Yivo Institute for Jewish Research.

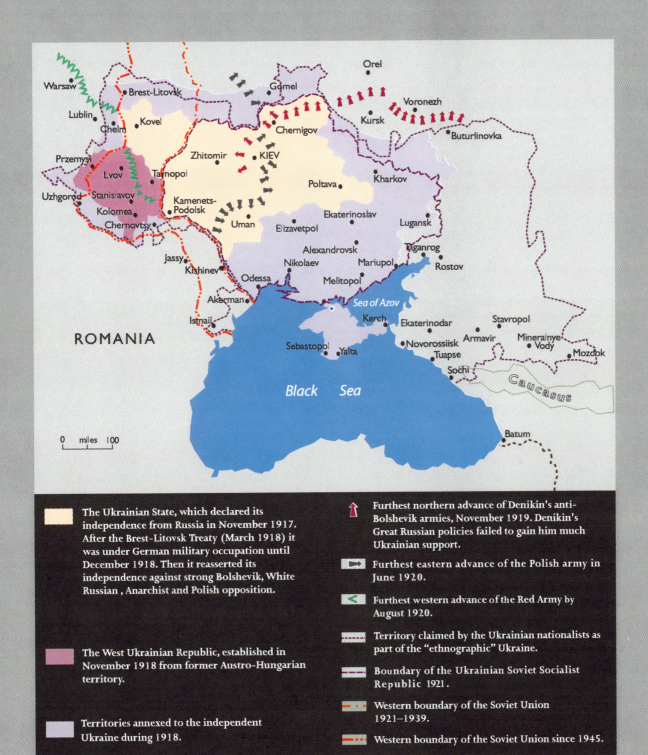

The Ukrainian State, which declared its independence from Russia in November 1917. After the Brest-Litovsk Treaty (March 1918) it was under German military occupation until December 1918. Then it reasserted its independence against strong Bolshevik, White Russian, Anarchist and Polish opposition.

The West Ukrainian Republic, established in November 1918 from former Austro-Hungarian territory.

Territories annexed to the independent Ukraine during 1918.

Furthest northern advance of Denikin's anti-Bolshevik armies, November 1919. Denikin's Great Russian policies failed to gain him much Ukrainian support.

Furthest eastern advance of the Polish army in June 1920.

Furthest western advance of the Red Army by August 1920.

Territory claimed by the Ukrainian nationalists as part of the "ethnographic" Ukraine.

Boundary of the Ukrainian Soviet Socialist Republic 1921.

Western boundary of the Soviet Union 1921–1939.

Western boundary of the Soviet Union since 1945.

Ukraine, 1917–1921

Map 3

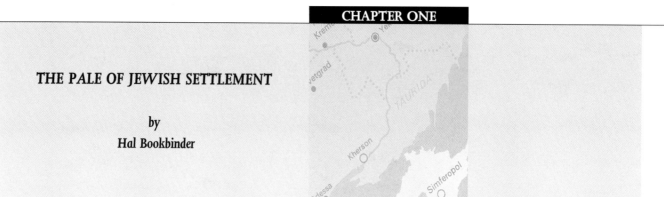

THE PALE OF JEWISH SETTLEMENT

by

Hal Bookbinder

The Pale of Jewish Settlement was the western area of the Russian Empire in which Jews were allowed to live. It began with the first partition of Poland in 1772 and survived until the beginning of World War I in 1917. This area is of special interest to Jews, as the vast majority of their ancestors lived there. This timeline provides a chronology of significant events related to the Pale. For further background, the reader may wish to refer to the *Encyclopedia Judaica* (New York: Macmillan, 1971–1972), Simon Dubnow's *History of the Jews in Russia and Poland from the Earliest Times Until the Present Day* (New York: Ktav, 1975), and Salo Baron's *The Russian Jew Under Tsars and Soviets*, 2nd ed. (New York: Macmillan, 1976).

TIMELINE OF THE PALE OF JEWISH SETTLEMENT (1770–1820)

1770 · 1780 · 1790 · 1800 · 1810 · 1820

1772: First partition of Poland. 27,000 Jews in Vitebsk (then Polotsk) and Mogilev are incorporated into Russia.

1791: Free movement is allowed only in Vitebsk, Mogilev, Yekaterinoslav, Kherson and Taurida (these last three provinces make up New Russia, and the government is interested in their colonization). Jewish merchants are no longer allowed to travel to Smolensk and Moscow.

1801: Paul I is killed; Alexander I becomes tsar.

1804: The study initiated by Paul is completed, and a decree is issued aiming to better integrate Jews into general society by causing them to use civil languages and dress. It also calls for the uprooting of all Jews from small villages to towns by 1807. Astrakhan and the Northern Caucasus are added to the Pale.

1774: The formerly Turkish areas of New Russia are added to the Empire. This area contains few Jews, mostly Karaite.

1793: Second partition. Minsk, Volhynia (then Izyaslav), and Podolia (then Bratslav), Kiev, Chernigov and Poltava (then Novgorod-Seversk) are added to the area in which Jews can reside. Russia now contains about 200,000 Jews.

1807: Uprooting is begun but then abandoned due to its economic impact and concerns about Napoleon. Napoleon creates the Grand Duchy of Warsaw and gives Russia the Bialystok area, which is incorporated into Grodno.

1786: A decree is issued limiting to one-third the number of town councilors in any town who can be Jewish. In practice, few Jews become councilors at all.

1795: Third partition. Grodno, Kovno and Vilna are added to the Pale. Russia now contains about one million Jews. Decrees are issued endeavoring to move Jews from villages to towns to restrict their movement.

1809: The Grand Duchy is expanded to include Western Galicia.

1812: Bessarabia is taken in an agreement with Napoleon on spheres of influence and added to the Pale.

1796: Tsar Catherine II (the Great) dies and Paul I becomes tsar. Paul initiates studies on how to deal with the Jews.

1815: The Grand Duchy of Warsaw is dissolved, with most of its territory incorporated into the Russian Empire as Congress Poland, comprised of 10 provinces. Technically, Poland and the Pale are separate entities whose Jews live under different rules.

1799: Famine ravages portions of the Pale. Jewish innkeepers are blamed, and many are dispossessed. Courland is added to the Pale.

1817: Alexander I issues a decree forbidding the unfounded spreading of blood libels. But such accusations continue to be made and pursued. Government efforts are initiated to get Jews to convert. Converts are promised land in New Russia. The effort fails and is abandoned in 1823.

■ *A distraught father tends to family members killed during a pogrom in Russia, c. 1917* 24

TIMELINE OF THE PALE OF JEWISH SETTLEMENT (1820–1870)

1820 **1830** **1840** **1850** **1860** **1870**

1820: Jews comprise 1.6 million of Russia's 46 million inhabitants.

1827: Jewish life in Kiev is severely circumscribed. In addition to a 25-year military obligation for draftees, the Cantonist program for Jewish youth is initiated. Under it, Jewish boys as young as 12 are taken away from the community to be educated in military schools and then to begin their 25 years of military service at age 18. Up to 60,000 Jewish males are impressed into this program between 1827 and 1856, when it is effectively ended. Many die from the harsh conditions, and many others convert to lessen their persecution.

1827–1856: Cantonist program inducts 60,000 Jewish males into the military.

1829: Courland is removed from the Pale.

1830: Poles rise in rebellion against tsarist rule. The rebellion is quickly put down, and there is little immediate impact on Polish Jews.

1835: A comprehensive decree concerning the Jews is promulgated. It bans settlement in border areas, small villages and some cities. It imposes travel restrictions, dress and language codes, and a minimum age at which Jews can marry. It also formalizes the Pale, specifically identifying what provinces make it up and removing Astrakhan and the Northern Caucasus from it. The Pale now consists of Belorussia (Minsk, Mogilev and Vitebsk), Bessarabia, Lithuania (Kovno, Grodno and Vilna), New Russia (Kherson, Taurida and Ekaterinoslav), and Ukraine (Chernigov, Kiev, Podolia, Poltava and Volhynia). Poland, which was not technically part of the Pale, consists of Kalisz, Kielce, Lomza, Lublin, Piotrikow, Plock, Radom, Siedlce, Suwalki and Warsaw.

1843: Jews are ordered expelled from 33 mile-wide western border areas of the Pale. This was modified in 1858 to exclude only Jews who had not previously resided in the border area.

1851: Jews comprise 2.4 million of Russia's 61 million inhabitants.

1855: Tsar Nicholas I dies and is succeeded by his son, Alexander II, who is favorably disposed toward the Jews and wishes them integrated into the Empire.

1856: The Cantonist program is suspended, although it remains on the books.

1855–1859: Schools and then universities are opened to Jews, and their participation is encouraged.

1859: Merchant members of the first estate are allowed to reside in the inner Russian provinces.

1861: A decree bans the conversion of Jewish children under age 14 without their parents' permission. University graduates and physicians with medical degrees are allowed to reside outside the Pale.

1865: Skilled craftsmen are allowed to reside outside the Pale, as long as their movement is approved by their home province and they remain gainfully employed.

1863: As a result of the Polish uprising in 1863, laws concerning the Jews of the Pale are extended to Jews of Congress Poland, giving them more freedom of movement, the right to own property and the right to testify in court on an equal footing.

1820–1870: A total of 7,500 Russian and Polish Jews emigrate to the United States

Hal Bookbinder has been writing and lecturing on genealogical and Jewish historical topics for over a decade. He has served as chair of an annual Seminar on Jewish Genealogy (Los Angeles, 1990), president of the Jewish Genealogical Society of Los Angeles (1991–1993), and treasurer and then vice-president of the International Association of Jewish Genealogical Societies (1994 to present). He has extensively researched his own family, tracing several lines into the early nineteenth and late eighteenth centuries, when they lived in the area known as The Pale of Jewish Settlement. Mr. Bookbinder was raised in the Catskills of New York State, absorbing its unique "Borscht Belt" experience. After obtaining degrees in mathematics and operations research from New York University and in business from the University of Northern

Colorado, he and his wife, Marci, settled in the Los Angeles area. Their four adult children live in or around Los Angeles. Mr. Bookbinder manages computing and telecommunications for UCLA Healthcare and is an instructor of mathematics and statistics at the University of Phoenix.

Editor's Note: The foregoing article was adapted from an article that originally appeared in *Roots-Key*, vol. 15, no. 3 (Fall 1995): pp. 11–13.

TIMELINE OF THE PALE OF JEWISH SETTLEMENT (1870–1917)

1870   1880   1890   1900   1910   1920

1871: A massive pogrom occurs in Odessa. A tsarist commission blames the Jews.

1874: The 25-year conscription and Cantonist laws are repealed. Jews are now to be drafted with obligations similar to those imposed on the rest of the population.

1875: Jewish youth across Russia, including Congress Poland, are registered for military service.

1879: Medical professionals (dentists, nurses, midwives) are allowed to reside outside the Pale, with or without university degrees.

1881: Tsar Alexander II is assassinated on March 1 and is succeeded by Alexander III, a vehement anti-Semite.

1881–1884: Pogroms begin in Elizavetgrad, and spread across South Russia, Ukraine, and even to Warsaw. Over the next few years, violence occurs across the breadth of the Pale. Jewish emigration is encouraged.

1882: "May laws" are promulgated prohibiting Jews from conducting business on Sundays and Christian holidays, from moving between villages, and allowing for their expulsion from villages where the Christian community so wishes it.

1884: Decrees are issued limiting Jewish participation in the schools and universities and in land ownership.

1887: The towns of Rostov and Taganrog are excluded from the Pale.

1888: Constantin Petrovich Pobedonostsev, Tsar Alexander's confidant, writes that the only solution for the Jewish question in Russia is that "one-third should emigrate, one-third become Christian, and one-third should perish."

1889: A decree is issued that severely restricts Jewish lawyers, allowing few to practice law.

1890: Jews comprise 4 million of Russia's 86 million inhabitants.

1891–1892: Thousands of Jewish craftsmen and their families are expelled from Moscow.

1893: The town of Yalta is excluded from the Pale.

1894: Alexander III dies and is succeeded by Nicholas II, who will be the last tsar of Russia.

1897: A census of the Pale shows 4,899,300 Jews. They constitute one out of every nine residents; 99% claim Yiddish as their native tongue.

1903: Several hundred villages that had grown in size are declared towns, allowing Jews to reside in them.

1903–1906: Horrific pogroms across the Pale take place in 64 towns and 626 villages. These are supported by the government as a way to combat revolutionaries. There are no pogroms in Poland or Lithuania. About 1,000 Jews die, thousands are injured, and tens of thousands are ruined.

1905: Jewish veterans of the Russo–Japanese War are allowed to settle outside of the Pale (later, when these veterans are drafted for service in World War I, their families are forced to move to the Pale).

1905–1916: Some 2,837 anti-Semitic books and pamphlets are published in Russia, with the tsar underwriting much of the cost.

1910: Jews comprise 5.6 million of Russia's 130.8 million inhabitants. The four Jewish members of the Duma (the Russian legislature) propose a bill to disband the Pale. It is ignored.

1911: Mendel Beilis is accused of ritual murder in Kiev. He is acquitted in 1913.

1914–1915: World War I begins and the territory of the Pale is invaded by a foreign army for the first time in 100 years. The destruction results in tens of thousands of Jews moving from the Pale into old Russia. Though still a legal entity, the Pale has, de facto, ceased to exist.

1917: The Pale, along with all anti-Jewish statutes, is abolished by the Provisional Government of Russia, led by Prince Georgi Lvov and Alexander Kerrenski.

1871–1880: 4,000 Russian and Polish Jews emigrate to the United States.

1881–1890: 135,000 Russian and Polish Jews emigrate to the United States.

1891–1900: 280,000 Russian and Polish Jews emigrate to the United States.

1901–1910: 704,000 Russian and Polish Jews emigrate to the United States.

1911–1920: 350,000 Russian and Polish Jews emigrate to the United States.

The Pale of Jewish Settlement at the End of the Nineteenth Century

Map 4

THE RUSSIAN GUBERNIYA
AT THE TURN OF THE CENTURY

by
Hal Bookbinder

Understanding the geographic history of an ancestral town can provide us with clues as to where to search for records, how they might be organized and in what languages they may have been written. It may also shed light on the environment in which our ancestors lived.

Consider Volhynia. The oldest records of Jews in Volhynia date to the twelfth century, when the *Volhynian Chronicles* note that resident Jews mourned the death of a prince of Volhynia. At that time, Volhynia was an independent principality. In 1452, Volhynia was absorbed by the Grand Duchy of Lithuania. In 1569, it was transferred to the Kingdom of Poland. In 1793, the eastern portion of Volhynia was incorporated into the Russian Empire; in 1795, Russia took the rest. In 1917, Volhynia became part of an independent Ukraine. By 1921, Poland had taken the western two-thirds of Volhynia. The 1939 partition of Poland between Nazi Germany and the Soviet Union resulted in all of Volhynia being incorporated into the Ukrainian Soviet Socialist Republic (SSR). Finally, with the 1991 breakup of the Soviet Union, Volhynia became a part of independent Ukraine.

The borders of Volhynia have not been static either; they have tended to shift to the east over the centuries. In the thirteenth century, the principality of Volhynia included lands that are currently in eastern Poland. The eastern portion of Volhynia, including the city of Zhitomir, was joined to it only in the 1790s, after the partition of Poland. Prior to the partition, Lutsk was the traditional capital of Polish Volhynia. Under Russia, Zhitomir became the capital. From 1921 to 1939, Lutsk was the capital of Polish Volhynia (Wolyn), while Zhitomir was the capital of Soviet Volhynia.

When Polish Volhynia was incorporated into the Ukrainian SSR in 1939, it was divided into two oblasts. The western portion was designated Volhynia Oblast, and the eastern portion became Rovno Oblast. They, with Zhitomir Oblast,

which had been a part of the Ukraine since 1917, comprise most of historic Volhynia. These three oblasts remain today, with their respective capitals of Lutsk, Rovno and Zhitomir. Some smaller portions of Volhynia were included in other oblasts. For example, the town of Kremenets went to Tarnopol Oblast, and the town of Shepetovka went to Khmelnitskiy Oblast (formerly Proskurov).

My ancestral town of Dubno is currently in Rovno Oblast, Ukraine. So it might be logical to look for records in Rovno or in Kiev, the Ukrainian capital. However, recognizing that Dubno was in Russian Volhynia from 1795 to 1917, I should not overlook Zhitomir and Moscow. And, since Dubno was in Polish Volhynia from 1569 to 1795 and from 1921 to 1939, I probably should not overlook Lutsk and Warsaw either.

The information that follows provides an overview of the political geography of the Pale of Jewish Settlement in the 1890s, when most of our ancestors were living there.

The Pale of Jewish Settlement consisted of the vice-regencies of Belorussia, Bessarabia, Lithuania, New Russia and Ukraine (Poland was a separate legal entity). Each vice-regency was composed of one or more guberniyas (provinces). Each guberniya was made up of a number of *uezdy* (districts). Normally, the name of a *uezd* was the same as its chief town. When the town had a different name, it is shown as "uezd/town" (see facing page). The population figures are from the 1897 Russian census, as shown in the *Atlas of Modern Jewish History* by Evyatar Friesel (New York: Oxford University Press, 1990). The list of *uezdy* by guberniya is from the *Great Soviet Encyclopedia*, A. M. Prokhorov, ed. (New York: Macmillan, 1973–1983). The contemporary names shown in parentheses are from *Where Once We Walked*, by Gary Mokotoff and Sallyann Amdur Sack (Teaneck, NJ: Avotaynu, Inc., 1991).

	РЕВИЗСКАЯ СКАЗКА.					РЕВИЗСКАЯ СКАЗКА.	

List of inhabitants for the town of Dubno, 1850. Entry #3 is for Berko Bukhbinder (1786–1848), son of Shlomo. Also shown are Berko's son Abram Itsko (born 1823), married to Khava-Serla (born 1826), and their daughter, Ester (born 1848); and Berko's second son, Shimon (1832–1837).

25

THE PALE OF JEWISH SETTLEMENT
with 1897 Population Data

Vice–Regency; Jewish Population; Jews as Percentage of Total Population	Guberniya (Year Formed); Jewish Population	Uezd (Contemporary Name); * = Guberniya Capital
Belorussia 724,500 13.6%	Minsk (1793–1795, 1796) 345,000	Bobruisk, Borisov, Igumen (Cherven), *Minsk, Mozyr, Novogrudok, Pinsk, Rechitsa, Slutsk
	Mogilev (1773–1778, 1802) 203,900	Bykhov, Chausy, Cherikov, Gomel, Gorki, Klimovichi, *Mogilev, Mstislavl, Orsha, Rogachev, Senno
	Vitebsk (1802) 175,600	Drissa (Verkhnedvinsk), Dvinsk (Daugavpils), Gorodok, Lepel, Liutsin (Ludza), Nevel, Polotsk, Rezhitsa (Rezekne), Sebezh (Sebeza), Velizh, *Vitebsk
Bessarabia 228,500 11.8%	Bessarabia (1873)	Akkerman (Belgorod Dnestrovskiy), Beltsy, Bendery, Izmail, Khotin, *Kishinev, Orgeyev, Soroki
Lithuania 697,400 14.7%	Grodno (1801) 280,000	Bialystok, Bielsk, Brest Litovsk (Brest), *Grodno, Kobrin, Pruzhany, Slonim, Sokolka, Volkovysk
	Kovno (1842) 212,700	*Kovno (Kaunas), Novoaleksandrovsk (Zarasai), Panevezys, Raseiniai, Siauliai, Telsiai, Vilkomir (Ukmerge)
	Vilna (1795–1797, 1802) 204,700	Disna, Lida, Oshmyany, Svencionys, Trakai, Vileika (Nanjoji Vilnia), *Vilna (Vilnius)
New Russia 501,800 8.0%	Ekaterinoslav (1802) 101,100	Aleksandrovka, Bakhmut (Artemosvk), *Ekaterinoslav (Dnepropetrovsk), Mariupol (Zhdanov), Novomoskovsk, Pavlograd, Slavianoserbsk/Lugansk (Voroshilovgrad), Verkhnedneprovsk
	Kherson (1803) 339,000	Aleksandriya, Ananyev, Elizavetgrad (Kirovograd), *Kherson, Odessa, Tiraspol
	Taurida (1802) 60,800	Berdyansk, Dnepr/Aleshki (Tsyurupinsk), Feodosiya, Melitopol, Perekop, *Simferopol, Yalta, Yevpatoriya
Ukraine 1,425,500 9.7%	Chernigov (1796) 114,500	Borzna, *Chernigov, Glukhov, Gorodnya, Konotop, Kozelets, Krolevets, Mglin, Nezhin, Novgorod Severskiy, Novozybkov, Oster, Sosnitsa, Starodub, Surazh
	Kiev (1708–1781, 1796) 433,700	Berdichev, Cherkassy, Chigirin, Kanev, *Kiev (Kyiv), Lipovets, Radomyshl, Skvira, Tarashcha, Uman, Vasilkov, Zvenigorodka
	Podolia (1796) 370,600	Balta, Bratslav, Gaysin, *Kamenets Podolskiy, Letichev, Litin, Mogilev Podolskiy, Novaya Ushitsa, Olgopol, Proskurov (Khmelnitskiy), Vinnitsa, Yampol
	Poltava (1802) 110,900	Gadyach, Khorol, Konstantinograd (Krasnograd), Kovelyaki, Kremenchug, Lokhvitsa, Lubny, Mirgorod, Pereyaslav (Pereyaslav Khmelnitskiy), Piryatin, *Poltava, Priluki, Romny, Zenkov, Zolotonosha
	Volhynia (1796) 395,800	Dubno, Izyaslav, Kovel, Kremenets, Lutsk, Novograd Volynskiy, Ostrog, Ovruch, Rovno, Starokonstantinov, Vladimir Volynskiy, *Zhitomir

Editor's Note: The foregoing article was adapted from an article that originally appeared in *Roots-Key*, vol. 16, no. 2 (Summer 1996): pp. 11–12.

KARTOTEKA „ALIJI"

קרטוטיקה של החברים שנרשמו ועלו לא"י

Miejscowość *Kolomyja* המקום

בעלי-מקצוע				חלוצים		חקלאים		המלצות
rejestrowani Imię i nazwisko	data	data kwalifik. w U. Pal.	data „aliji"	Imię i nazwisko	data „aliji"	Imię i nazwisko	data „aliji"	Imię i nazwisko
Tarnopoler Dawid			10/IV. 935	Baumöhl Gusta W.	8/II 933			Reissman Moses Sam.
				Kriwitz Frima „	19/III 934			Friedler Jita
				Lautner Israel „	12/II 935			Pomeranz Jochewet
				Baumöhl Lina „	12/II 935			
				Dresler Bluma H.H.	24/II 36			
				Kanter Golda A.	10/III 36			
				Süsskind Lyla H.	3/II-36			
				Rosner Keila A.	14/II-936			

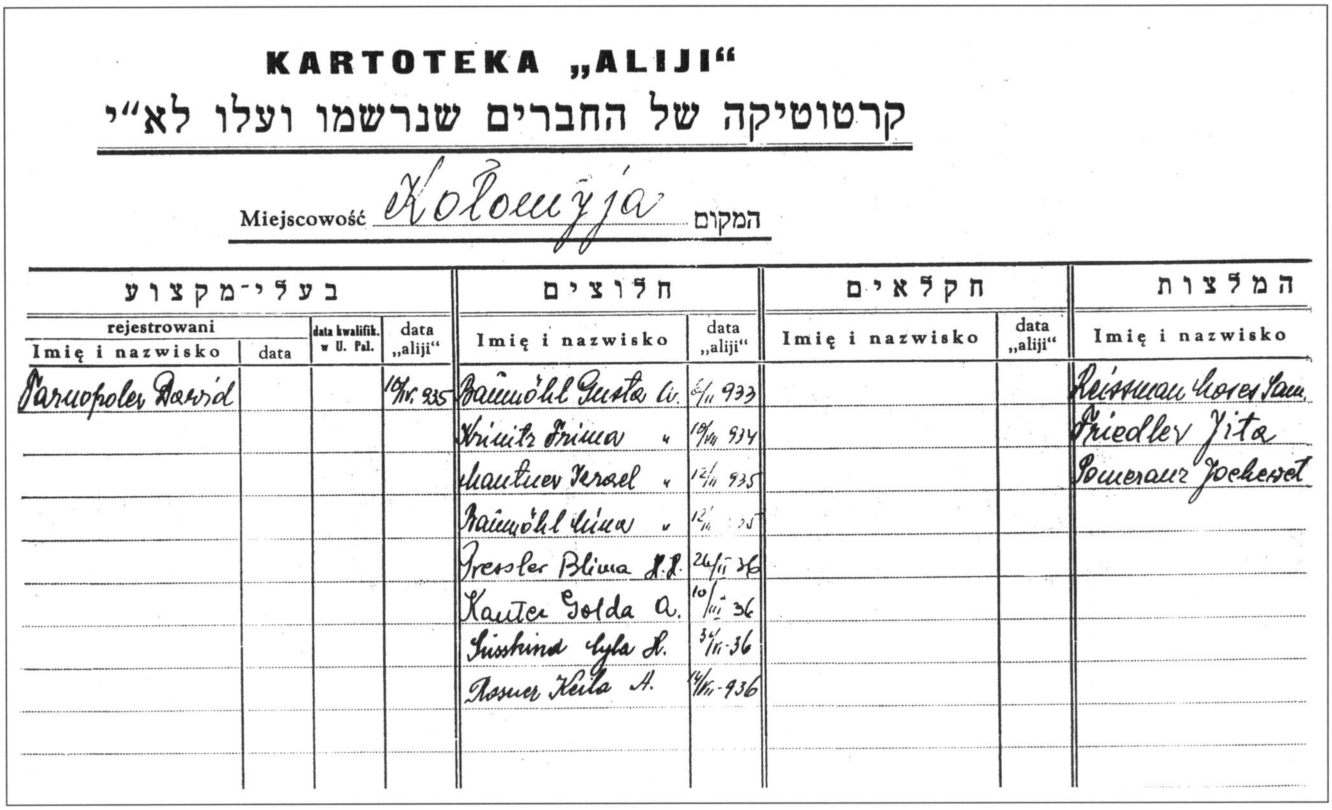

List of Jews in Kolomyja (Rus: Kolomiya; Ukr: Kolomyia) who plan to emigrate to Palestine, 1937 26

Zeugn. Prot. Nr. 652

Militärärztliches Zeugnis.

(Erforderlichenfalls:) Ausgestellt auf Grund des Befehles des Kommandos (Vorstandes) de ...

vom ... 19...

1. Truppenkörper, Unterabteilung, Charge (bei Personen des Reservestandes die tatsächliche berufsmäßige Beschäftigung), Vor- und Zuname, Assentjahrgang und Grundbuchblattnummer. Alter, allgemeine Körperbeschaffenheit.

K. u. k. Inf. Reg. Nr. 9. 2. Ersatz Kompagnie Ers. Res. Infanterist – Schreiber Israel Grünberg mittelkräftig.

13/96

2. Ergebnis der ärztlichen Untersuchung (Befund). Bezeichnung des vorgefundenen Gebrechens oder Krankheitszustandes und dessen Grades in Ausdrücken, die auch dem Nichtarzte verständlich sind (zur Erläuterung etwa notwendige wissenschaftliche Bezeichnungen sind einzuschalten); sind mehrere Gebrechen vorhanden, so ist das wichtigste zuerst anzuführen; Angabe der wesentlichen, das Gebrechen oder den Krankheitszustand charakterisierenden (pathognomischen) Erscheinungen; Anführung der objektiven Symptome; in jenen Fällen, in welchen sich die Diagnose nur auf subjektive Symptome stützt, ist dieser Umstand zum Ausdruck zu bringen.*)

Rechtes Ohr. Linkes Ohr.
1. Hörschärfe für akzentuierte Flüstersprache
0 m. 3 m.
2. Ohrenspiegelbefund.
Vollständige Zerstörung des Trommelfells, die Gehörknöchelchen glatt ausgegriffen. Getrübtes Trommelfell.
3. Sonstiger Befund.
4. Diagnose
Otitis media suppurativa chronica et Hypacusis acustica. Catarrhus tubae.

Künftiger Domizil

VI/44

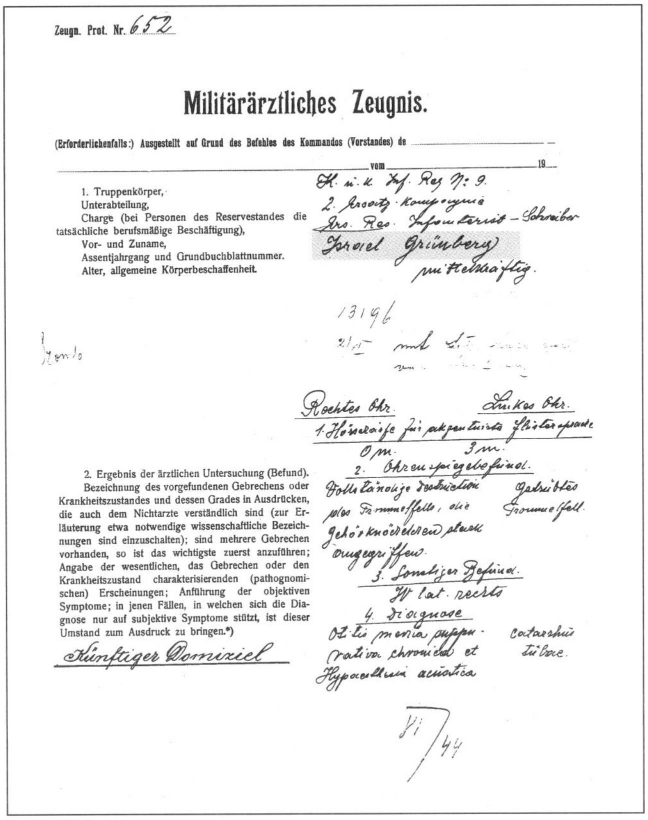

Military records (Austro-Hungarian Empire) of Israel Grünberg. This document was issued by the Lvov local office and is a medical certificate attesting to claims for exemption, 1915. 27

WHITE STAR LINE FILJA we LWOWIE

Do

Ekspozytury Urzędu Emigracyjnego

we LWOWIE

ul. Karmelicka 4

Ja niżej podpisany (a) Rosenberg Chula

urodzony (a) w roku 1894 zamieszkały (a) Drohobycz ul. Zavale 10

op ... powiat Drohobycz

w celu wyjazdu do Ameryki

z (wymienić osoby, które umieszczone być mogą na jednym paszporcie)

upraszam o wydanie mi zaświadczenia na bezpłatny paszport emigracyjny.

(Miejscowość) Drohobycz , dnia 11/9 1925.

Podpis Chula Rosenberg

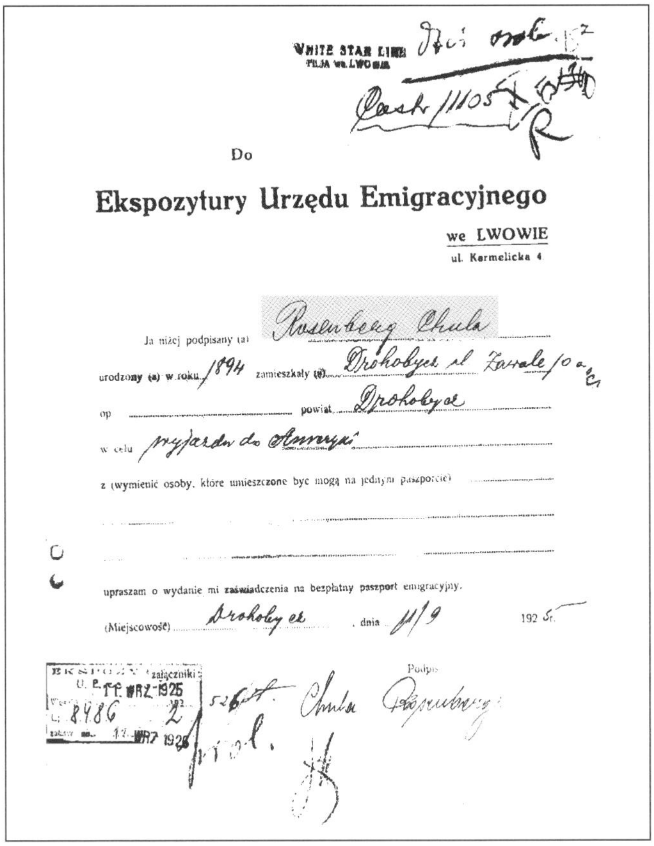

Emigration record from Lvov to the United States (White Star Line), dated 1925, for Chula Rosenberg, born 1894 in Drohobych 28

GENEALOGICAL RESOURCES OUTSIDE OF THE STATE ARCHIVES

by
Miriam Weiner

INTRODUCTION

The new opportunities created by the fall of communism have opened up endless resources for tracing Jewish roots.

A decade ago, there was virtually no possibility of tracing Jewish roots in the archives of the countries of the former Soviet Union and Eastern Europe, and the idea of strolling through the streets of ancestral towns was about as farfetched as the likelihood of being selected as an astronaut to visit the moon. Yet, today, travel agents routinely book trips to larger cities and arrange guides for visits to smaller towns in the region.

As a result of this literal onslaught of tourists and family historians visiting out-of-the-way places and striking up conversations with local historians and others they meet, a barrage of resources has come to light that, each in its own way, can be helpful to those who want to walk in the footsteps of their ancestors. The resources for information are virtually endless.

THE ADDRESS BUREAU

In each town in Ukraine, there is a government office called the *Adresnyi Stol* (Address Bureau). Several years ago, I visited the Address Bureau in Odessa, where I met with the director. After a discussion about my purpose there, he had his staff do a search of their records for a particular name. Within a few minutes, he was able to produce an index card for the exact person we sought. With the information on the card, we were eventually able to locate my friend's previously unknown second cousin, who had recently moved to St. Petersburg.

In Kiev, a visit to the Address Bureau produced a listing of a dozen of my family members named Odnopozov. Each index card included the full name of the individual (including the patronymic name [of father]), date and place of birth, current address and sometimes the occupation. If the person had died or emigrated within the past few years, that information was also noted.

These local offices maintain files on virtually everyone living within the town. Residents are required to register their addresses and, as a result, these offices are the best source of locating residents in a specific locality. (Although local telephone books might be the first source one would think of, because so many people in the former Soviet Union do not have telephones, there is a significant percentage of the populace that would be missed in a search of telephone books.)

Money wire-transfer receipt located in the Odessa Address Bureau, for Yulia Petrovna Balko, daughter of Leya Zavelskaya. This document lists the last three addresses where Yulia resided, 1991.   29

HOLOCAUST DOCUMENTATION IN UKRAINE AND MOLDOVA

Neither Ukraine nor Moldova had extermination camps on its territories (such as Auschwitz-Birkenau and Majdanek in Poland). Although there were ghettos and forced-labor camps throughout both Ukraine and Moldova where tens of thousands of Jews perished, there are no specific museums or repositories devoted to the Holocaust in these countries.

There are, however, significant documents throughout the archives of Ukraine and Moldova relating to the Holocaust period (see Chapter 7). In addition, certain local museums in both countries have small Judaic collections of whatever possessions were confiscated from the local Jews.

The United States Holocaust Memorial Museum in Washington, D.C., has microfilmed hundreds of thousands of documents relating to the genocide of Soviet Jewry during the Holocaust. This material is searchable both in person and on the Internet (catalogue only) <*http://www.ushmm.org*>. There is a place-name index to the record group *Extraordinary Commission to Document Nazi Atrocities on Soviet Territory*.

MEMORY BOOKS OF SOLDIERS KILLED IN WORLD WAR II

Within the last few years, a series of books has been published in Ukraine and Belarus (and probably in other countries in the former Soviet Union) consisting of "memory books" organized by oblast (district), with multivolumes within the oblast. These books include town-by-town lists of soldiers who perished during World War II. A typical entry includes the first and last name, patronymic name, year and place of birth, nationality (Jews were listed as *Evrei*) and where the person died.

The source of the data is listed as various archives, and these books can be found in some libraries and archives (in the country of publication) as well as some local bookshops.

---

515   **г. Нежин**

Похоронен г. Корэстень, Житомирская обл.

ФИЛОНЕНКО Павел Кузьмич, г. Нежин, украинец, рядовой.

ФИЛЬ Владимир Петрович, 1905 г., г. Нежин, украинец, рядовой.

ФИЛЬ Григорий Григорьевич, г. Нежин, украинец, рядовой.

ФИЛЬ Григорий Харитонович, 1905 г., г. Нежин, украинец, мл. сержант. Проходил службу в 429 минп 31 ад. Погиб 17.04.45 г. Похоронен в Германии.

ФИЛЬ Пантелей Александрович, 1919 г., г. Нежин, украинец, рядовой.

ФИЛЬ Сергей Иванович, г. Нежин, украинец, рядовой.

ФИНЕНКО Владимир Владимирович, 1908 г., г. Нежин, украинец, рядовой. Погиб 19.11.41 г. в плену, в Германии.

X

ХАЙКИН Борис Давыдович, 1907 г., г. Нежин, еврей, рядовой.

ХАЙКИН Зальман Абрамович, г. Нежин, еврей, рядовой.

ХАЙКИН Михаил Зиновьевич, 1911 г., г. Нежин, еврей, офицер. Проходил службу в 71 обс 251 сд.

ХАМКО Яков Силович, г. Нежин, украинец, ст. политрук.

ХАНИН Мордух Шмеркович, 1902 г., г. Нежин, еврей, ст. лейтенант. Проходил службу в 30 оср. Погиб 04.12.42 г. Похоронен Ленинградская обл.

ХАРИТОНОВ Михаил Михайлович, 1914 г., Одесская обл., украинец, рядовой.

ФОНТАЛИН Афанасий Григорьевич, 1918 г., г. Нежин, украинец, старшина. Проходил службу в 255 минп 238 сд. Проходил лечение в 397 омсб. Умер 20.04.45 г. Похоронен г. Шведт, в Германии.

ФОНТАЛИН Василий Григорьевич, 1923 г., Сумская обл., украинец, рядовой. Проходил службу в в/ч пп 61165. Погиб 10.11.43 г. Похоронен п. Иванков, Киевская обл.

ФОНТАЛИН Григорий Митрофанович, 1896 г., Сумская обл., украинец, рядовой.

ФОНТАЛИН Федор Григорьевич, 1919 г., г. Нежин, украинец, мл. сержант.

ФРАТКИН Григорий Самуилович, г. Нежин, еврей, лейтенант.

ФУРСА Николай Яковлевич, 1899 г., г. Нежин, украинец, рядовой.

ХАРИЦКИЙ Ефим Иванович, 1909 г., с. Титовка, украинец, рядовой.

ХАРИЦКИЙ Михаил Иванович, 1900 г., г. Нежин, украинец, рядовой.

ХАРЛАМОВ Иван Дмитриевич, 1893 г., г. Нежин, украинец, рядовой. Проходил лечение в 1913 сэг. Умер 10.04.44 г. Похоронен г. Киев.

ХАРМАЧ Павел Евсеевич, 1900 г., г. Нежин, украинец, рядовой. Проходил службу в 656 сап. Погиб 14.02.45 г. Похоронен в Польше.

ХАРЧЕНКО Иван Макарович, г. Нежин, украинец, рядовой. Проходил службу в 3 гв. осбр. Погиб 03.05.45 г. Похоронен в Чехо-Словакии.

ХАРЧЕНКО Федор Митрофанович, 1901 г., г. Нежин, украинец, рядовой.

Entry from the 1996 Memory Book of Chernigov Oblast, vol. 5 (*Kiev: Ukrainian Encyclopedia, 1996*), *listing veterans and those who died in World War II, including these men from the town of Nezhin, all listed as Evrei ("Jew"): Boris Khaikin (born 1907), son of David; Zalman Khaikin, son of Abram; and Mikhail Khaikin, an officer (born 1911), son of Zinovy*   30

JEWISH DOCUMENTS AND ARTIFACTS IN PRIVATE COLLECTIONS

Throughout Eastern Europe, there are private collections of Judaica and documents, collected for various reasons but often preserved with care by those who have chosen to become the trustees of this material. In the village of Korolovka, located in Ternopol Oblast, a local schoolteacher has meticulously reconstructed the Jewish community of the village with a hand-drawn map showing the location of each Jewish family by name and occupation. He also has a collection of school records dating back to 1899. The teacher permitted me to make photocopies of the map (16 pages in total, taped together) and also to make copies of some pages from the school records.

In Luboml, a Ukrainian town near the Polish border, a young man in his 30s has become the town's Jewish historian. Since Luboml was primarily Jewish before the Holocaust, virtually any history of the town focuses on the Jews who lived there. Mikola Dzei is proud of his collection, which he has amassed from local residents, archival research and other resources. Among the items in his archive are documents (both originals and copies), Judaica, photographs and maps.

During a walking tour of the town, Mr. Dzei points out various Jewish sites and simultaneously maintains a running commentary on the historical significance of the places. He has old photographs of many of the streets in the town. Even though he was not alive during World War II, he interviewed local Ukrainians who were eyewitnesses to the extermination. He is among hundreds of Ukrainians who have chosen to preserve the Jewish history of their communities and to share the information with those who come seeking their roots.

In September 1998, Mr. Dzei's article entitled "The Tragedy in the Fall of 1942– Black Pages of Our History" was published in the regional newspaper *Our Lives* in Luboml. Following a brief description of the German invasion of Luboml, Mr. Dzei quotes numerous survivors who witnessed the atrocities.

Report card (with grades) of Hindie Gottesfeld (born 1921), living in Korolovka, daughter of Mortko Izak Gottesfeld, 1928–1929 school year

31

LOCAL TOWN-HALL RECORDS (ZAGS OFFICES)

In cities and towns throughout Ukraine and Moldova, the vital records were maintained by the *kahal* and stored in Jewish vital registration offices, which had their seats in the local administration building. Very small villages were members of a *kahal* in nearby larger towns and registered there. The particular office for recording births, marriages, deaths and divorces is officially known as the *Otdel Zapisi Aktov Grazhdanskogo Sostoyaniya* (more commonly known as the ZAGS office or archive). These offices are under the jurisdiction of the Ministry of Justice (13 Horodetskoho Street, 252001 Kyiv, Ukraine), and each local ZAGS office reports to an oblast ZAGS archive. Jewish vital records registered after World War II were incorporated into the general registrations of the entire town.

By law, the metrical books are retained in the ZAGS offices for a period of 75 years. Books older than 75 years are to be transferred to the appropriate state archive. When the record books include multiple years, the books are retained in the local ZAGS office until all documents in the book are more than 75 years old. This regulation often causes confusion as to where documents are actually kept. However, it is important to bear in mind that metrical books, which should be transferred to the state archive, are often retained in the ZAGS office for various reasons (*e.g.*, insufficient space in the state archive, or restoration work needs to be done on the books prior to their transfer).

Public access to ZAGS documents is regulated by law, which prohibits on-site access and research by individuals looking for multiple records for genealogical purposes. It is not uncommon to find a sympathetic clerk in a local ZAGS office who will cooperate to varying degrees in order to accommodate the visitor. However, this is a courtesy response and not available upon demand.

It is possible to write to the Ukrainian Consulate (240 E. 49th Street, New York, NY 10017) or the Ukrainian Embassy (3350 M Street NW, Washington, D.C. 20007) and request a search for a few specific vital records. This is a time-consuming process; it may take months to receive a response. If the search is successful, a letter will be sent to the requestor advising him or her to forward a sum of money to the consulate's office; in return, a certified extract of the document (on a typed form) will be sent out by mail.

SOME METRICAL BOOKS ARE KEPT IN POLISH ARCHIVES

An exception to the foregoing concerns Jewish metrical books from the area of the former Lwów, Stanisławów and Tarnopol Provinces (now Lviv, Ivano-Frankivsk and Ternopil Oblasts). These record books are held in a collection known as the Zabużański ("East of Bug River") Archive and are housed in the Urząd Stanu Cywilnego, Warszawa-Śrómieście (P.O. Box 18, 1/3 Jezuicka Street, 00-950 Warsaw, Poland). The contents of these records are generally written in Polish, but the books have column headings in German. In the area formerly known as Galicia (included in the Austro-Hungarian Empire), the Polish language was accorded equal official status with the German language, *e.g.*, in vital-statistics registrations. However, some books between October 1939 and mid-1941 are written in German or Ukrainian. It is possible to visit this office and request a document search, which will be done by the staff.

The metrical books in these archives generally date from 1898. Access to this material is possible by making a written request directly to the office or through Polish consulate offices in the United States. Older books are transferred to the Polish State Archives, Archiwum Główne Akt Dawnych (AGAD), 7 Długa Street, 00-263 Warsaw, Poland. Access to this material may be achieved by writing to AGAD, requesting a search by archivists. Due to the poor condition of these books (in AGAD), currently they are neither available to the general public nor have they been microfilmed.

Birth record of Aron Bichek, born February 11, 1905, in Berezno, Ukraine, son of Yankel Bichek (son of Idel) and Khana Polishuk (daughter of Moishe-Mordko), document #10 in the Rovno ZAGS Archive

Книга Староконстантиновской синагоги за 1884 г.

Архивный № 50

Запис акта про народження № 100

від «____» _____ 1884 г. _____ 199____ року

(перший, другий, примірник)

Штамп органу загсу

Відомості про дитину

1	Прізвище	Винокур	2	Ім'я	Аврум – Мордко
3	По батькові		4	Стать	син

5 | Час народження «17» июня 1884 г. 199___ р.

6 | Місце народження — місто (селище) _____ район _____ область (край, республіка) _____

7 | Скільки народилося дітей: одно, двійня, трійня

8 | Живим народжений чи мертвим народжений

9 | Яка за рахунком дитина народилась у матері, включаючи новонароджених (враховуючи померлих і не враховуючи мертвонароджених)

10 | Документи, що підтверджують факт народження дитини

Відомості про батька		Відомості про матір
11	Прізвище	Винокур	
12	Ім'я	Аврум	Рухель
13	По батькові	Ицхокович из Грицева	Мордковна

14 | Час народження «____» _____ 199__р. «____» _____ 199__р.
Вік: минуло _____ років минуло _____ років

15 | Національність

Birth record of Avrum-Mordko, dated June 17, 1884, in Starokonstantinov, son of Avrum Vinokur from Gritseva and his wife, Ruchel (daughter of Mordko), registration book in the Khmelnitskiy ZAGS office   33

У. С. Р. Р

НАРОДНИЙ КОМІСАРІЯТ ВНУТРІШНІХ СПРАВ

ЗАЦС при _Ново-Ушицькій_ сільраді (виконк.) Книга Ч. 1

Н.-Ушицького району Кам'янецької округи 192 8 р.

ЗАПИС ПРО ШЛЮБ Ч. 1

1. Запис складено: „3" дня _Січня_ міс. 1928 р.

Відомости про молодих	Про молодого	Про молоду
2. Прізвище, ім'я та по батькові перед шлюбом	Ройзенблім Берко Ицко-Волькович	Бланк Малка-Рива Шмульовна
Прізвище після шлюбу	Ройзенблім	Ройзенблім
3. Вік (скільки повних років має)	24 роки	27 років
4. Національність	Єврей	Єврейка
5. Де постійно живе (округа, район, село або місто, вул. ч. буд.)	Кам'округа, Ново-Ушицького району м. Нова-Ушиця	он. Нова-Ушиця
6 Котрий раз бере шлюб	Перший	Перший
7. Сімейний стан перед шлюбом	Парубок	Дівчина
8. Скільки дітей в попередніх шлюбах	народилося — живі і тепер —	народилося — живі і тепер —
9. Як здобуває прожиток? (з якої саме роботи, ремества, промислу, посади чи з прибутків од майна або живе коштами рідні, держави та инш.)	Промислу тютю поб плантатор	Коштами батьк.
10. Де служить? (назва підприємства або установи) чи господарює у себе?	У себе	У себе
11. Становище в зайнятті, що дає прожиток?	Хазяїн або одинець, член артілі службовець, робітник, помічн. у зайнятті член сем'ї (підкреслити)	Хазяйка або одиначка, член артілі службовка, робітниця помічни. зайнятті член сем'ї (підкреслити)

Marriage record of Berko Roizenblim (age 24, son of Itsko-Volko) and Malka-Riva Blank (age 27, daughter of Shmul), both living in Novo (Novaya) Ushitsa, recorded in the local ZAGS office in 1928   34

Transcript of birth record of Dvoira, dated December 25, 1939, in Novograd-Volynskiy (registered January 3, 1940), daughter of Yankel Ios Baru (son of Srul Moshko) and Rozaliya Baru (daughter of Leib)   35

Birth record of Sara Milztein, dated 1920 in Soroki, daughter of Peretz Milztein (son of Sliomo from Dombroveni) and Sura (daughter of Boruh)   36

In 1991, the author gave a fax machine to the Ministry of Justice in Kiev. In this 1992 photo, Emilia M. Sych (right), then director of the ZAGS offices for all of Ukraine, laments that her office does not have enough fax paper to accommodate genealogy requests. In this photo, she shows one 17-page genealogy research request.   37

1.	Айзенштейн	
2.	Айзенштейн	
3.	Айзенштейн	
4.	Абельман	
5.	Абельман Абрам	
6.	Абельман	
7.	Абельман	
8.	Абельман Нахем	1883 г.
9.	Абельман Сруль	1921 г.
10.	Адимашек Дуся – парикмахер	
11.	Айзенберг	отец
12.	Айзенберг	мать
13.	Айзенберг	сын
14.	Айзенберг	дочь

Б

1.	Букимер Лиза		
2.	Балагула Рахиль Мордхолне и ее семья		
3.	Бирбраер Сруль		
4.	Бирбраер шмил		
5.	Бирбраер Берко		
6.	Бородавка	отец	
7.	Бородавка	жена	
8.	Бородавка	дочь	
9.	Бородавка	сын	
10.	Бельфер		
11.	Брандвайн Аврум		
12.	Брандвайн Мойше		
13.	Брандвайн Енте		
14.	Бабер	отец	владелец магазина
15.	Бабер	жена	
16.	Бабер	дочь	
17.	Бабер	сын	
18.	Бабер	отец	владелец кинотеатра
19.	Бабер	жена	
20.	Члены семьи		
21.			
22.	Букимер	отец	
23.	Букимер	мать	
24.	Букимер Александр	сын	
25.	Букимер Борис	сын	

List of people shot during World War II in Ostrog, 38
compiled by the surviving Jewish community,
listing names, family members and relationships,
some dates of birth and occupations, 1950

List of 61 men and women born and residing in Ostrog since 39
1941, including name, year of birth, father's name and year of
death (post-Holocaust). This list was provided by the head of
the local Jewish community in Ostrog, Ukraine, 1950.

СПИСОК
...ТЕЛІВ НОВОТ УЛИЦІ ЄВРЕЙСЬКОТ НАЦІОНАЛЬНОСТІ.
СТАНОМ НА 1.01.1974 р.

№п/п	Фамілія, ім,я та по батькові	Посада	Освіта	Домашня адреса	Зв"язки за гранцею	Примітка
1.	Айзін Борис Бенціонович	пенсіонер	початкова	Бул.Дзержинського	син в Ізраїлі	2 дітей
2.	Айзін Лізавета Моісеєвна	пенсіонерка	початкова	"	"	"
3.	Юсім Абрам Семенович	пенсіонер	початкова	вул.Шевченка 34	сестра в Америці	2 дітей
4.	Юсім Броня Абрамівна	пенсіонерка	початкова	"	сестра,брат в Америці	
5.	Видельман Самуіл Бенціонович	Голова горпо	початкова	вул.Жовтнева		4 дітей
6.	Видельман Геня Хаймівна	утриманка	початкова	"		
7.	Фрумкін Самуіл Бенціонович	контролер	семирічна	вул.Шевченка		2 дітей
8.	Фрумкін Марія Гершківна	пенсіонерка	комунгоспу	"		
9.	Грімберг Марія Йосипівна	пенсіонерка	середня	вул.Дзержинського		1 дитина
10.	Явіна Діна Миронівна	медсестра	середня	вул.Дзержинського		1 дитина
11.	Малах Волько Іхельович	завторг горпо	початкова	вул.Дзержинського		
12.	Бельдерман Слува Анкелівна	пенсіонерка	початкова	вул.Дзержинського		
13.	Фільштинська Ася Ушірівна	вихователька	вища	вул.Дзержинського		2 дітей
14.	Іткін Абрам Йосимович	заготовач	семирічна	вул.Дзержинського		2 дітей
15.	Фільштинська Махля Шоилівна	пенсіонерка	початкова	вул.Дзержинського		5 дітей
16.	Фільштинський Нюня Ушірович	пенсіонер	семирічна	вул.Леніна		
17.	Фільштинська Марія Борисівна	вчителька	вища	вул.Леніна		
18.	Сирота Михайло Якович	заготовач МСТ	семирічна	вул.Леніна		1 дитина
19.	Іткін Ісак Нусимович	конюх учг.тех.	початкова	вул.Шевченка		2 дітей
20.	Крушельницька Галина Йосипівна	пенсіонерка	середня	вул.Леніна		1 дитина

Two-page list of Jews living in Novo (Novaya) Ushitsa (as of 1974), compiled by the mayor's office. The list includes 40
name, status (pensioner or occupation), level of education, street address, relatives in Israel or the United States, and
number of grandchildren.

BUSINESS DIRECTORIES

From the mid-1800s through World War I, a series of directories was published in Russia that included business directories, address calendars, almanacs and other books listing local government officials, occupations and businesses.

In the Russian Empire at the end of the nineteenth century, business directories entitled *Vsia Rossiya* ("All Russia") were published. Some of these directories have been filmed by the Library of Congress (including 1895, 1899, 1903, 1911–1912 and 1923). Some of the books are indexed by name. These directories are generally arranged by guberniya, by town and then by business. For a description of the directories, see Harry D. Boonin, "Russian Business Directories," in *Avotaynu*, vol. 6, no. 4 (Winter 1990): pp. 23–31; and James Rhode, "Russian Business Directories as Aids in Genealogical Research," in *Avotaynu*, vol. 4, no. 2 (Spring 1988): pp. 3–8. Copies of these directories may be found in the Microform Division of the Library of Congress, the Slavic and Baltic Division of the New York Public Library and Widener Library at Harvard University. Originals and copies of these directories may be found in libraries and archives throughout the world, including Moscow and St. Petersburg. In Ukraine, various forms of these business directories can be found in the State Archive of Kiev Oblast, the Central State Historical Archive in Lvov and throughout various oblast archives.

A typical town entry includes an alphabetical list of occupations or industries, followed by the names of people within those categories. The name entry includes the family name, first and patronymic names (these names are often abbreviated), street location and the name of the person who owned the home or business.

In the Austro-Hungarian Empire, business directories covering Galicia were published as early as the 1850s. Some of these directories are arranged by town, while others are arranged by business or occupation. Generally, these directories include full names of proprietors and full street addresses. The Slavic and Baltic Division of The New York Public Library and the Library of Congress have copies of some of the following directories: *Handels-und Gewerbe Adressenbuch der österreichischen Kaiserstaates* ("Commercial and Business Directory of the Austrian Imperial State"); *Adressenbuch für Handel, Gewerbe und Actien-Gesellschaften der Oesterreichisch-Ungarishchen Monarchie* ("Directory of Trade, Business and Stock Companies for the Austro-Hungarian Monarchy"); *Kaufmännisches Adressbuch für Industrie, Handel und Gewerbe der Osterreichisch-Ungarischen Monarchie* ("Commercial Directory for Industry, Trade and Business for the Austro-Hungarian Monarchy"); and *Księga Adresowa Przemysłu* ("Directory of Galician Industry").

"All Russia" business directory, 1902   41-A

Sample page entry from 1902 business directory, with entries by guberniya (province)   41-B

Title page from "Commercial Directory for Industry, Trade and   42-A
Business for the Austro-Hungarian Monarchy," 1891

Sample page from 1891 "Commercial Directory"   42-B

List of people in the mining and petroleum industry   43-A
in western Poland, 1938

Sample page entry for Borislav, including an entry   43-B
for S. Wiksel, with the firm of F. Rajchel & Tow

SYNAGOGUE RECORDS AND PINKASSIM

Many Jewish communities in Eastern Europe kept internal records that supply considerable historical and genealogical information. The communities usually created *pinkassim* (register books) or *księgi duchowne* (community books) to record births, marriages, deaths, community tax rolls, synagogue-seat ownership, community charitable contributions and other information. Although the majority of these invaluable books were either destroyed in the Holocaust or ritually buried by the community to preserve them from profanation after becoming unusable, many have survived. The Central Archives for the History of the Jewish People in Jerusalem has one of the largest collections of extant *pinkassim*. For a partial listing of the *pinkassim* available at the Central Archives, see A. Teller, H. Volovici and H. Assouline, eds., *Guide to the Sources for the History of the Jews in Poland in the Central Archives* (Jerusalem: Central Archives for the History of the Jewish People, 1988). The Jewish Theological Seminary Library in New York and the Jewish National Library in Jerusalem also have collections.

In a recent meeting with Irina Sergeyeva at the Vernadskiy National Library of Ukraine, she described the extensive collection of *pinkassim* now held in the library's Manuscript Department. Among the 100,000 books and 8,000 manuscripts, there are some 100 *pinkassim*. It is believed to be the largest collection of Eastern European *pinkassim* in the world.

Pinkas from Sudilkov, Ukraine, published by Pinkas Hevrah Malbish Arumim, a society for providing clothes for the poor; entries begin in 1858 (56 pages)

44-A

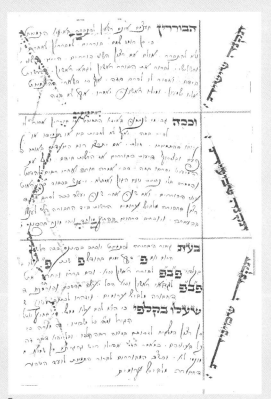

Sample pages from the Sudilkov pinkas in the Vernadskiy Library in Kiev

44-B

"These are the men whose contributions supported the new Sefer Torah [5664], 1903–1904"

44-C

JUDAIC DISCOVERIES IN OTHER REPOSITORIES

During my travels in Ukraine (since 1991) and Moldova (since 1992), I have not only worked in archives but have also made inquiries about Jewish documents and Judaica in the hundreds of towns I have visited. Throughout both countries, I have encountered Jewish documents and Judaica in private collections and several local museums; some items are well preserved, others in deplorable condition.

The local museum in Ostrog, Ukraine, offers exhibits depicting artifacts devoted to folklore and customs in Ukraine. In addition, there is a significant collection of Yiddish and Hebrew books, more than 50 Torahs and many civil record books with valuable documents for anyone with roots in Ostrog (the latter is not part of the museum exhibits).

Normally, these civil record books are housed in the Ukrainian State Archives and, therefore, one would expect to find them in the State Archive of Rovno Oblast in Rovno.

Among the record books in the Ostrog Museum (5 Academicheskaya Street, 265620 Ostrog, Rovno Oblast, Ukraine) are school records, lists of inhabitants and family lists. In addition, the local Jewish community in Ostrog maintains lists of former residents, Holocaust victims and survivors (see samples on page 41). These books are in relatively good condition and appear to be well preserved.

There are no photocopy facilities in this museum, and the office space is very limited. Access to this material is granted (selectively) by permission from the museum director.

Family list in Ostrog for Zelman Munish Boskis (son of Abram-Volf), listing eight children; spouses; one grandchild; brother and wife and their four children; with age of each person, military service and some occupations, 1886

45

THE RABBI IN IVANO-FRANKOVSK

In the early 1990s, I visited Ivano-Frankovsk (formerly Stanisławów), where I met Rabbi Moishe Leib Kolesnik. Rabbi Kolesnik spent hours showing me his remarkable archival collection of documents, photographs, maps and books. Through the years, Rabbi Kolesnik has continued to seek out, preserve, copy and collect material about the Jews of Ivano-Frankovsk region. Throughout the area, people know of his work and make valuable contributions to his collection. He is a remarkable man with infinite patience and dedication to his projects and goals.

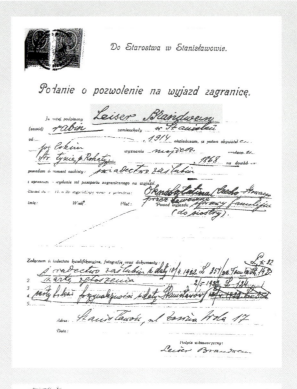

Three-page passport application, dated 1922, for Rabbi Leizer Brandwein (born 1868), son of Nuchim and Malka Blima Brandwein, residing at Zosina Wola 17 in Stanisławów

46

THE JEWS OF STANISŁAWÓW PROVINCE

by

Rabbi Moishe Leib Kolesnik

The Synagogue
7 Stregeny Street
284000 Ivano-Frankivsk
Ukraine

Tel: 380/3422/2-30-29

Since 1989, I have been the rabbi of Ivano-Frankovsk Oblast. In that role, I have traveled to towns and villages throughout the region, meeting with local Jews in their homes, prayer houses and synagogues. Many Jews have had questions or problems, and I have tried to help them. During our conversations, people frequently have mentioned old Hebrew books they have in their homes, often handed down through several generations. Also, when people were ready to emigrate, they left their family books with friends and neighbors.

Since many of the Jews in Ukraine today do not read Yiddish or Hebrew, they asked me about the handwritten notes on some of the pages. After seeing so many of these books, it was clear that grandparents and great-grandparents had studied from these books and recorded family data in them, in neat and meticulous notes. In one book, I found notes made by the book's owner during 1941–1943, recording the birth of a daughter in January 1941 and a son in January 1943. These events were recorded when the Jews of Stanisławów were imprisoned in the ghetto, probably at a time when they did not have money even for bread. As of today (December 1998), I have more than 1,000 unique books.

When the word spread that I was collecting prayer books, the Jews of Ivano-Frankovsk region began giving me documents and photographs, some concerning very well-known and prominent individuals.

Former residents of this region or people with ancestral roots here write letters to me asking for help in tracing their family history. I try to help these people, and if I do not find information in my collection, I often go to the archives and do research there. For example, once I looked for Holocaust documents for someone, and when I realized how interesting and important the archival documents were, I began making copies of as many documents as possible.

Sometimes old houses are destroyed in order to build new ones. I remember one situation where I received a telephone call explaining that during the demolition of the house, the person had found many Hebrew documents but did not know what they were. The documents had been sent to the local garbage dump. When the caller told me the location, I immediately rescued these papers, consisting of passport applications for Jews planning to emigrate. Many of these documents include photographs of the entire family.

When I travel in Ivano-Frankovsk Oblast, I visit many Jewish cemeteries that are unfenced, devastated and devoid of tombstones. I speak with the local people about the cemeteries, and with this information I have drawn maps of many cemeteries. Of course, these maps are incomplete, but the information includes the earliest and most recent burial date, size of cemetery, number of tombstones, names of prominent personalities and rabbis, and what happened to the cemetery during World War II.

During these village visits, many people tell me about Jewish cultural and religious life. I note this information and mark the location of Jewish sites on maps. I also photograph these sites as much as possible. As a result, I have detailed information about Ivano-Frankovsk and nearby towns.

Editor's Note: Rabbi Kolesnik does not speak English. He welcomes visitors and may be contacted at the synagogue (see above).

Rabbi Moishe Leib Kolesnik, with sample passport documents discovered during the reconstruction of a house in Ivano-Frankovsk and rescued by him from discarded trash (photo, 1998)

47

Selected Items (by Town) from the Archive of Rabbi Moishe Leib Kolesnik

BOLEKHOV

- List of Jews killed in Bolekhov Ghetto, 1941–1944 (8 pages)
- Photocopy of synagogue photo, 1957

BOLSHOVTSY

- General correspondence from synagogue members, 1934
- Testimonials from survivors after the Holocaust, 1945
- List of victims, 1945 (20 pages)

BUKACHEVTSY

- Testimonials from survivors, 1945

BURSHTYN

- Testimonials from survivors, 1945
- Protocols (memorandums) from the Jewish community, 1935
- Private documents of Rabbi Gersh Landau, 1933

DELYATIN

- Announcement in Hebrew from the Talmud Torah
- List of people killed by the Nazis (31 pages and 1,748 names) from Delyatin, Yaremche and Stanisławów (c. 1945)
- Holocaust documents, 1941–1943

DOLINA

- Correspondence from Rabbi Osias Halberstam to the education minister in Warsaw regarding voting procedures for electing rabbis, 1937
- Photo of synagogue from the village of Broshnev Osada, 1954

GALICH

- KGB report listing number of Jews killed in Galich, 1944

GORODENKA

- Voters' list in Polish (9 pages and 1,168 names), 1938
- List of victims (11 pages)

GVOZDETS

- List of taxpayers, 1937
- Map of Jewish cemetery (no names)

KALUSH

- Metrical book, 1832–1848 (987 people, 72 pages)
- Map of Jewish cemetery (no names), 1977
- Map of Kalush, including Jewish cemetery
- Map of Kalush, in Polish
- Photographs of the Jewish cemetery (1990, 1993); Holocaust monument; destroyed tombstones; the 1995 dedication of a Holocaust monument to 6,000 Jews killed in Kalush District, including photograph of attendees

KOLOMIYA

- Local newspaper article, 1997: the government returned the synagogue to the local Jewish community (formerly a sports center and now a prayer house)
- Agreement regarding the rental of a house to be used as an office for the Jewish community, 1997
- Letter from the Jewish society Merkaz Ruchanee about voting procedures, 1933

- General correspondence from the Jewish society Agudath Israel, in Polish, 1938
- Autobiography of Rabbi N. L. Jeczes from Kuty, 1933
- Family tree of Orenshtein
- Architectural drawing of synagogue at 19 Asha Street
- Many private documents from individuals
- Letter from the chief of the Jewish community to the Stanisławów local government, including a list of workers in the Jewish hospital and their salaries, 1936

LANCHIN

- Map of Jewish cemetery, 1997

NADVORNAYA

- Metrical book in Polish, 1850–1865
- Topographical plan of the electric plant, 1937
- Map, 1860
- Map in Hebrew (region of Jewish cemetery)
- List of taxpayers (Jewish community, 333 names), 1932
- Maps of the Jewish cemetery, 1947 and 1996
- Topographic map of Nadvornaya and surrounding towns, 1950
- Map of Jewish cemetery (in Polish), late 1800s
- Map of stadium (adjoining the Jewish cemetery)
- Aerial photograph of Nadvornaya, 1969
- Aerial photograph of Nadvornaya, 1947; the Jewish cemetery is visible
- Map showing property lines, late 1800s
- Map of Nadvornaya, 1847
- Documents from the Jewish community, 1933, 1935
- Correspondence from Jewish community to Stanisławów local government regarding taxes, 1936
- Correspondence from Nadvornaya to Stanisławów local government regarding voting in the Jewish community, 1933
- Voters' list, 1933
- Correspondence from Jewish community to Stanisławów local government regarding a protest of the Jews from Nadvornaya about a tax; court documents on this dispute, 1934
- Documents from Rabbi Kolesnik and the Nadvornaya mayor's office regarding the Jewish cemetery (erecting a fence)

OBERTYN

- List of people who were sent to German labor camps for work
- Holocaust documents: postwar lists of property and list of victims

OTTYNIA

- Jewish community documents (budget, salaries), 1926
- Private documents

ROGATIN

- Local maps

SOLOTVINA

- Letter from the rabbi to the president of the Polish Republic, 1936
- Letter from Jonas Olivera, a merchant, to the local government, objecting to the rabbi's assistant, 1934
- Letter from the Jewish community to the Nadvornaya local government requesting that the villages of Maidan and Prislup be combined with the Solotvina Jewish community, undated

STANISŁAWÓW

Stanisławów and Stanisławów Province

- Documents from Agudath Israel Society (7 pages)
- Documents relating to the towns of Galich, Mariampol, Yezapol (now Zhovten) and Stanisławów, in Polish, 1927
- Report from the police department with a list of members of the Jewish community and a list of Jewish buildings (synagogues, schools, etc.)
- Correspondence from the Stanisławów Jewish community to the Starostat (government office), listing which Jewish communities in surrounding towns were a part of the Stanisławów Jewish community (giving statistics from 1921 and names)
- Letter from the Yezapol Jewish community to the Starostat office listing the Jews (statistics) in their region, 1923
- Documents including statistics about the number of Jews in surrounding villages, in Polish, 1924
- Passport applications of individual rabbis (22 files)
- Numerous twentieth-century documents and photographs relating to individuals; maps of towns; plans of synagogues; correspondence between the Jewish community and the local government; photos of Jewish sites and town views

Holocaust Period/Document Copies

- List of 1,086 Jews killed in Stanisławów in August 1941
- List of 4,911 Jews who died in Stanisławów with ages, names of family members and addresses
- Numerous survivor testimonies from the period 1941–1944
- Report from the Jewish community to the local government listing losses (people killed; synagogues and homes destroyed)
- Witness testimonials (methods of killing and destruction)

- Concentration-camp documents in Stanisławów about medical experiments on November 29, 1944
- Map of Stanisławów Ghetto, 1942
- Photographs of ghetto entrance
- Newspaper articles
- Photograph of monument in the Jewish cemetery commemorating where 120,000 Jews died

Jewish Cemetery

- Map of cemetery, dated 1994 (more than 4,500 graves documented by Rabbi Kolesnik)
- Plan of cemetery, showing size
- Alphabetical list of those buried in the cemetery and date of death
- Map showing the location of graves
- Correspondence between the Jewish community and the mayor's office, 1996
- Letter from the Jewish community to the mayor's office requesting a new Jewish cemetery; correspondence continued from 1913 to 1924 until the new cemetery was established

TATOROV

- Private documents of Rabbi Gersh Matus Fischer, consisting of correspondence to the local government regarding his application for examination in a foreign language
- Correspondence between Rabbi Fischer and the local government about voting, 1936

TLUMACH

- List of 200 contributors to the Jewish community, 1936
- Photographs of the dedication of the Holocaust monument

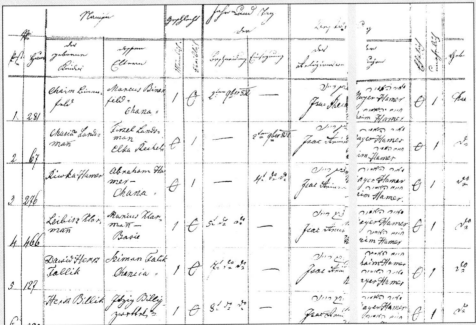

Birth record from Kalush metrical book, 1832–1848 (Yiddish version recorded on right-hand page)   48

Current Borders of Ukraine

Map 5

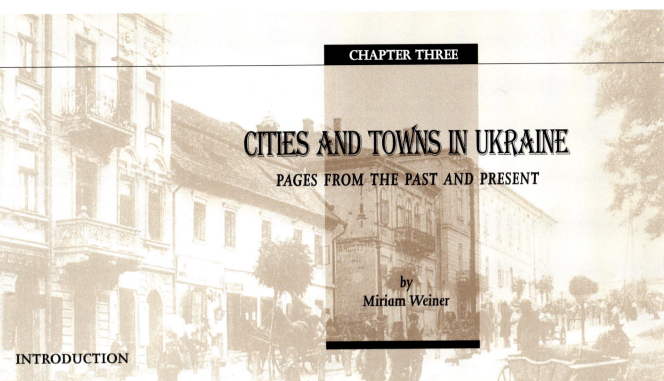

CITIES AND TOWNS IN UKRAINE

PAGES FROM THE PAST AND PRESENT

by
Miriam Weiner

INTRODUCTION

In the 1990s, increasing numbers of Jews from all over the world are traveling to their ancestral towns in Eastern Europe.

The travel agencies and organizations now offering "Jewish roots tours" provide a valuable option for those who feel the need to walk the streets of their ancestors. As an alternative to organized group tours, customized private family tours to Eastern Europe are becoming increasingly popular. Special planning and concern for security, however, are necessary when traveling in the republics of the former Soviet Union.

Before the Holocaust, approximately 1.5 million Jews lived in the area within the current borders of Ukraine. An estimated 486,000 Jews were counted in the last official Soviet census in 1989. Due to emigration and other factors, it is believed that about 200,000 Jews remain in Ukraine (see Chapter 5). They can be found in the largest cities and in the smallest villages. The uncertainty of the population range results from many factors, including the fact that some people are only now discovering their Jewish origins, while others have kept them hidden for many years for fear of becoming targets of repression and anti-Semitism.

This chapter focuses on 56 cities and towns within the current borders of Ukraine. An additional 23 towns in Ukraine are featured in Chapter 11 in *Town Clips* (one-page pictorials).

CHAPTER RESOURCES

A typical town entry in this chapter includes a map showing the specific locality and surrounding towns, the Jewish population (pre-Holocaust), the percentage of the Jewish population based upon the general population, the latitude/longitude and a reference to a nearby larger town. Within each town entry are a number of photographs, both current and historic views.

Spelling Variations

Alternative names and some spelling variations of town names are shown above the map in each town entry. As explained in the *Introduction* of this book, each town name is transliterated from its former Russian spelling. The current Ukrainian spelling is the first one shown above the map. Some photos of town signs were taken prior to Ukrainian independence in 1991 or prior to the signs being changed. The spelling of town names is a difficulty encountered by numerous researchers due to the many changes caused by shifting borders and changing names. Alternative spellings of town names can also be found in publications listed in Appendix 1, *Selected Bibliography*, as well as in other reference books.

Mukachevo (Munkács), c. 1918   49

The sources for the current spellings of the town names and the latitude/longitude are:

- Mokotoff, Gary and Sallyann Amdur Sack. *Where Once We Walked* (Teaneck, NJ: Avotaynu, Inc., 1991).
- A series of gazetteers published by the U.S. Board on Geographic Names.
- Map "Roads of Ukraine," 1995.

Sources consulted for population figures:

- *Black Book of Localities Whose Jewish Population Was Exterminated by the Nazis* (Jerusalem: Yad Vashem, 1965).
- Gutman, Israel, ed. *Encyclopedia of the Holocaust.* 4 vols. (New York: Macmillan Publishing, 1990).
- *Jewish Towns in Ukraine: Podoliya* (Jerusalem and St. Petersburg: Jerusalem Center for Documentation of the Diaspora Heritage, 1997). (R)
- Klevan, Avraham, ed. *Jewish Communities Destroyed in the Holocaust* (Jerusalem: Yad Vashem, 1982).
- *Pinkas Hakehillot: Poland. Vol. 2* (Jerusalem: Yad Vashem, 1980). (H)
- *Pinkas Hakehillot: Poland. Vol. 5* (Jerusalem: Yad Vashem, 1990). (H)
- Published local and regional histories.
- Roth, Cecil, ed. *Encyclopaedia Judaica* (Jerusalem: Keter Publishing House, 1971–1972).
- Yizkor books.

The source for the map shown in each town entry is:

- *Ravenstein Verlag GmbH,* a publisher of maps in Germany.

Sources consulted regarding data for synagogues, cemeteries and Holocaust memorials include:

- *Encyclopaedia Judaica.*
- Jan Jagielski, director of the Department for Documentation of Monuments at the Jewish Historical Institute in Warsaw, Poland.
- Eleonora Bergman, a researcher in the Department for Documentation of Monuments at the Jewish Historical Institute in Warsaw, Poland.
- Data gathered from numerous on-site visits by the author to towns in Ukraine and Moldova during the period 1991–1999.
- Reports and photographs from travelers and researchers.
- Yizkor books.
- The Vaad of Ukraine (the Association of Jewish Organizations and Communities of Ukraine).

Sources for historic and present-day photographs:

- Many of the old photographs included in this chapter and elsewhere in the book are reproductions of antique, hand-tinted postcards from private collections.
- Some photographs were found in various archives and institutes throughout Ukraine, Poland, Moldova and the United States.
- The present-day photographs were taken by both private individuals and professional photographers. In some cases, it was possible to show a contemporary photograph side-by-side with a pre–World War II view of the same site.

Konotop, Ukraine, c. 1922   50

*H*olocaust memorial erected in 1970 by a local Jewish committee in memory of the Jews murdered by the Germans in the town of Pechora in Vinnitsa Oblast. The Hebrew text reads: "Memorial Stone, Here lie the Jewish dead, brutally killed by the fascist murderers, whose hands are full of blood. Thousands of men, women and children died for kiddush haShem from 1941–1945 in the town of Pechora. May the Lord look kindly upon them and avenge the blood of His servants."

The Russian text reads: "Reflect, O Man! Thousands of these miserable people did not live to see the victory over the German fascist hangmen and their helpers, who bestially cut short the breath, voice, thoughts and life of women, children and old men. Words cannot describe their death. They were your mother, your father, your brothers and sisters. They perished so that you could live in happiness.

Do not suffer, but fill yourself with hatred and swear that you will never again allow this to happen. Perpetuate a living memory of them through your descendants.

Do Not Forget!

This Is Their Testament."

51

BELAYA TSERKOV

Location

84 km S of Kiev
49°47´/30°07´

Oblast

Kiev

Jewish Population, Pre-Holocaust

15,624 (36% of general population in 1926)

| Street view of market square with a social club in the center, c. 1915   53

| Plaque in memory of Yiddish author Sholom Aleichem, who lived and worked in Belaya Tserkov from 1883 to 1887. The plaque is on a house built on the site of his former home.   52

| Jewish cemetery with more than 1,000 tombstones, mostly from the twentieth century, with a few older ones that were relocated from their original locations where they had been heavily damaged, 1993   54

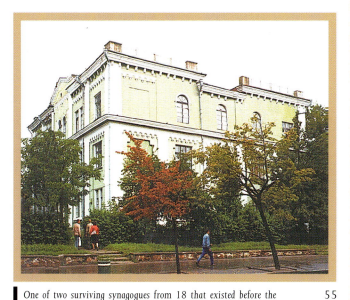

One of two surviving synagogues from 18 that existed before the   55
Holocaust. This synagogue, known as "The Great Synagogue," was closed
in 1960; until recently, it served as an agricultural secondary school,
1993.

Holocaust memorial to the 7,000 Jews killed in Belaya Tserkov   56
on September 6, 1941; dedicated in September 1991

Market square, 1915   57

BERDICHEV

BERDYCHIV (UKR); BERDYCIV (ALT)

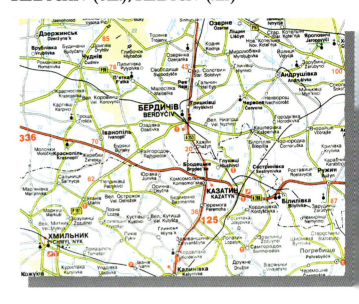

Location

43 km S of Zhitomir

59° 54´/28°35´

Oblast

Zhitomir

Jewish Population, Pre-Holocaust

30,812 (55.6% of general population in 1926)

▌ *Former synagogue, now utilized as a glove factory, 1998*   58

▌ *Interior of Great Synagogue, c. 1918*   59

■ *Artist's rendering of the Great Synagogue, based upon a photograph from the 1890s* 60

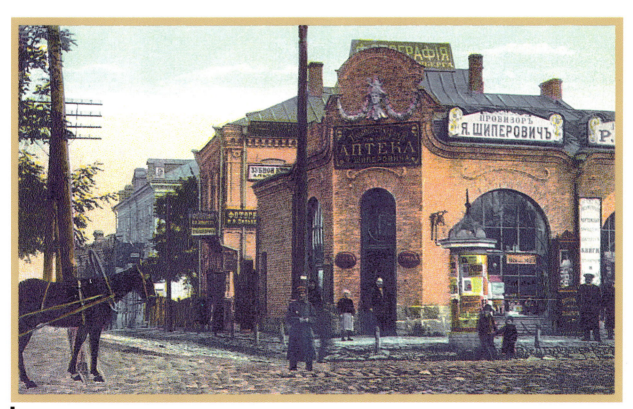

■ *Pharmacy owned by Ya. Shiperovich, c. 1917* 61

Entrance to Jewish cemetery, Lenina Street
(Holocaust memorial in the background), 1995

62

Holocaust memorial in Jewish cemetery in memory of the Jews of
Berdichev and surrounding towns killed between 1941 and 1943
(photo, 1995)

63

Makhnovskaya Street; view of Choral Synagogue at left rear and furniture store of I. Nirenberg at right, c. 1917

64

Belopolskaya Street, c. 1917   65

Jewish cemetery with more than 5,000 tombstones dating from the   66
18th century, 1997

Jewish cemetery, 1996   67

Makhnovskaya Street, synagogue at center, c. 1925 (since destroyed)   68

Ohel of Rabbi Zvi *Aryeh* Twersky from Makarov, died 1835. His son
and grandson are also buried here, 1994.

70

Jewish cemetery, 1994   69

Holocaust memorial in memory of 3,000 Jewish children killed in 1941   71

Ohel in Jewish cemetery. Burial site of Rabbi Levi Yitzhak (1740–1809),
student of the Maggid (popular preacher) of Mezhirich and son of Rabbi Meir, 1996

72

The only currently operating synagogue in Berdichev, 1997   73

Synagogue interior, 1997   74

Only operating synagogue, view from the northeast, 1994   75

BRODY

Location

93 km SW of Rovno
50° 05′/25° 09′

Oblast

Lvov

Jewish Population, Pre-Holocaust

7,702 (66.5% of general population in 1921)

BRODY (UKR)

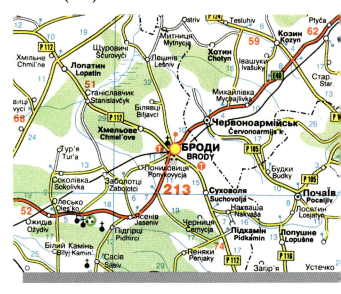

Bet ha-knesset, pre-1939

Local view, 1995

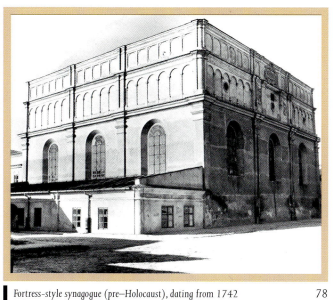

Fortress-style synagogue (pre–Holocaust), dating from 1742
and partially destroyed by the Nazis in 1943, with further
destruction by the Soviets (see photo below)   78

 A marketplace, 1914   79

Synagogue in ruins (see above photo), 1995   80

A marketplace, 1995   81

 Jewish cemetery, 1995 82

 Jewish cemetery, 1995 83

Holocaust memorial in the Brody forest at edge of the Jewish cemetery, 1995. "In the memory of 84
the holy martyrs—Jews who were ruthlessly killed by the Nazi murderers"

▌ Police checkpoint at the Austrian-Russian border, c. 1918   85

▌ Jewish cemetery with more than 5,000 tombstones dating   86
from the 1800s (photo, 1995)

▌ A former Jewish street, 1993   87

▌ Train station, 1909   88

BUCHACH

BUCHACH (UKR); BUCZACZ (POL)

Location

72 km SW of Ternopol
49° 04′ / 25° 24′

Oblast

Ternopol

Jewish Population, Pre-Holocaust

3,858 (51.5% of general population in 1921)

Town view, 1992

89

Entering the center of town, school on the left, c. 1930

90

Former synagogue, dating from the 18th century, 1998　　　　91

Former Jewish district, 1992　　　　93

Jewish cemetery, 1992　　　　92

Local view, c. 1930　　　　94

Jewish cemetery with several hundred tombstones dating from the 19th century. Many tombstones are toppled and damaged, 1992.　　　　95

CHERNIGOV

CHERNIHIV (UKR)

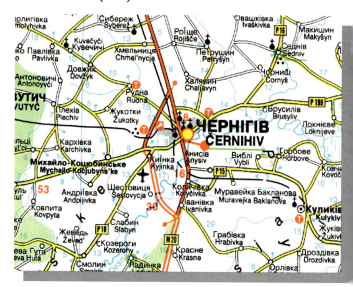

Location

140 km NNE of Kiev
51° 30´/31° 18´

Oblast

Chernigov

Jewish Population, Pre-Holocaust

10,607 (30% of general population in 1926)

Former Choral Synagogue, now an office building, 1998   96

Town view, c. 1990   97

Town view, c. 1920

98

Town view. Cinema on the left and a hotel on the right, 1998

99

Upper: "Here are buried approximately 1,500 Soviet citizens, who were tortured to death by the German-Fascist invaders in 1941. Let us remember the sacrifices that the people endured in winning the freedom and independence of future generations."

Lower: "On November 18, 1941, the German Fascists shot 800 Jewish residents of Chernigov and surrounding towns."

101

Holocaust monument in memory of 800 Jews killed at this site by the Nazis in 1941 (photo, 1998)   100

Jewish cemetery, 1998

102

Entrance to Jewish cemetery, where the earliest tombstone dates from 1863.
There are several thousand tombstones in this cemetery, 1998.

103

CHERNOVTSY

CHERNIVTSI (UKR); CERNAUȚI (ROM); CZERNOWITZ (GER)

Location

176 km SSE of Ternopol

48° 18´/25° 56´

Oblast

Chernovtsy

Jewish Population, Pre-Holocaust

46,000 (40% of general population in 1930)

The Great Synagogue, constructed in 1853–1878 and severely burned by the Nazis in 1941, c. 1917 (see current view at right)

104

Bet Tfila Benjamin Synagogue, 1992. Only functioning synagogue now in Chernovtsy, out of more than 20 before the Holocaust. This synagogue was constructed between 1923 and 1938 (photo 105-A, 1994; photo 105-B, 1995; photo 105-C, 1992).

105-B

105-C

105-A

Formerly the Great Synagogue, this building now functions as a cinema and is known among the locals as the "kinagoga," 1995.

106

▌ *View of Herrengasse-Kochanowskiego Street, c. 1915* 107

▌ *Belle Vue Hotel and Restaurant, c. 1918* 108

A main street, c. 1915

Jewish People's House, c. 1925   109

Old market square with town hall in the center, c. 1918   112

Former Jewish district, 1992   110

Town hall (center) and restaurant/hotel (right), c. 1920   113

G.S. Atlas (left), 1933-1965, and Sh.M. Polyak (right), 1905–1965 (photo, 1991)   114

Jewish cemetery with more than 5,000 tombstones at Zelonaya   115
Street dating from the 18th century, 1995

Jewish cemetery, 1995   116

Memorial to 29 Jews murdered by the Nazis in July 1941   117
(photo, 1995)

Prayer house in the Jewish cemetery, 1991   118

Yoma Golda Frimmel, daughter of Aizyk Yehuda
Luttinger, died 1923 (photo, 1995)
119

Jewish cemetery, 1998
120

Jewish cemetery, 1998
121

Former Jewish district in Chernovtsy, 1994
122

CHORTKOV

Location

74 km S of Ternopol
49° 01′/25° 48′

Oblast

Ternopol

Jewish Population, Pre-Holocaust

5,869 (30.7% of general population in 1935)

CHORTKIV (UKR); CZORTKÓW (POL)

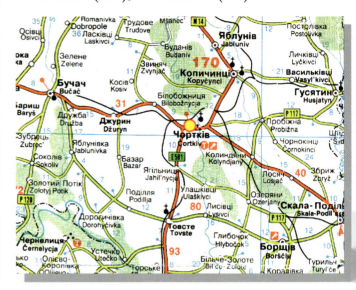

Town square, 1914   123

Synagogue interior, Aron ha-Kodesh, c. 1908   124

Jewish cemetery, 1992   125

Tombstones dating from 1927 in the Jewish cemetery, 1994   128

Local view, 1912   126

View of eastern wall of synagogue, now used as a hospital's   129
warehouse, 1998

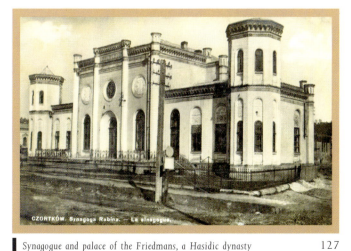

Synagogue and palace of the Friedmans, a Hasidic dynasty   127
of Sadgora, 1938

Former synagogue and palace of the Friedmans, 1992   130

Jewish cemetery, established in the 17th century. A few hundred   131
stones remain, but many are severely damaged or toppled.
Tombstones date from the early 20th century (photo, 1992).

Jewish cemetery, 1998   133

Tombstone for Gitel, daughter of Zvi, died 1933   132
(photo, 1994)

Local view, 1998   134

Jewish cemetery, 1998

135

Jewish cemetery, 1998

136

Jewish cemetery, 1992

137

Local view, 1998

138

DNEPROPETROVSK

DNIPROPETROVSK (UKR); EKATERINOSLAV (ALT)

Location

183 km SSE of Poltava
48° 27´/34° 59´

Oblast

Dnepropetrovsk

Jewish Population, Pre-Holocaust

80,000 (16% of general population in 1939)

L'Avenue Pushkin, c. 1915

Ekaterininskiy Prospekt, c. 1920

140

A former synagogue, 1994

141

Общій видъ   Екатеринославъ

▌ Town view, c. 1915   142

▌ Choral Synagogue, c. 1915   143

Former synagogue, now a cultural center, 1994   144

Street map at the edge of town, 1994   145

Former Jewish hospital, now a dental clinic, 1994   146

DOLINA

DOLYNA (UKR)

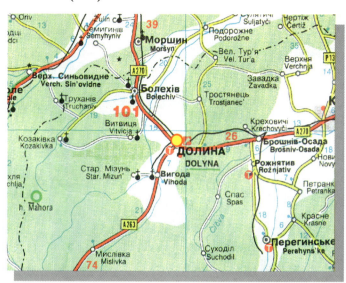

Location

112 km S of Lvov
48° 58´/24° 01´

Oblast

Ivano-Frankovsk

Jewish Population, Pre-Holocaust

2,014 (23% of general population in 1921)

Fragment in the Jewish cemetery, 1992   148

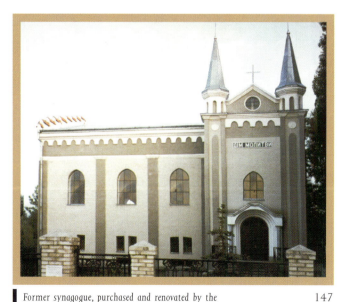

Former synagogue, purchased and renovated by the   147
Baptist Church, 1997

Former synagogue, now a Baptist church, 1997   149

▮ *Former synagogue, 1992*   150

▮ *Jewish cemetery. Fewer than 100 tombstones remain dating from 1920, and none are upright, 1997.*   151

DROGOBYCH

Location

69 km SSW of Lvov
49° 21´/23° 30´

Oblast

Lvov

Jewish Population, Pre-Holocaust

15,000 (40% of general population in 1939)

Stryjska Street, 1909

152

Mickiewicza Street, 1912

153

Choral Synagogue, built between 1847 and 1865. This photo was taken 154
in 1992, when the synagogue was being utilized as a furniture factory.

Choral Synagogue, recently returned to the Jewish community, 1997 155

Synagogue on Stryjska Street, c. 1909 156

Entrance to Jewish cemetery (near the bus station), 1991   157

Memorial plaque in memory of Bruno Schulz   159
(1915–1941), a famous writer and painter, who
lived in this house in the years 1915–1941 (photo, 1995)

Left: Samuel Schiffman, 1847–1933   158
Right: Chaim Luzer Hirschhorn, 1867–1934 (photo, 1994)

Jewish cemetery, with tombstones dating from the 1870s (photo, 1992)   160

Holocaust memorial in nearby Bronitsa Forest, where 450 Jews from the   161
Drogobych Ghetto were murdered on February 15, 1943 (photo, 1992)

■ Jewish cemetery, 1995   162

■ Pharmacy on Mickiewicza Street, 1917   163

■ Mickiewicza Street, 1992   164

Drohobycz   Ogólny widok — Totalansicht

■ Local view, c. 1915   165

DUBNO (UKR)

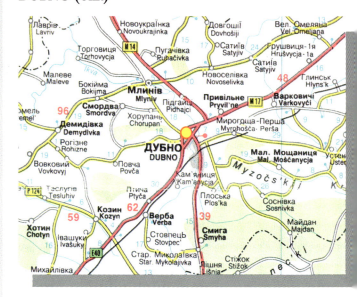

Location

48 km SW of Rovno
50° 25´/25° 45´

Oblast

Rovno

Jewish Population, Pre-Holocaust

7,000 (47% of general population in 1937)

Local view, c. 1917   166

Former Jewish district, 1998   167

Synagogue constructed in 1782–1784 (photo, pre-1936) 168

Synagogue, 1995 169

Tsarina Aleksandra II Street, c. 1917 170

Jewish cemetery where only a few tombstones remain
from the 20th century, 1995   171

Jewish cemetery (with the oldest tombstone dating from 1581)   172
before the massive destruction during the Holocaust, 1995

View of bimah and Aron ha-Kodesh, c. 1939   173

The Jewish hospital, pre-Holocaust   174

Former Jewish district, 1998 175

Holocaust memorial, 1995 "On this territory (in the region of the so-called Shibana Gora) Hitler's aggressors shot more than 6,000 peaceful citizens of Jewish nationality in 1941–1942, from the town and region of Dubno as well as three other regions in Rovno Oblast. Let's bow our heads in mourning in memory of the people whose blood so profusely soaked our earth. In eternal memory of the victims of the Nazis."

176

Holocaust memorial to 6,000 Jews from Dubno and surrounding towns who were shot by Nazis in 177
1941–1942 (photo, 1995)

GLUKHOV

HLUKHIV (UKR)

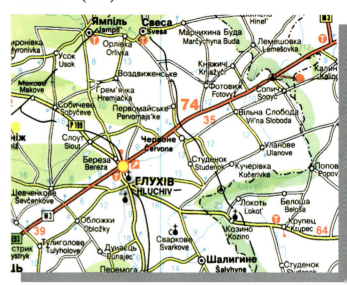

Location

130 km NW of Sumy
51° 41´/33° 55´

Oblast

Sumy

Jewish Population, Pre-Holocaust

2,551 (16% of general population in 1926)

Local view, 1993   178

Local view, c. 1900   179

Jewish cemetery, with tombstones dating from 1823 (photo, 1993) 180

Jewish cemetery, with approximately 1,000 remaining tombstones, 1993 182

Memorial plaque for Holocaust victims erected in 1995 by Alan and Marjorie Goldberg in memory of their Zavelskiy ancestors and the Jews of Glukhov who perished during World War II 183

Former Jewish district, 1993 181

Holocaust memorial, 1997 184

IVANO-FRANKIVSK (UKR); STANISŁAWÓW (POL); STANISLAU (GER)

Location

135 km SE of Lvov

48° 56´/24° 43´

Oblast

Ivano-Frankovsk

Jewish Population, Pre-Holocaust

24,823 (41.3% of general population in 1931)

Rabbi Moishe Leib Kolesnik with the Tanne family from the United States and Israel, 1992   185

Rabbi Moishe Leib Kolesnik with parokhet (ark covering) donated by the Neiman family and Shrage Feitel Fuks, 1997   186

Scenic view of Ivano-Frankovsk (Stanisławów), 1918   187

The Temple, constructed in 1893 (photo, 1933)   188

One of just seven synagogues remaining from before the Holocaust,   189
when there were more than 50 synagogues and prayer houses.
See earlier photo of the same synagogue at left, 1992.

Jewish cemetery, 1992   190

Holocaust memorial in the Jewish cemetery in memory of the Jews who   191
were murdered by the Nazis between 1941 and 1944 (photo, 1992)

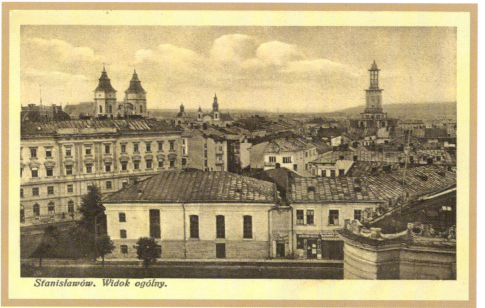

Stanisławów. Widok ogólny.

View, 1936   192

Former Jewish district, 1995   193

Holocaust memorial in the forest where the Nazis killed 120,000   194
citizens and prisoners, including Jews, from 1941 to 1944 (photo, 1992)

100

Tombstones used for paving sidewalks. 195
Hirsch Hoffman, died 1922 (photo, 1992)

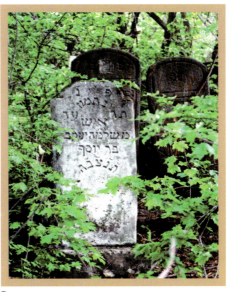

Tombstone of Shlomo Yakov, son of Josef 196
(photo, 1992)

Ohel of Rabbi Chaim Chager, son of Boruch from Otynya, died 1932 197
(photo, 1998)

Center of town, c. 1990 198

IZYASLAV

Location

69 km SE of Rovno
50° 07´/26° 48´

Oblast

Khmelnitskiy

Jewish Population, Pre-Holocaust

3,820 (33% of general population in 1926)

IZYASLAV (UKR); ZASLAV (ALT)

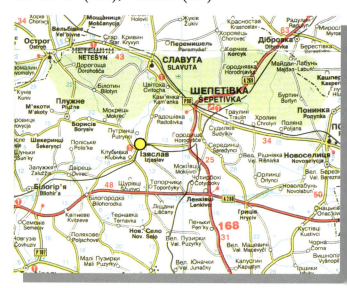

Former Talmud Tora, 1996   200

Local view, c. 1916   199

Former synagogue, now a furniture factory, 1996   201

Jewish cemetery, 1996   202

Left: *Abram Nakhmanson, son of Isaak, 1886–1956*   203
Right: *M. P. Nakhmanson (photo, 1996)*

Jewish cemetery, 1996   204

Local view, 1909   205

KALUSH

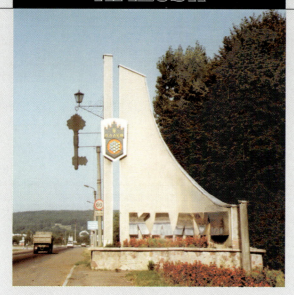

KALUSH (UKR)

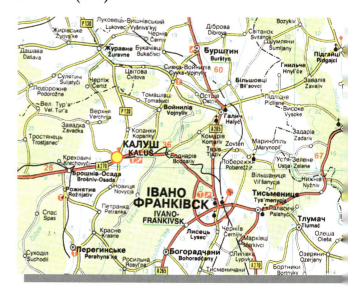

Location

32 km NW of Ivano-Frankovsk
49° 01´/24° 02´

Oblast

Ivano-Frankovsk

Jewish Population, Pre-Holocaust

6,000 (33% of general population in 1938)

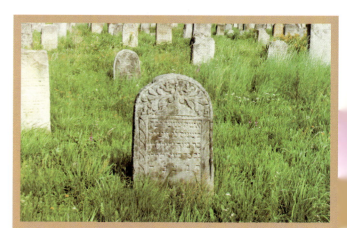

Jewish cemetery, 1997

206

Jewish cemetery, 1997

207

Jewish cemetery, 1997   208

Former Jewish community offices, now local government offices,   209
1997

Holocaust memorial, 1997   210

Holocaust memorial, 1997   211

KAMENETS-PODOLSKIY

KAMIANETS-PODILSKYI (UKR)

Location

103 km SSW of Khmelnitskiy
48° 40´/26° 34´

Oblast

Khmelnitskiy

Jewish Population, Pre-Holocaust

12,774 (29.9% of general population in 1929)

General view, c. 1917

Holocaust memorial in memory of the 23,600 Jews 213
from Kamenets-Podolskiy and surrounding towns who
were murdered by the Nazis on August 27–28, 1941
(photo, 1992)

Former synagogue, now a restaurant, 1994 214

Town view, c. 1917 215

General view, 1994 216

Jewish cemetery, 1998 217

Jewish cemetery, 1998 218

Jewish prayer house, 1995 219

"Let the generations remember 220
our fathers and mothers, brothers
and sisters, the best sons and
daughters of our people—who
were murdered on the fifth day
of Elul [August 28] in the
year 1941 by the German
fascists."

Holocaust memorial, 1998 221

Fortress in the background, c. 1917   225

"In memory of the victims   222
of fascism in *World War II*,
1941–1945" (photo, 1998)

Holocaust memorial, 1998   223

View of the fortress from the Kamenets-Podolskiy City-State Archive, 1994   224

Town view, c. 1917   226

KHARKOV

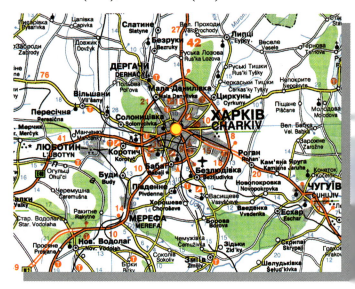

Location

487 km E of Kiev
50° 00´/36° 15´

Oblast

Kharkov

Jewish Population, Pre-Holocaust

130,200 (16.7% of general population in 1939)

Bazaar, c. 1918   227

Local view, 1997   228

Tombstone of Inna Ita Sivak, 1882–1938, daughter of Aron Zelik (photo, 1997)

229

Local view in Kharkov, 1997

230

Plaque at entrance gate to synagogue (see below right), 1997

231

This synagogue, constructed c. 1910, functioned as a sports center in the 1960s. On August 31, 1998, the synagogue was heavily damaged by fire (photo, 1997).

232

Харьковъ.—Kharkoff. № 57.
Торговая площадь.—Place de commerce.

Commercial Square, 1906

233

Харьковъ. Сумская улица. Сѣверный банкъ.

Sumskaya Street, c. 1917

234

Former synagogue, now the Jewish cultural center, 1996   517-A

Plaque on the Osher Schvartsman   517-B
Jewish Cultural Center, 1996

Market scene, 1939   518

Holocaust memorial, 1996   519

ТУТ БРАТНЯ МОГИЛА 17500 РОВЕНСЬКИХ ЄВРЕЇВ-СТАРИКІВ, ЖІНОК І ДІТЕЙ БЕЗВИННО ЗАМУЧЕНИХ РОЗСТРІЛЯНИХ ЖИВЦЕМ ЗАКОПАНИХ НІМЕЦЬКО-ФАШИСТСЬКИМИ КАТАМИ 6 ЛИСТОПАДА 1941 РОКУ. ВІЧНА ШАНА ІХ СВІТЛІЙ ПАМ'ЯТІ.

Monument in memory of the 17,500 Jews from
Rovno and surrounding towns who were murdered
by the Nazis on September 6, 1941 (photo, 1996)   520

Steps to the Holocaust memorial, 1996   521

Segment of list of Rovno's Jews who
were murdered by the Nazis, 1996   522

Jacquelyn Seevak Sanders visits the Holocaust memorial and looks for the   523
Seevak family name, 1996

Portion of the Holocaust memorial, 1996   524

Portion of the Holocaust memorial, 1996   525

SAMBOR

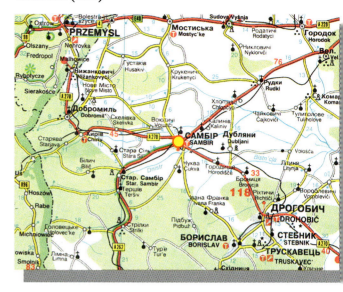

SAMBIR (UKR)

Jewish cemetery, 1992   526

Location

65 km SW of Lvov
49° 31´/23° 12´

Oblast

Lvov

Jewish Population, Pre-Holocaust

6,068 (31.3% of general population in 1921)

Trybunalska Street, 1915   527

One of the few remaining tombstones
in the Jewish cemetery, 1992   528

Rynok (market square), c. 1920   530

Synagogue dating from c. 1730; now used for storage, 1992   531

Plaque on the wall in Jewish cemetery   529
in memory of the Jews of Sambor
who were murdered by the Nazis
between 1941 and 1944
(photo, 1995)

Kopernika Street, c. 1920   532

SATANOV

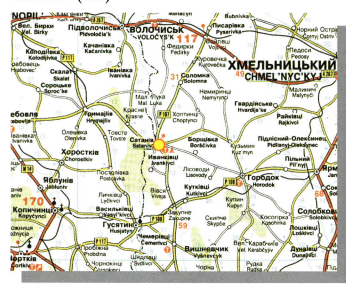

Location

107 km N of Chernovtsy
49° 15´/26° 16´

Oblast

Khmelnitskiy

Jewish Population, Pre-Holocaust

2,359 (58% of general population in 1926)

▌ Jewish cemetery, 1995

533

▌ *Local view from the Jewish cemetery, 1995*

534

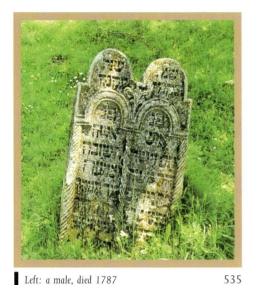

Left: a male, died 1787
Right: a female, died 1795
(photo, 1995)

535

Stone and brick synagogue dating from the 17th century; currently used for storage purposes, 1995

536

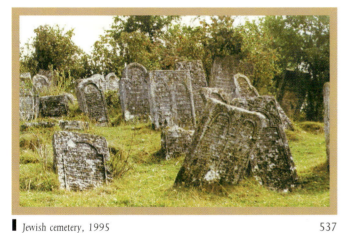

 Jewish cemetery, 1995

537

Synagogue, 1995

538

Jewish cemetery, 1995

539

Location

56 km SSW of Vinnitsa
48° 45´/28° 05´

Oblast

Vinnitsa

Jewish Population, Pre-Holocaust

2,697 (55.9% of general population in 1926)

SHARHOROD (UKR)

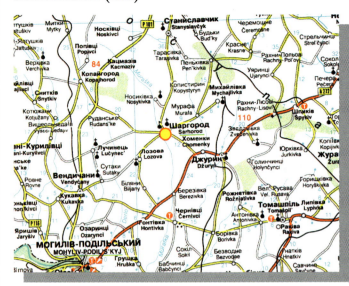

Local view, 1994   540

Local view, c. 1918   541

Synagogue constructed in the 16th century, now used as a
workshop, 1994

542

Entrance to the New Jewish Cemetery, 1994

545

New Jewish Cemetery, dating from the 18th century, 1994

543

Old Jewish Cemetery, dating from the 17th century, 1994

546

New Jewish Cemetery, 1994

544

A former Jewish street, 1994

547

SHEPETOVKA

SHEPETIVKA (UKR)

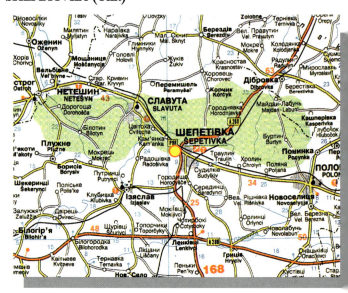

Location

86 km N of Khmelnitskiy
50° 11´/27° 04´

Oblast

Khmelnitskiy

Jewish Population, Pre-Holocaust

3,916 (26.7% of general population in 1926)

Local hotel, 1991

548

Interior of synagogue, 1991

549

Memorial in the forest near Shepetovka where the Jews of
Shepetovka and surrounding towns were murdered by the Nazis
(photo, 1998)

550

Synagogue (see below), used as a sport center until 1991,
when one room was returned to the Jewish community
(photo, 1991)

551

Synagogue, closed down by the authorities in the early 1960s (photo, c. 1935)

552

Rededication ceremony celebrating the return of one room of the synagogue to the Jewish community, 1991   553

The graves of Rabbi Pinchas of Korets and his sons, who were rabbis in Shepetovka and Slavuta.   554
Rabbi Pinchas, 1726–1791, was one of the foremost rabbis during the generation of the
Baal Shem Tov's students, 1991.

■ Rivka Shuster, daughter of Arye
(1894–1973) photo, 1991

555

■ Three members of the Shnaider family
are buried here, 1991

556

■ The Jewish community of Shepetovka poses in front of the new cemetery gate funded by the Shepetovka landsmanshaftn society in New York, c. 1920

557

SKALA PODOLSKAYA

Location

100 km SE of Ternopol

48° 51´/26° 12´

Oblast

Ternopol

Jewish Population, Pre-Holocaust

1,555 (38.6% of general population in 1921)

View of main street and local transportation, 1993   558

This monument is in memory of the 3,000 Jewish men, women and children from Skala, Ozeryany, Korolovka, Borshchev (site of the massacre), Melnitsa and neighboring villages massacred by the Nazis in the spring of 1943. The monument was erected on the site of the destroyed Jewish cemetery in nearby Borshchev, 1998.   559

 Ruins of a 17th-century Turkish castle, a local historic landmark, 1992   560

The Beth Am Jewish Community Center, constructed   561
1921–1922. The building housed the Hebrew
school, Jewish library and various Zionist youth clubs.
The second floor was a large hall for public meetings,
weddings, shows and parties, c. 1935.

Former Jewish community center, now used for   562
private residences, 1993

Funeral procession of Rabbi Nute Drimmer, the scion of a 563
prominent rabbinic dynasty who served the local Jewish
community for more than 100 years (photo, c. 1930s)

Among the surviving tombstones (dating from the 16th 564
century) is that of Rabbi Nute Drimmer, third from right,
1991.

Restored Jewish cemetery with new wall and 565
gate entrance, 1997

Plaque on gate entrance to Jewish cemetery: "Fence erected 566
in 1997 by Holocaust survivors in the USA in memory
of the martyred Jewish community of Skala that lived
here since 1570. Perished in 1942" (photo, 1997)

The Port-Arthur Synagogue in Skala, constructed in 1903, one of
seven that existed between the two world wars, named after the Port
Arthur Fortress made famous the next year in the Russo-Japanese
War, 1927

567

Partial view of the main street. Houses in the foreground
are all former Jewish homes, 1997.

568

Motie, the oldest water carrier, 1927

569

SNYATYN

SNIATYN (UKR); ŞNIATYN (POL)

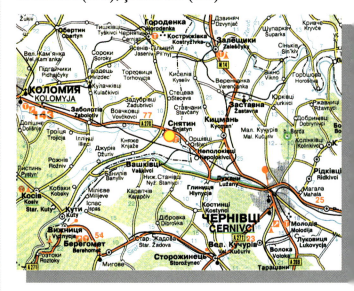

Location

32 km WNW of Chernovtsy
48° 27′/25° 34′

Oblast

Ivano Frankovsk

Jewish Population, Pre-Holocaust

3,248 (31% of general population in 1921)

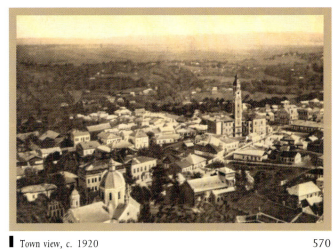

Town view, c. 1920   570

Jewish cemetery, 1993   571

Tombstone used in constructing sidewalks, 1997 — 572

Segment of town square, 1997 — 574

Former synagogue constructed in the 1930s; now used as a workshop, 1997 — 575

Main Street, c. 1920 — 573

Jewish cemetery, 1993 — 576

227

STAROKONSTANTINOV

STAROKOSTIANTYNIV (UKR)

Location

49 km N of Khmelnitskiy
49° 45´/27° 13´

Oblast

Khmelnitskiy

Jewish Population, Pre-Holocaust

4,837 (33% of general population in 1931)

Street scene, c. 1920

577

Jewish cemetery, 1994   578

New housing development, 1993   580

Jewish cultural center, 1998   581

Jewish cemetery, 1993   579

Jewish cemetery where tombstones date from 1860 (photo, 1993) 582

Fortress dating from the 16th century, c. 1985

583

Torah fragment (displayed upside down) in the local museum, 1993

584

Holocaust memorial, 1993

58

230

Exhibition in the local museum, 1993   586

Jewish cemetery established in the 16th century, 1993   587

STOROZHINETS

STOROZHYNETS (UKR)

Location

23 km SW of Chernovtsy
48° 10′/25° 43′

Oblast

Chernovtsy

Jewish Population, Pre-Holocaust

2,600 (26% of general population in 1924)

Local transportation, 1994

588

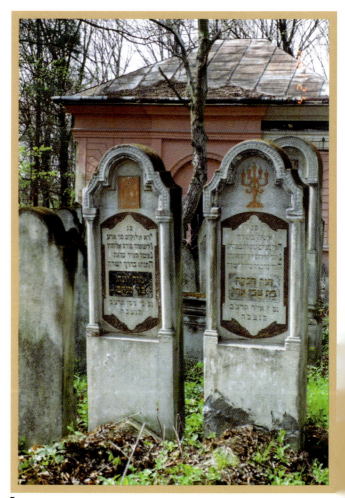

Jewish cemetery, 1994

589

232

Local view from the mayor's office, 1994   590

Former synagogue, now used as a sports club, 1994   592

Etel Lobel, died 1918, daughter of Zvi Dov (photo, 1994)   591

Jewish cemetery with tombstones dating from the 18th century, 1994   593

Local view of Czernowitz Street, c. 1922   594

233

STRYY

STRYI (UKR); **STRYJ** (POL)

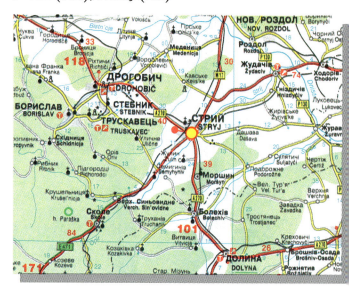

Location

69 km S of Lvov
49° 15´/23° 51´

Oblast

Lvov

Jewish Population, Pre-Holocaust

10,980 (40% of general population in 1921)

Former Jewish district, 1994

595

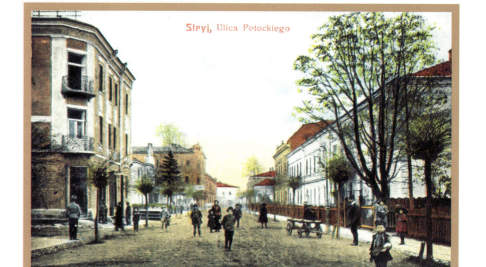

Potockiego Street, c. 1917

596

▌ Synagogue constructed in the early 19th century, now in ruins, 1994   597

▌ Apartment buildings now occupy the site of the Jewish cemetery, 1994   600

▌ Surviving wall of the former synagogue, 1994   598

▌ Local transportation in downtown Stryy, 1994   601

▌ Former synagogue, 1994   599

▌ Third of May Street, 1915   602

Third of May Street, c. 1920

603

View of town, 1916

■ Rynok (market square), c. 1920

604

605

SUDILKOV

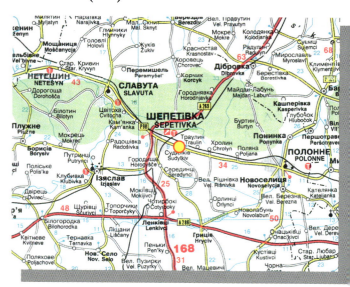

Location

89 km N of Khmelnitskiy
50° 10′/27° 08′

Oblast

Khmelnitskiy

Jewish Population, Pre-Holocaust

1,200 (15.7% of general population in 1925)

Site of the grain mill formerly owned by the Winikur family, 1991   606

Jewish cemetery, 1991   607

The local market, 1991   608

Jewish cemetery, 1994   609

The Sudilkov Synagogue, destroyed during the Holocaust (illustration, c. 1948)   610

One of the few surviving tombstones in the Jewish cemetery, 1991   611

Jewish cemetery, 1993   612

TALNOYE

TALNE (UKR); TOLNA (ALT)

Location

220 km SE of Kiev
48° 53′/30° 42′

Oblast

Kiev

Jewish Population, Pre-Holocaust

4,169 (39% of general population in 1926)

Jewish cemetery (new section), 1998

Former Jewish district, 1998

Jewish cemetery (old section), 1998   615

Holocaust memorial, 1998   616

Local traffic in front of the government offices for the region, 1994   617

This tombstone is among many lying in the grass, 1994   618

TERNOPOL

TERNOPIL (UKR); TARNOPOL (POL)

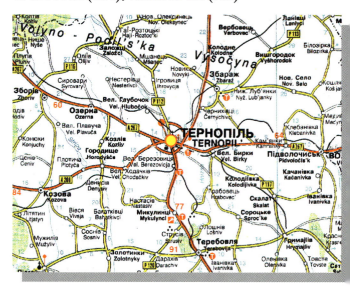

Location

127 ESE of Lvov
49° 33′/25° 35′

Oblast

Ternopol

Jewish Population, Pre-Holocaust

14,000 (39.3% of general population in 1931)

Tarnopol. Ul. Agenora Gołuchowskiego

Agenora Gołuchowskiego Street, 1915

619

620

621

622

Nukhim Rapoport, 1849–1924, son of Shmuel 623
(photo, 1997)

Jewish cemetery, 1997 624

Jewish cemetery established in the 19th century, 1997 625

Ruska Street, c. 1918

626

Mickiewicza Street, c. 1920

627

UMAN

UMAN (UKR)

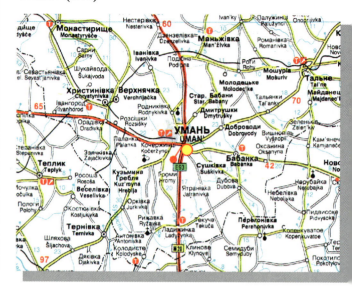

Location

212 km S of Kiev

48° 45´/30° 13´

Oblast

Cherkassy

Jewish Population, Pre-Holocaust

22,179 (49.5% of general population in 1926)

General view, 1903

628

General view, 1998

629

Former Jewish district, 1998

630

Former Jewish district, 1998

631

The tomb of Rav Nakhman of Bratslav, 1772–1811 (photo, 1996)　　　632

Plaque at site of Rav Nakhman's tomb, 1996　　　633

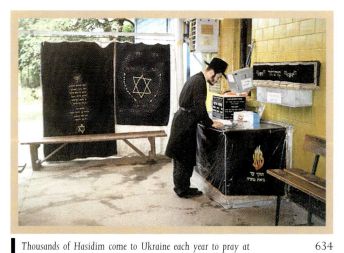

Thousands of Hasidim come to Ukraine each year to pray at　　　634
Rav Nakhman's tomb, 1996

Jewish communal center for Hasidim pilgrimages, 1998　　　635

על פי עדות זקני אומן
נשטיו פה לפני המלחמה
נטמנו במקום חזון
רב' **אברהם**
ב"ר נחמן הלוי
חזן ד"ע
בעל וזה"אור הליקוטים
ולב"ע כ"ט בכסלו תרע"ח
וליד ו
רב' **אליקום געציל**
(המכונה רב' געצ')
ב"ר אברהם ד"ע
ולב"ע שביעי של פסח תרע"ח
ת נ צ ב ה

אותר רשומך ע"י דרך צדיקים

Tombstone of Rabbi Avraham ben Nakhman HaLevi Hazan, author of a book of commentaries, who died in 1917; and next to him, Rabbi Elyakum Getsil (known as Rabbi Getsi), son of Avraham, who died in 1918. The tombstone was erected by Derekh Tsadikim (Path of the Righteous), 1998.   636

❚ Jewish cemetery, 1998   637

UZHGOROD

UZHHOROD (UKR); UNGVAR (HUN)

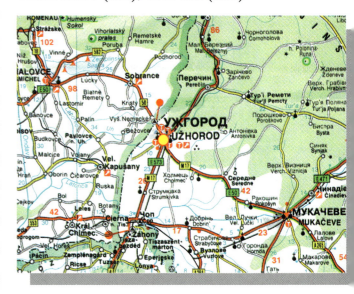

Location

178 km SW of Lvov
48° 37´/22° 18´

Oblast

Zakarpatskiy

Jewish Population, Pre-Holocaust

7,357 (33% of general population in 1930)

▌ Radvanska Street, c. 1920   639

▌ Local view, 1995   638

▌ Local view, 1995   640

Local view, 1995   641

Synagogue, c. 1920   642

Synagogue, 1995   643

Jewish cemetery, 1995   644

Torahs in the synagogue, 1995   646

Outside the synagogue, 1995   647

Synagogue interior, 1995   645

Entrance to the Jewish cemetery, 1995   648

to 1921 and 1941 to 1945. But pogroms against the Jews during the Russian Revolution and Civil War—when anarchy, destruction, banditry and crises of power reigned supreme in the Ukraine—did not resemble the pogroms of the tsarist period. In Podolia, the Jews were killed en masse—about 25,000 Jews were killed; approximately 19,000 Jewish children were orphaned. The Minister of Jewish Affairs of the Ukrainian People's Republic organized an All-Ukrainian Central Committee to help those who had suffered from pogroms. Its fonds, kept in Kiev's Central State Archive of the Higher Bodies of Power and Administration, include many letters, complaints about pogroms, requests for help and registration books of people who suffered in pogroms.

In the State Archive of Vinnitsa Oblast, fonds include both lists of those killed during pogroms in the towns and villages of Podolia and lists of those who survived and subsequently received food, clothing or other assistance. (An active campaign to assist the Jewish population was carried out by the Committees of Help for the Jews.) All of this material, tragic in content but rich in genealogical information, is kept in our archives. In the State Archive of Vinnitsa Oblast, for example, there are nine fonds with 300 files. The documents basically concern issues of food and clothing, and a serious researcher will find many valuable pieces of information in them. For example, on the list of people who received clothing and food from the American Jewish Joint Distribution Committee (the "Joint") is the name Mottel Malid. Alongside a list of the food and clothing that he received, one reads that Mottel Malid was born in 1880, that he was a blacksmith and that he had three children: Pinya, 17; Zisya, 11; and Nyuma, 10. His mother, Sura Malid, was 75 and in the hospital. Thus, a single item provides information about an entire family. Unfortunately, although their genealogical and historical importance is considerable, not many genealogists have researched these fonds.

As mentioned earlier, most Jews occupied the left wing of the political spectrum. After the victory of the Bolsheviks in 1917, some Jewish parties and organizations (the left faction of the Bund, the Poalei Zion and the Jewish Communist Party) disbanded. Those remaining found themselves under rigid control from Soviet political organs and soon ceased their activities. Their records (lists and letters of these parties and organizations) are kept in the fonds of the corresponding guberniya party committees and the Central Committee of the Ukrainian Communist Party.

The 1920s were characterized by the beginning of socialist reconstruction, which was reflected adversely in the life of the Jewish people. A large number of petty owners (merchants) and craftsmen went bankrupt and their businesses were ruined. The number of unemployed grew and Jewish young people were in

an especially difficult position because of bleak prospects for the future. The protocols (memoranda), reports, accounts and certificates of that time held in local bureaus of the Jewish section of guberniya committees (and later of the committees of the Ukrainian Communist Party) give detailed information.

In the early 1920s, two national Jewish districts were established (Novozlatopol in Zaporozhe Okrug [District] and Stalindorf in Krivoy Rog Okrug). All the information on the demographic, economic and cultural developments of these regions is kept in the fonds of the Novozlatopol and Stalindorf departments of the Communist Party of Ukraine. Documents of these and other fonds in the Ukrainian archives testify most convincingly that Jews took an active part in the socialist reconstruction and the sociopolitical life of the Soviet Union. The archives have numerous questionnaires; lists of delegates

Lp	Imię i nazwisko	Wiek	Charakter rodzinny	zawód	data za- mieszkania	Uwagi.
135	Sternberg r.Brett Itte	1868	gł.rodz.	grajzlerka	od ur	
6	" Sara	1903	córka		".	
7	" Bina	1904	"		"	
8	" Józef	1906	syn		"	
9	" Zelman	1912	syn		"	
140	Wiksel Markus	1868	gł.rodz.	pośrednik hand.	od ur.	
1	Feiga	1872	żona		"	
2	" Dawid	1906	syn		"	
3	" Antonina	1907	córka			
4	" Berta	1909	"			
5	Deligtisch Sluwe	1850	gł.rodz	grajzlerka	1866	1866
6	Dr Deligtisch Selig Uszer	1835	syn	adwokat	od ur.	
7	Hessel Anna	1877	córka	przy matce	od ur.	
8	Hessel Ernestyna	1906	wnuczka	przy babce	"	
9	Hessel Jerzy	1907	wnuk	przy babce	"	
150	Nacht Regina	1871	gł.rodz.	wł.młyna	1879	
1	" Herman	1893	syn	piekarz	od ur.	
2	" Ida Berta	1900	córka	p rzy matce	"	
3	" Debora	1906	"	"	"	
4	Forst Adolf		gł. rodz.	pryw.urz.	1930	br.dat.ur.
5	" Hania		żone	--	"	"
6	Henne Jakób	1879	gł.rodz.	zarobnik	1905	
7	" Rebeka	1880	żona	em.fabr.	od ur.	
8	" Balomea	1912	córka		"	
9	" Marja	1914	"		"	
160	" Oskar	1919	syn		"	
161	Rapa Maks	1894	gł.rodz.	dentysta	1927	
2	Kahane Maurycy, Edmund	1889	gł.rodz.	radjotechnik	1929	
3	" Elsa	1892	żona		"	
4	" Herbert	1920	syn		"	
5	" Rut	1922	córka		"	

List of Jews dated 1932, from villages in the Lvov region, with name, year of birth, relationship to head of household, occupation and length of residence in the village. Nos. 140–144 include five members of the Wiksel family: Markus, born 1868; his wife, Feiga, born 1872; son Dawid, born 1906; and daughters Antonina, born 1907, and Berta, born 1909.

693

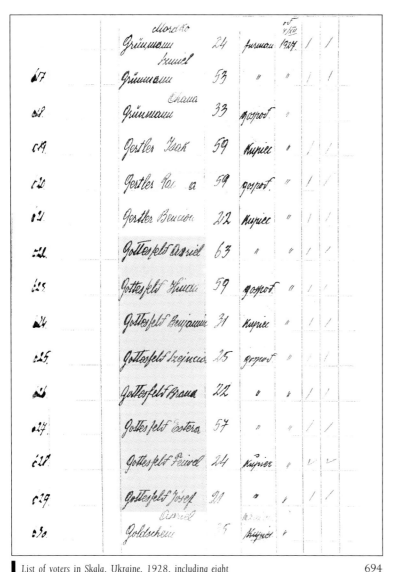

List of voters in Skala, Ukraine, 1928, including eight entries for the Gottesfeld family. Each entry includes the person's name, age and occupation.

694

of the occupation. Materials that can help to locate data about individuals include transcripts of interviews with witnesses, testimonials of survivors, and information given by the Jews who were saved by some miracle.

Following a recent decision of the Ukrainian Parliament, our archives have just completed accessing the personal files of the NKVD camps kept in the KGB archives. This collection includes more than 1 million files—one for each person (typically not Jewish) taken to Germany by the Nazis. After liberation, each was required to undergo an investigation by organs of the NKVD (secret police). There are lengthy stories of the experiences of each person, including detailed autobiographies. Some of those interviewed were Jews.

The archive of the former Communist Party of Ukraine is the final major source for Jewish genealogists studying the period since 1917. This archive includes a great body of documents, with much genealogical information. The Communist Party controlled all spheres of the economic, socio-political, cultural and spiritual life of the entire population throughout the country. Virtually inexhaustible genealogical sources can be found in the personal files of Communists and in the materials of control and party committees.

For the time being, however, ethical and privacy considerations make these documents from the KGB and former Community Party archives inaccessible for genealogical research. However, by law, persons whom the documents concern directly, as well as the court procurator's office, may have access to these documents.

SUMMARY AND CONCLUSIONS

I wish to draw some conclusions and offer practical recommendations for research in Jewish genealogy in our archives. In volume and content, the Ukrainian archives possess rich and vast information about almost every person who ever lived in the territory of our state, including the Jewish population. Unfortunately, this information is scattered among many fonds and is not well developed from the viewpoint of genealogical research.

During the Communist years, the elaboration of the theoretical and methodological foundations of genealogy as a science had, in fact, ceased. Our historians did not study individuals but, rather, processes created by individuals. Alphabetical (by name) catalogs were made only at the initiative of archivists who understood professionally the importance of this kind of work. Nevertheless, these catalogs cannot help very much in genealogical research, because they contain very few names from the documents in the archives. Instead, a researcher working in the Ukrainian archives must have not only intuition but also must know the history of Ukraine, the

and deputies at different levels; lists of members of the bureaus of party bodies; and lists of participants in all sorts of congresses, conferences and meetings that were held in those days. All of these have valuable information for researchers.

Little research has been done on the documents of the period of German occupation (1941–1945). From the very first days after occupying Ukraine, German authorities began a registration of Jewish passports and a census of the Jewish population, allegedly with a view toward organizing ghettos, but in reality in preparation for the mass extermination of the Jews. Ukrainian archives have some of these documents, but this material is most fully represented in the fonds of the oblast commissions for the registration and calculation of the damage done (Extraordinary Commission to Document Nazi Atrocities on Soviet Territory) by the German invaders. These commissions, formed immediately after each community was liberated, did a great deal of work to document the tragedies

structure of the state organs of power and administration in each historical stage of its development, and the modern network of archives in the country.

A researcher studying the genealogy of workers, clerks, craftsmen, businessmen, and so forth has far fewer sources than a researcher searching the genealogy of the aristocracy. Our archives do not have private fonds of such "average" individuals from prerevolutionary times. The family fonds of merchants are poor also. Their lives were reflected only in documents of the state or countryside estates.

A researcher working in Ukrainian archives must carefully devise methods of extracting genealogical data and must determine their degree of reliability. These problems are still to be solved by the study of genealogical sources. Currently, the Ukrainian archives have few trained specialists in the field of genealogical research. We cannot produce the results that would be possible if genealogy were to be placed on a more professional basis throughout our archival system.

Since Ukraine's independence, our archives have received an increasing number of inquiries about doing genealogical research, especially about Jewish ancestors. As a result of this demand, we have made great strides toward training professional genealogists at Kiev State University and at the Kiev Cultural Institute. Such departments have been created

Application of Moses and Leiser Wasserman of Skala Podolskaya for membership in the Keren Hajesod society, 1938 — 695

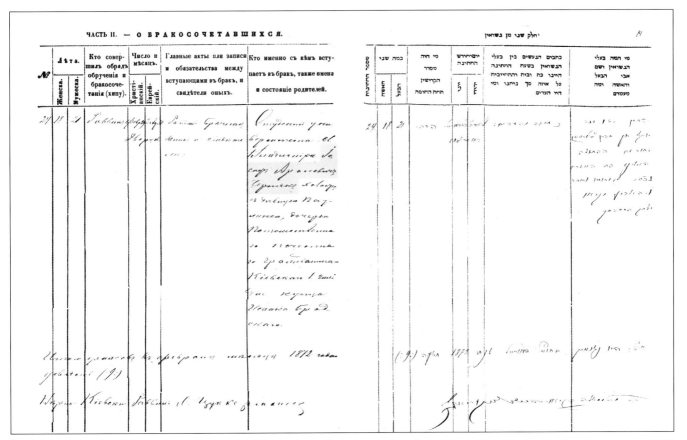

Marriage of Josef Chernyak in Kiev, a student at St. Vladimir University, age 21, son of Aron, and Paulina Brodskaya, age 18, daughter of Isaak Brodskii, an honorary citizen and merchant in the first guild. The marriage was performed in 1872 by Rabbi E. Tsukerman and witnessed by Shumin Bogaturov and Yankel Alevskii. — 696

and would-be archivists are being trained. Among other subjects, we plan to teach a course on genealogy as an auxiliary historical discipline. Specialists in the field of Jewish genealogy will be critical, particularly if we remember that approximately half of all the Jews in the Soviet Union counted in the 1970 census lived in Ukraine.

This situation brings to mind the need to computerize our archives and create a bank of information for facilitating research in the field of genealogy (some work is already being done). By order of the Ukrainian government, the Main Archival Administration has established a special department of archival computerization in the Ukrainian Research Institute of Archives and the Study of Documents. Our initial focus has been on people who were under reprisals in Josef Stalin's time and the so-called *Ostarbeiter* (mostly non-Jewish Russians, taken as slave laborers to Germany during World War II). This is a colossal undertaking that will continue far into the future.

Dr. Volodymyr S. Lozytskyi is deputy director of the Main Archival Administration of Ukraine. Dr. Lozytskyi teaches at Kiev State University of Culture and Art, where he is the chairman of the archival department and teaches a newly established course in genealogy for archivists and researchers. He holds a doctorate in history and is the author of more than 30 works on the history of Ukrainian national culture.

Editor's Note: This article was adapted from an earlier version that appeared in *Avotaynu*, vol. 10, no. 2 (Summer 1994): 9–14.

From left: Irina Antonenko, archivist, and Boris V. Ivanenko, then the director of the Main Archival Administration, try out a fax machine presented by Miriam Weiner, 1991.

697

MAIN ARCHIVAL ADMINISTRATION UNDER THE CABINET OF MINISTERS OF UKRAINE

by
Dr. Ruslan Y. Pirig, Director

24 Solomyanska Street
252601 Kyiv
Ukraine

Tel: 380/44/277-4522
Fax: 380/44/277-3655

Long before Ukraine became a newly independent state in 1991, the Ukrainian people could celebrate a rich history. Ukrainians' outstanding achievements are reflected in the numerous sources found in the country's archival fonds—a part of its national and world historical–cultural heritage. At present, these fonds consist of more than 50 million items of different types of archival documents.

State archival services have a strict and established structure regulated by the law of Ukraine entitled "About the National Archival Fond and Archival Regulations" (1993).

Seven central state archives are the national repositories of valuable archival documentation, organized by certain historical periods and by the kinds of institutions and documents that are stored there.

The Central State Archive of the Higher Organs of Power and Management of Ukraine preserves the documents of the administration of the president, the Supreme Rada, the Cabinet of Ministers, ministries and administrations of Ukraine. It also holds documents of institutions and organizations that have sought state power in Ukraine (since February 1917).

The Central State Archive of Public Organizations of Ukraine was established from the archive of the former Communist Party. It houses documents of public societies founded after 1917 whose activities were of national importance, including materials of political parties and movements, volunteer societies and social organizations.

The Central State Historical Archives of Ukraine in Kiev and Lvov hold unique sources that reflect the national history from the fourteenth century until February 1917 (in Lvov, until 1939).

The fonds of the Central State Cinema and Photo Archives of Ukraine contain videotapes, photographs and audiovisual materials.

Scientific-technical documents that characterize major developments in agriculture, science and technology are kept at the Central State Scientific-Technical Archive of Ukraine, located in Kharkov.

Materials on Ukrainian culture are stored at the Central State Archive and the Museum of Literature and Arts of Ukraine. Valuable items related to famous cultural figures are kept also at other museums, including the one in Plyuti (a branch of the Museum of Literature and Arts of Ukraine).

State archives at the Ministry of the Autonomous Republic of Crimea, state regional archives, and archives of the cities of Kiev and Sevastopol also store national archival fonds and are the executive bodies of archival management. Together with 485 archival departments of regional state administrations and 146 local archives, they preserve documents of regional history and fonds of famous Ukrainians.

The archival system employs more than 3,000 archivists and other staff members who ensure the safety of some 49 million files, 74,000 video documents, more than 1 million photo documents, 30,000 audio documents and 613,000 items of scientific-technical documentation. Archivists work on the improvement of the storage system, the preservation of archival sources and the utilization of retrospective information for the benefit of the country and the people. Archival workers have their own organization—The Society of Archivists. The National Archival Services of Ukraine is a member of the International Society of Archives, under the leadership of UNESCO.

Researchers are welcome to write to or visit our archives at the above-listed address.

Dr. Ruslan Y. Pirig was born in 1941 in Poltava region. He is a graduate of Kharkov State University, with a degree in history. Upon graduation, he became a teacher. Dr. Pirig has published more than 200 articles on the modern history of Ukraine. In March 1997, the president of Ukraine appointed Dr. Pirig to his current position as director of the Main Archival Administration of Ukraine.

Dr. Ruslan Y. Pirig, director of the Main Archival Administration, in his office with a map of Ukraine, 1998

698

CENTRAL STATE HISTORICAL ARCHIVE OF UKRAINE IN KIEV (KYIV)

by

Olga Marushak, Director

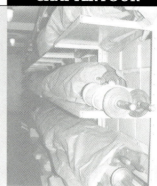

24 Solomyanska Street
252601 Kyiv
Ukraine

Tel: 380/44/277-3002

The Central State Historical Archive of Ukraine located in the city of Kiev is one of the oldest archival repositories in the country. The foundation of the documentary collection consists of the fonds of the Kiev Central Archive of Ancient Acts, Kharkov Central Archive of the Revolution and the State Archive of Kiev Oblast. The collection in this archive increased substantially upon receipt of documentary materials from a branch of this archive, located in Kharkov, that was liquidated in 1971. At the present time, more than 1,600 fonds and approximately 1.5 million files are kept at the archive in Kiev.

Unique written documents kept at the archive reflect the long history of Ukraine, with items dating from the fourteenth century until 1917. They are preserved in fonds of central and local institutions that operated during the occupation of Ukrainian lands by the Great Lithuanian Principality and Polish *Shliahkta* (nobility), institutions of the Cossack administration and the tsarist institutions established after Ukraine was annexed by Russia.

The most valuable part of the documentary collection of the Central State Historical Archive of Ukraine in Kiev consists of record books of the courts and estate institutions of the right-bank Ukraine (west of the Dnieper River); city, district

and confederate courts (which resolved issues between jurisdictions within the Russian Empire); and city governments. This collection is a priceless resource for studying the history of Ukraine in general and, more specifically, the Jewish history of Ukraine.

The most important resources for studying Jewish genealogy in Ukraine are the metrical books of synagogues of Kiev Province, kept at the archive. Unfortunately, many towns were able to preserve only fragments of books (for certain years). They total approximately 1,500 units dating from the mid-nineteenth century to 1917.

In addition to the foregoing, some archival fonds contain information regarding specific topics. For example, fonds of the administration office of the Board of Education include information about Jewish education and lists of students; fonds of the administration office of governor and governor-general include census information for certain towns and estates; and fonds of police and prison documents include information about pogroms against the Jews (including lists of names of victims and perpetrators).

Unfortunately, research for specific last names for the purpose of genealogy is very difficult because of the absence of research tools. The creation of a name index (made possible by the development of computerized databases at the Central State Historical Archive of Ukraine in Kiev) is a matter to be considered in the future.

Olga Marushak, director of the Central State Historical Archive in Kiev, with one of dozens of Torahs in the archive's collection, 1998

699

Olga Marushak (née Muzichuk) is the director of the Central State Historical Archive in Kiev. She was born in 1965 in Kiev. In 1987, Ms. Marushak graduated from Shevchenko University in Kiev with a degree in history. That year, she also began working as an archivist in the Central State Historical Archive and continued her studies. She then became chief of her section. Ms. Marushak studied archival procedures in France, where she graduated from the International Technical Archive School in Paris. In addition to her duties in the archive, she is now a postgraduate student in the Hrushevskii Institute in the subject of ancient documents.

CENTRAL STATE HISTORICAL ARCHIVE OF UKRAINE IN LVOV (LVIV)

by
Dr. Orest Y. Matsuk, Director

3a Plaza Soborna
290006 Lviv
Ukraine

Tel: 380/322/72-30-63

The Central State Historical Archive of Ukraine in Lvov has a large collection of historical documents about the Jewish people who have lived in the territory of Western Ukraine for many centuries. Related documents can be found in nearly all of the collections of this archive. However, they are scattered, and thus the research is tedious and very time-consuming. Most of the material is not indexed, so a researcher looking for information based upon specific family names in specific towns would need to research many different files. To further complicate the matter, these files are arranged not by town name but by subject matter.

There are more than 30 fonds (some 12,000 files) for the period from the mid-seventeenth century through the early twentieth century, including documents about religion, science, culture, art and education among the Jewish population of Galicia. The largest collection (and least studied as of December 1998) is the documents of town and local courts as well as the city administrations of Lvov and other towns (1,382 fonds dating from the early twentieth century), in addition to hundreds of other fonds. Almost all of these fonds contain interesting materials about the Jews of Galicia and its environs. Important documents for genealogical research are kept not only in our archive but also in most oblast archives in Ukraine.

In our archive, Fond 701 is of great interest to Jewish genealogists. It is the largest Jewish collection in the archive and includes birth, marriage and death registrations for towns throughout Galicia. The earliest records in the fond date from 1784. These registers (commonly known as metrical books or *kehillah* records) are not indexed. One must search page by page and line by line to find specific names.

Miriam Weiner has undertaken a gigantic project in collecting information and compiling inventories about documents in the archives throughout Ukraine. It is not an easy task because most of the materials regarding the Jewish population were inaccessible during Soviet times.

Ms. Weiner's book will promote the study and use of these documents and will be of great help for those people searching for relatives or information about relatives who were dispersed and scattered throughout the world as a result of World War II and the Holocaust.

We have worked with Ms. Weiner since her first visit in 1991. Most recently, we have verified the material that she has collected; at the same time, we have added new material to the inventories. When we first discussed this many years ago, I made arrangements for one of my archivists (a specialist in Jewish documents) to travel to Ternopol, Chernovtsy and Ivano-Frankovsk in connection with this survey, and he was able to collect inventory data from these archives as well.

I fully endorse this research project and the publication of this book, which represents the most comprehensive description of the documents in our archives to date.

Orest Y. Matsuk was born in 1932 in the town of Truskavets, in Lvov Oblast, to a teacher's family. In 1955, he graduated from the Economic Department of the Lvov Agricultural Institute. He then attended and graduated from the Moscow Historical-Archival Institute; thereafter he was employed as an economist in the town of Zolochevo. Since 1960, Dr. Matsuk has occupied various positions at the Central State Historical Archive in Lvov; in 1991, he was appointed its director. He is a member of numerous professional organizations and societies and the author of more than 200 scholarly works, including eight monographs.

Dr. Orest Y. Matsuk, in his office at the Central State Historical Archive of Ukraine in Lvov, 1998   700

JEWISH DOCUMENTS IN THE KAMENETS-PODOLSKIY CITY-STATE ARCHIVE

by
Sergei A. Borisevich, Director
and
Zinaida M. Klimishina, Archivist

14 Frantsiskanska Street
Kamyanets-Podilsky
Khmelnytskyi Oblast
281900 Ukraine

Tel: 380/3849/2-10-25

The Kamenets-Podolskiy City-State Archive in Khmelnitskiy Oblast holds many documents about the Jewish residents of Podolia Guberniya from 1793 to 1917. There are also many documents from the Soviet period, including information about education, the occupations of the local population and other documents that describe the social, political and economic life before World War II. Most of the documents from the Soviet period are located at the State Archive of Khmelnitskiy Oblast. In the Kamenets-Podolskiy City-State Archive, we have documents describing events in both the city and region prior to 1941.

Statistics on the Jewish population of Podolia Guberniya can be found in different files. Only a small quantity of metrical books survive, primarily those for Kamenets-Podolskiy and Starokonstantinov (Volhynia Guberniya) for the period 1870 to 1913, and for the town of Zbarizh and a few others. According to the laws of the Russian Empire, Jews were permitted to settle only in shtetls and to work as craftsmen or merchants. They were generally not allowed to work on the land; to do so, it was necessary to have special permission from the governor. Jewish agricultural colonies were established in only specific regions. There were a few in the Balta and Vinnitsa regions as well as Letichev region. However, agricultural colonies survived for only 10 years, regulated by a specially established Jewish migration committee. A few documents (with general information) from the committee fonds have survived, such as petitions from Jews for permission to join the colonies and lists of farmers and their families (in Podolia Guberniya and other regions of the Russian Empire).

Jews worked primarily in commercial businesses. They rented land and owned mills, inns and shops. Sometimes they were stewards at landowners' estates, plants and factories, or were professionals, such as doctors and lawyers.

Most of the documents can be found in the following fonds:

Fond 228   Podolsk governor (passport desk)
Fond 227   Podolsk City Hall (metrical books of
              births, marriages, deaths and divorces)
Fond 226   Podolsk Treasury (economic department
              and inventory reports)

The inventory reports have information on family members, family lists and lists of Jewish soldiers in the Podolsk region. However, prior to 1840, the last name of the father was not always mentioned. It was only in the early nineteenth century that the emperor issued a law that required the use of last names in metrical books. Therefore, it is often difficult to follow relationships between generations during the research process.

Information on births and lists of Jewish citizens of towns and shtetls are kept in different fonds. For example, regional courts and city-hall fonds hold various criminal files, purchase agreements and petitions for different years. The Podolsk City Hall also kept information on elections, the opening of prayer houses and schools, and the assignment of rabbis in small towns.

Many Jews came from other lands. Therefore, they had to obtain permission to live in and become citizens of the Russian Empire. In this situation, a petition would be sent to the governor of Podolsk requesting permission to enter the city boundaries and to obtain a residence permit.

All citizens were listed in the inventory reports (revision or census lists) for tax purposes, but many people tried to avoid registration (in an attempt to evade the draft), resulting in incomplete census lists. Accordingly, supplementary revision lists were created. By law, these revision lists were to be created every 10 years, but in reality, that schedule was not adhered to.

Although Jews had permission to rent property, they could do so only in specified regions. Often a family was registered in one place but lived somewhere else. Very often the family record was incomplete (for example, the wife and small children were reported in one place, while the father and older children, usually sons, were registered in another location). In most of the revision lists, men and women are listed separately, on facing pages.

This archive also has documents about Jewish families in the military lists until 1917. There were many cases of males avoiding military service (because of the 25-year term and harsh conditions). In this situation, the parents had to pay a fine in money or in kind. If the family did not have the money, the court could confiscate their house or other property in order to satisfy the fine.

Although Jews were not legally permitted to live in villages, but only in towns or shtetls, there were many violations of this rule. For example, a shtetl would be divided into several sections, and one section would resemble a village. If a Jewish family settled in that section, the neighbor might send a letter to a judge, and the Jewish family would be ordered to leave. Such cases could last for years, as the Jewish families might be able to bribe the authorities and thereby avoid expulsion.

Until the mid-nineteenth century, the majority of the shtetl population was Jewish. There were many disputes between the Jews and other nationalities, resolved by the Podolsk County Board, Podolsk Treasury Department, county courts and the townships themselves.

Thousands of files bear Jewish surnames. In almost every record book of the Podolsk County Board, it is possible to find information about the life of the Jewish community. There is also a great deal of information in the fonds of the Podolsk court, notary offices, records of public colleges, boys' and girls' gymnasiums (high schools), the Proskurov and Kamenets City Halls, the Kamenets and Proskurov townships and the city boards of these towns.

Jews were allowed to settle no closer than 30 miles from the borders of the Russian Empire. Podolia and Bessarabia Guberniyas were considered frontier guberniyas. Jewish colonization of the Russian Empire began from the southwest, which is why most violations of the settlement law took place in this region. The same kind of violations also occurred during the census registration.

Kamenets-Podolskiy was the center of Jewish population from where Jews spread north through the Russian Empire. Many Jews resided in Podolia Guberniya as foreigners. They, as opposed to citizens, could change the place of their residence as often as they wanted, which resulted in significant migration within the guberniya.

Many Jews obtained passports and consequently moved abroad. About 300 emigration documents of Jewish families have survived.

Research in the Jewish documents of Podolia Guberniya is just beginning. There is a wealth of information to be discovered about the Jews and Jewish life in the region among these many records.

Zinaida M. Klimishina was born in 1953 in the village of Kosikovtsy, in Novaya Ushitsa region, Khmelnitskiy Oblast. From 1976 to 1984, Ms. Klimishina was a teacher at various levels in the school system. Since 1984, she has worked for the state archive.

Sergei A. Borisevich was born in 1959 in Kamenets-Podolskiy. He worked as a history teacher in the local high school for eight years. In 1993, Mr. Borisevich began working in the Kamenets-Podolskiy City-State Archive, where he is now the director.

From left: *Vitaly Chumak, Miriam Weiner's associate, in Ukraine and Moldova; Zinaida M. Klimishina, archivist; and Sergei A. Borisevich, director of the Kamenets-Podolskiy City-State Archive; 1995*

701

JEWISH DOCUMENTS IN THE STATE ARCHIVE OF VINNITSA OBLAST

by
Faina A. Vinokurova, Vice-Director
and
Oleksander S. Petrenko, Chief Archivist

17 Soborna Street
287100 Vinnitsa
Ukraine

Tel: 380/4336/32-20-93

The State Archive of Vinnitsa Oblast holds documents dating from the eighteenth century to the present. Among these documents are 5,900 fonds, consisting of 1,433,573 files. Due to the former administrative-territorial division of Vinnitsa Oblast, documents in this archive cover towns from other districts, including Cherkassy, Kiev, Zhitomir, Khmelnitskiy, Odessa and Kirovograd, along with some areas of the Republic of Moldova.

The history of Jewish settlement in the eastern part of Podolia (Bratslav region) dates back to the end of the fifteenth century. The settlers were Ashkenazi Jews, persecuted by Emperor Maximilian and forced to move to Poland and Lithuania. Thus, an intensive Jewish settlement of Bratslav region began only in the second half of the sixteenth century, in connection with the rapid growth in farming.

A considerable part of the Jewish population was annihilated during the liberation war of the Ukrainian people against the Polish gentry in 1648–1654. In the postwar period, the survivors emigrated to Poland.

Eastern Podolia was populated by Jews from the beginning of the eighteenth century. The archival documents include 300,000 files (which include information about Jews) and cover the period from 1725 to the present time. The number of strictly Jewish fonds is comparatively small. There are fonds of some synagogues, educational establishments, Jewish societies and national town councils. The fonds of the Jewish public committees contain information about the pogroms of 1918–1920, the political views of the participants, the number of victims and the results of the pogroms. For example, the testimony of a witness of the pogrom in Trostyanets in May 1919 describes the events, participants and number of deaths. The testimony also reports where victims were buried. From a genealogical viewpoint, these documents are valuable in doing research on pogrom victims and on those people given subsidies by the American Jewish Joint Distribution Committee and other public organizations.

The fonds of the town councils of Ladyzhin and Samgorod for 1920 to 1930 shed light upon the so-called "small town problem" (Jews had no work because of the bad economy and, therefore, had to move somewhere else). They deal with the migration of Jews to the southern regions of Ukraine and to Birobijan. The many electoral rolls and lists of those who

lost electoral rights, immigration records and other official documents in Yiddish are also resources for genealogists.

More than 600 metrical books of birth registrations by state rabbis contain valuable genealogical material. There are records of births, marriages, divorces and deaths that are not evenly preserved in different populated areas. The birth registrations of Vinnitsa and Yuzvin date back to 1834. There are also birth registrations for Khmelnitskiy region (Izyaslav, Novyi Konstantinov, Staraya Sinyava) and Rashkov (in Moldova).

The majority of the Jewish documents can be found in the general fonds as follows:

1. The documents of the state councils, local authorities, and financial, tax and military-service organizations (Bratslav vice-regency, the town dumas, police departments, public fonds and revision committees). Among them are the revision lists (1795–1858), family lists (1874–1913), tax lists on Jewish property, and lists and photographs of men called up for military service in the late nineteenth and early twentieth centuries; documents about synagogues, schools and home construction; and electoral rolls to the State

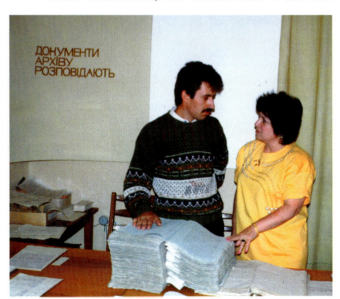

Oleksander S. Petrenko, vice-director of the Research Department in the State Archive of Vinnitsa Oblast, with Miriam Weiner, explaining the difficulty of making photocopies from a book of this size, 1993

702

Dumas (1905–1907). The earliest documents, dating from 1795, consist of the revision lists from Eastern Podolia covering Skvira, Lipovets and Mogilev Districts.

2. The documents of legal-administrative and notary offices (regional courts and magistrates from 1796 to 1872), Vinnitsa regional court of 1909–1920 and notary records from 1880 to 1920. Numerous documents, among them the decree of Prot Pototskii about the Jewish settlement in Yampol in 1792 and the names of those who wished to move there, are represented. The traditions and customs of the Jews of Podolia region can be found in the testaments and marriage contracts. One can find interesting information about pogroms before World War I and the October Revolution, such as the judicial-inquiry documents about the pogrom in Bogopol in 1905.

3. The documents of educational establishments—especially non-elite ones—in the late eighteenth and early nineteenth centuries. For example, one can find documents from the Mogilev Podolskiy specialized commercial school, where Jews were the overwhelming majority. Lists of advanced pupils and their personal files are displayed here.

4. The fonds of various state and public organizations (local authorities, regional and district executive committees) contain numerous documents about Jewish life for the period 1920 to 1930, a time of national cultural revival. The documents that contain the lists of electors and those who lost electoral rights testify to the social origin and status of adult Jews. Materials about the political campaign of the 1920s

in Vinnitsa, Tulchin, Gaysin and Mogilev Podolskiy are also kept in the State Archive of Vinnitsa Oblast.

5. Documents of Jewish agricultural cooperatives include membership lists of the collective farm of Shpikov, the cooperative FJAC, the collective farm Khliborob in Yanov, the Komintern in Khmelnik and others.

6. Jewish migration to southern Ukraine and to Birobijan is reflected in the documents of the regional executive committees and in the fonds of the regional agricultural departments and the Society of Jewish Migration Assistance. For instance, in Illintsy, a society for migration to Dzhankoy (Crimea region) was organized in 1929. The full list includes 57 members. The fonds of administrative departments (*administrativnyi otdel*) of the regional executive committees are other important sources of genealogical information. They contain registration files of the Jewish religious communities, including lists of synagogue members (with personal signatures) and personal files of rabbis and cantors of the synagogues.

7. The activities of the Jewish National Schools and the Pedagogical Technical School are reflected in the documents of Podolia Province and the district educational inspections. The judicial-inquiry documents on the reprisals against Jews from 1920 to 1950, especially those arrested as members of the underground Zionist organization in Tulchin District in July 1924, represent an interest for academic research.

The State Archive of Vinnitsa Oblast contains a massive number of documents on the Holocaust (see Chapter 7). These are of great genealogical significance and deserve extensive research.

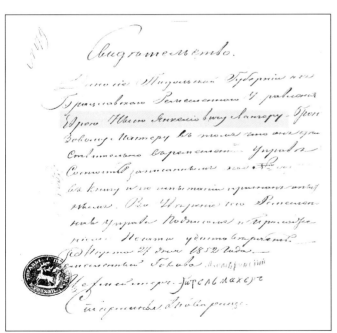

Application for a business license (bronze worker) by Aron Nison Langer, son of Yankel, living in Bratslav, 1852

703

Faina A. Vinokurova is a professional historian-archivist. She graduated from the Moscow Historical-Archival Institute in 1973. She is currently vice-director of the State Archive of Vinnitsa Oblast. She has participated in more than a dozen international and local conferences on Jewish history and has lectured at several of them. Ms. Vinokurova is a specialist in the history of the Jews of Podolia and the author of the forthcoming monograph *The Repressed Generation: From the History of Jews in Podolia in the 1920s–1930s*. She is co-editor (with Iosif Maliar) of the first Ukrainian/Israeli selection of testimonies and recollections of Holocaust survivors from Vinnitsa Oblast, *The Catastrophe and the Resistance* (Tel Aviv/Kiev: Ghetto Fighters' House, 1994). The results of her archival research on the Holocaust are represented in document examples to be published by Anthex Publishing in 1999, under the title *The Jews of Vinnitsa Oblast During the Holocaust*.

Oleksander S. Petrenko was born in 1968 and graduated from the Historical Faculty of Vinnitsa Teachers' Training Institute in 1992. He then began working for the State Archive of Vinnitsa Oblast, where he is currently chief archivist and the vice-director of the Research Department. Mr. Petrenko has a special interest in the feudalism of Eastern Podolia and the history of Jewish towns in the late eighteenth century and first half of the nineteenth century.

The following pages are samples of documents from throughout Ukrainian archives

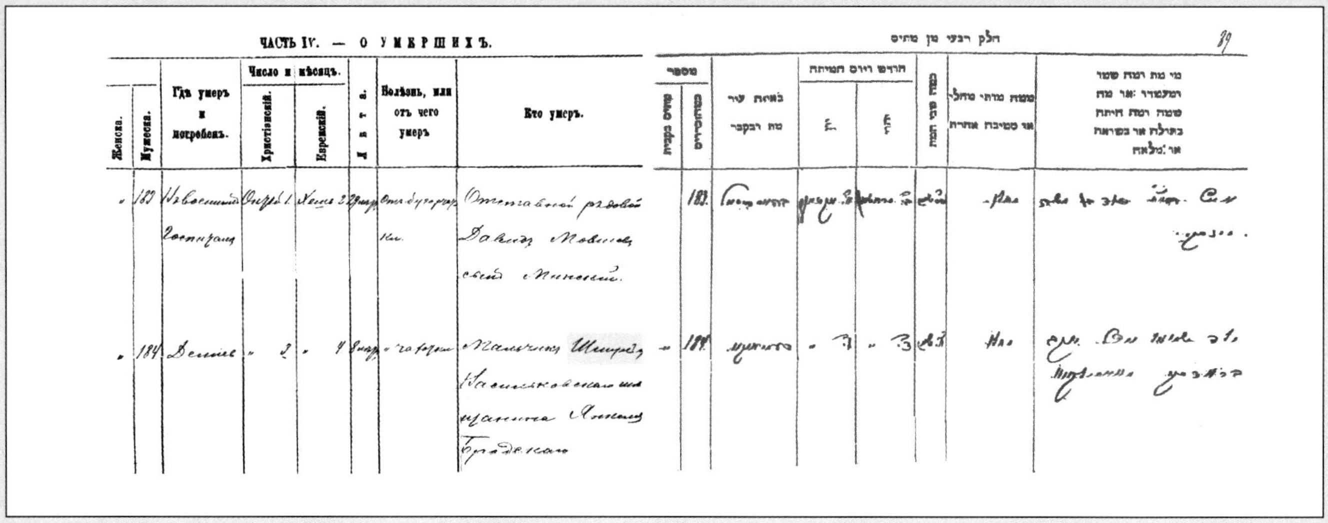

Death record No. 184 of Shmuil, age eight, son of Yankel Brodskiy, a citizen of Vasilkov. Shmuil was buried in the Demevskoe cemetery, 1874.

704

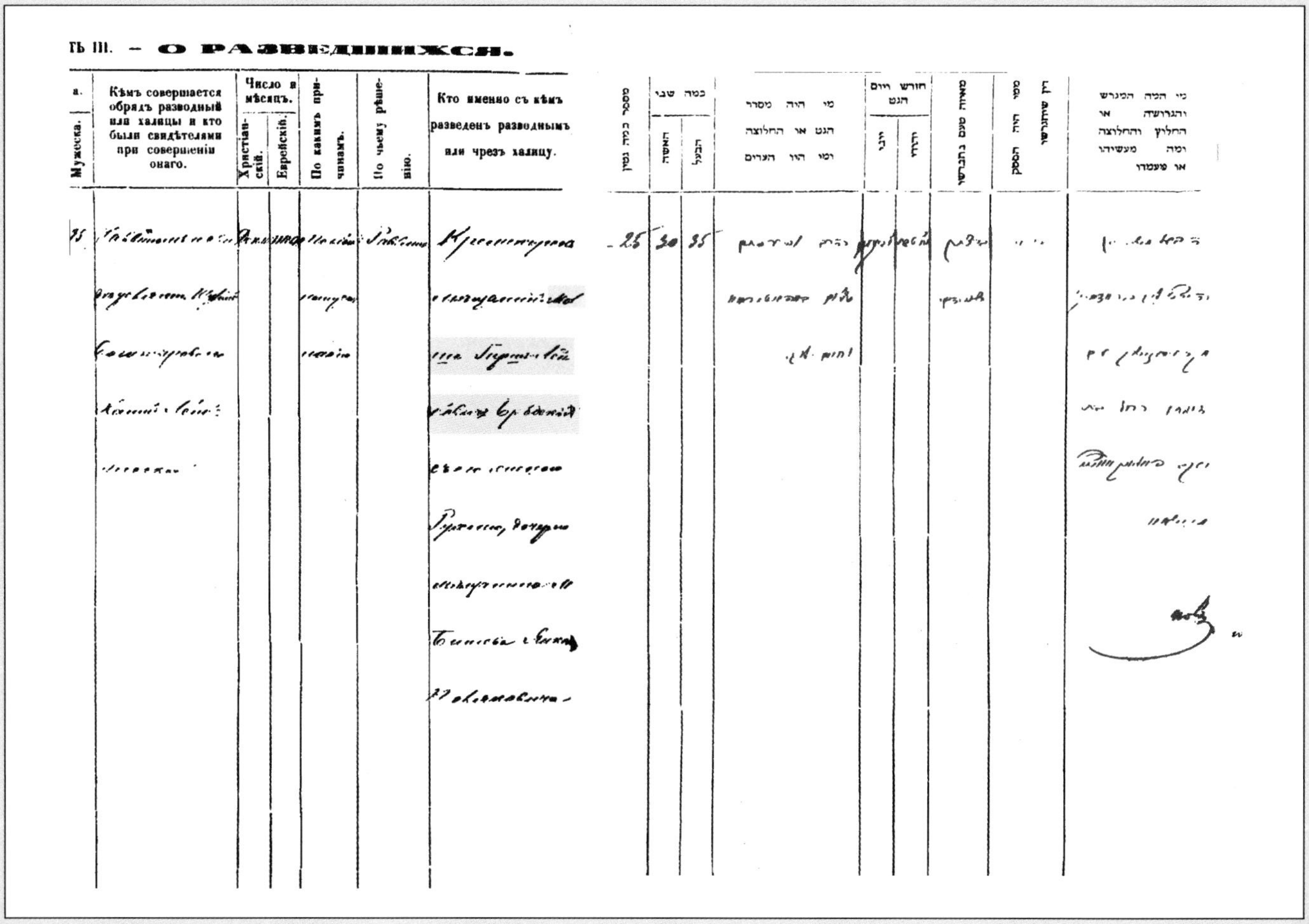

Divorce record No. 35 of Moishe Brodskiy, age 35 (son of Gersh-Leib) and his wife, Rukhlya Bushev, age 30 (daughter of Yankel Povyakovich). The divorce was by mutual consent and was witnessed by Shumin Bagaturov and Khaim Leib Ploskiy, 1869.

705

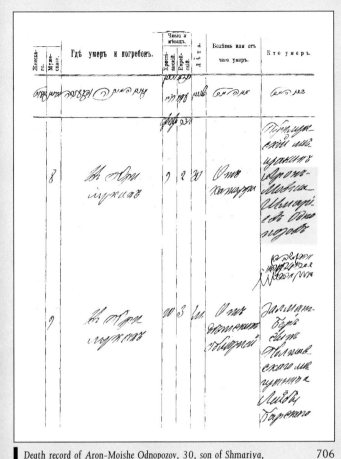

Death record of Aron-Moishe Odnopozov, 30, son of Shmariya, from Priluki, 1901

706

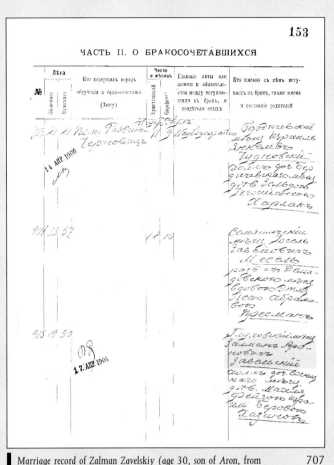

Marriage record of Zalman Zavelskiy (age 30, son of Aron, from Glukhov) and Makhla Feiga Khazanov (age 19, daughter of Israel-Ber, from Sosnitsa), 1901

707

Birth record of Samuil, son of Yankel Brodskiy from Vasilkov and his wife, Mirits. The circumcision was performed by Aron Shtraiman from Zhitomir, 1868.

708

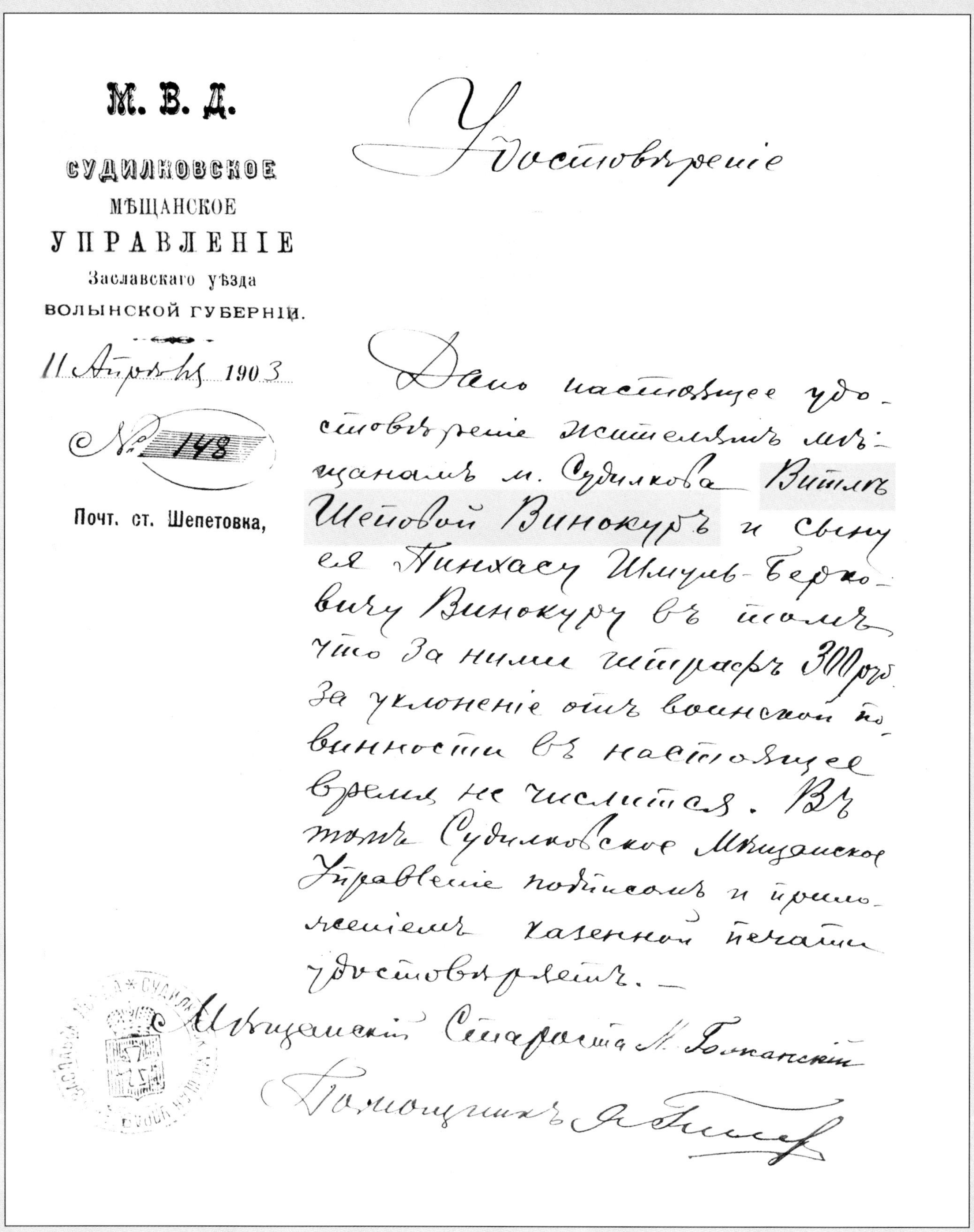

М. В. Д.

СУДИЛКОВСКОЕ
МѢЩАНСКОЕ
УПРАВЛЕНIЕ
Заславскаго уѣзда
ВОЛЫНСКОЙ ГУБЕРНIИ.

11 Апрѣля 1903

№ 148

Почт. ст. Шепетовка,

Удостовѣренiе

Дано настоящее удостовѣренiе жительнымъ мѣщанамъ м. Судилкова Витлѣ Шевовой Винокуръ и сыну ея Пинхасу Шмуль-Берковичу Винокуру въ томъ что за ними штрафъ 300 руб. за уклоненiе отъ воинской повинности въ настоящее время не числится. Въ томъ Судилковское Мѣщанское Управленiе подписомъ и приложенiемъ казенной печати удостовѣряетъ. —

Мѣщанскiй Староста М. Боканскiй

Помощникъ Я. Шиндъ

Certification from the Sudilkov town administration that a 300-ruble fine (for evasion of military service) has been paid by Vitla Vinokur, wife of Shmuel-Ber Vinokur, on behalf of her son, Pinkhas, in 1903

Translation of a Letter from Sudilkov

Dear Ms. Weiner: My name is Zinaida Samuelovna Sandler (née Pugach) and I am a resident of Sudilkov. Yesterday, my neighbor visited me and told me about your interest in the history of Sudilkov. I am very sorry we did not meet when you were here. I have very interesting and valuable information for you—the memoirs of my father. The tragic fortunes of Sudilkov's Jews deeply concerned him and in the last years of his life, he compiled lists of residents of our town. I have nine notebooks with the lists and historical information, including the Vinokur family, which may interest you.

His notes contain lists of the Jewish residents, street by street and house by house. There is also a map of the streets and buildings, and the history of the Jewish community in Sudilkov. Yesterday, I spent a few hours with the oldest resident of Sudilkov (87 years old) who remembered some names. He studied the photographs that you left here and thinks that the tall man with black hair and a mustache could be Ukel Winokur. I will talk with other older residents about what they remember. I plan to leave for Israel by the end of the year and hope to see you there. If you are interested, I can give the notebooks to you that tell so much about the life and times of the residents of Sudilkov and their tragic fate during the German occupation. It could be wonderful material for a book. I also have a picture of Sudilkov's young residents taken in the 1920s. I wish you all the best. You can write to me at the following address. (signed) Zinaida Sandler, May 3, 1991

Introductory Excerpt from the Sudilkov Memoirs

"During the Nazi invasion (1941–1945), virtually the entire Jewish population of Sudilkov was destroyed. Only a few emigrated and a few still live in Shepetovka or other cities in Ukraine. Other survivors were young people who were in the army during the war and did not die. All citizens of Sudilkov were held by the Germans in the Shepetovka ghetto, located in the region near the synagogue. Only two girls escaped from Sudilkov: Fanya Pugach and Klara Korol. The houses where Jews once lived are destroyed now, the cemetery is ruined, and stones from the cemetery were stolen by local citizens for the foundations of future houses. Only a few remaining monuments remind us about the Jews of Sudilkov."

711 ▶

A page from the Sudilkov Memoirs showing a list of the Jewish residents of Sudilkov. Page 24 (see highlighted entry): Avrum Vinokur; his wife; his sons Shmiluk and Yukel; and his daughters Ida, Gosya and Esya

At the Shepetovka cemetery entrance, Zinaida Sandler gives Miriam Weiner a book of memoirs about Sudilkov's Jews, 1991. ▲ 710

Excerpt from the Sudilkov Memoirs

"The Germans entered Sudilkov on July 4, 1941. The Jews of Shepetovka and nearby villages were executed in three stages (actions) in the forest on the road to Klimentovichi: July 21, 1941; June 20, 1942; and August 10, 1942."

Metrical books of the Priluki Jewish community
in the local ZAGS (vital-records registrations) office
in Priluki, 1991

712-B

712-A

Above: Miriam Weiner (left) with archivist Ludmila N. Chumak
in the Priluki Archive, a branch archive of the State Archive of Chernigov
Oblast, 1991

Above: Title page of 1875 birth records of the Priluki Jewish community
Right: Birth record of Miriam Odnopozov (maternal grandmother of Miriam Weiner), daughter of Israel and Huda, born in Priluki, 1875

713

Family list from the town of Priluki, two-page listing of the Odnopozov family, listing 41 relatives. The document dates back to Yankel-Isak Odnopozov, born c. 1800, and covers family members spanning six generations, with the latest entry for Leizor Odnopozov, the great-great grandson of Yankel-Isak. Although the family list was compiled in 1889, additional data were added as various births occurred.

714

List of inhabitants (revizskie skazki) from Novograd Volynskiy, entry #167 for Moshko Goldman (son of Mikhail), born c. 1840; and Moshko's three sons, Abramko, Michel and Nukhim. Names of spouses and Moshko's grandson are also listed, 1816.   715

1943 Lvov Ghetto registration card for Pesach Grünberg, born 1903   716

Marriage record of Berko Zolotarov (age 26, son of Nokhim, a rabbi's assistant) and Rokhel Matsa (age 20, daughter of Elli), married in Priluki in 1897   717

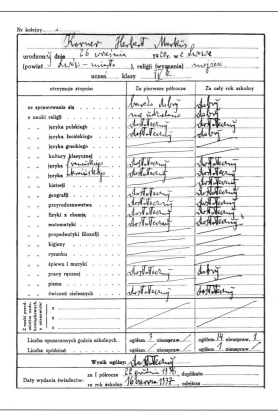

The 1936 school records in Lvov for Herbert Markus Korner, born 1920

718

Ordainment of Rabbi Benzion Schachter from Zborov, 1938

719

1829	Feldman Mojżesz i Salomea	Janowska 36	wł.realn.	400
1830	Feldschuh Adela	Sykstuska 54	wdowa	80
1831	Feldschuh Józef	Lwowska 45	kupiec	50
1832	Felika Herman	3-go Maja 12	dentysta	16
1833	Dr.Fell Bolesław	Kopernika 14	lekarz	40
1834	Fell Jakób	Ormiańska 30	urzędnik	16
1835	Dr.Fell Marek	Halicka 19	adwokat	50
1836	Feller Arnold Józef	Kotlarska 11	kupiec	6
1837	Feller Henryk	Pasaż Fellerów	wł.realn.	100
1838	Feller Ignacy v.Izak	Teatyńska 11-12a	kupiec	12
1839	Feller Jetti	pl.Strzelecki 1.	restaurat.	6
1840	Feller Józef	Lelewela	malarz pok.	6
1841	Dr.Feller Leon	Legjonów 35	lekarz	450
1842	Feller Luzer i żona Basia	Lwowska 13	kupiec	24
1843	Feller Majer	Szpitalna 84	wł.realn.	20
1844	Dr.Feller Norbert Ignacy i Salomea	Na Skałce 3	lekarz	24
1845	Feller Zygmunt i żona Julja	Pordes,Łyczakowska 13	kupiec	12
1846	Fellig Lazar	Rappaporta 9	urzędnik	6
1847	Dr.Fels Izrael	Słoneczna 1	lekarz	20
1848	Fels Jakób	Kochanowskiego 4	kapelusznik	6
1849	Fels Joachim	Ossolińskich 14	kierownik	40
1850	Felsenstein Salomon Józef	Słoneczna 14	kupiec	18
1851	Fendrich Herman	Sobieskiego 23	rzeźnik	12
1852	Fenig Róża	Panieńska 20	wł.realn.	16
1853	Fenster Chiel	Nowy Świat	młynarz	40
1854	Ferbel Natan	Kotlarska 12	urzędn.kol.	6
1855	Fenster r.Kordon Jakób	Łyczakowska 22a	restaurat.	6
1856	Ferberl Leon	Kotlarska 12	urzędnik kolj.	6
1857	Färber Izak i żona Jüdes	Zamarstynowska 21	kupiec	6
1858	Fern Ire	Krasickich 18	kupiec	12
1859	Hern Jechil	Pasaż Fellerów 3	kupiec	18
1860	Fern Marek	Tarnowskiego 34	urzędnik	100

List of taxpayers in Lvov, including name, year of birth, address, occupation and amount of taxes paid. This entry includes three members of the Fern family: Ire, Jechil and Marek, 1936.

720

Do

Zarządu Żydowskiej Gminy Wyznaniowej

we Lwowie.

Podpisany stud.III roku Wydziału Mat.Przyrodn.U.J.K. prosi uprzejmie o łaskawe przyznanie mu subwencji na zapłacenie I raty taksy administracyjnej.

Prośbę swą motywuje następująco:

Ojciec podpisanego,oficjalista rolny zamieszkały na wsi, znajduje się obecnie bez posady tak,że nie może w żadnej mierze wspierać petenta materjalnie.

Podpisany utrzymuje się wyłącznie z lekcyj których to marny dochód /32.—zł./ nie wystarcza nawet na utrzymanie bardzo skromne,— tymbardziej na zapłacenie taksy.

Petent jest mieszkańcem Żydowskiego Domu Akademickiego.

Wobec powyższego prosi o łaskawe przychylne załatwienie jego prośby.—

Lwów, dnia 7.grudnia 1938.—

Appel Juljusz

stud. III r. mat.

Ż.D.A

TOW. ŻYD. STUD. FIL.

Wpłynęło dnia 7 XII 1938

L.p.

Wydział T-wa i porozentów stwierdza,że k. Appel Juljusz jest mieszkańcem ŻDA., utrzymuje się wyłącznie z lekcyj,że wzgędu na jego ciężkie położenie materjalne podanie jego zasługuje na uwzględnienie.—

Za Wydział

Mgr.B.Hirschhorn   D.Simelman

Letter to Jewish community of Lvov from Juliusz Appel, requesting financial assistance, 1938

721

Прилуки.

МИНИСТЕРСТВО ВНУТРЕННИХЪ ДѢЛЪ.

Предводитель дворянства. Милорадовичъ В. Р.

Полицейское управление. Исправникъ Юшкевичъ Я. М. Помощн. его Русаневичъ Ф. Е.

Городская управа. Городской Голова Кисловскій И. И.

Мѣщанская управа. Старшина Юнакъ Н. Я.

Земская управа. Предсѣдатель Маркевичъ Н. Н.

Почтово-телеграфная контора. Начальникъ Буяновъ А. П. помощн. его Фадѣевъ И. И.

МИНИСТЕРСТВО ВОЕННОЕ.

Воинскій начальникъ. Подполковникъ Ницкевичъ Н. А.

МИНИСТЕРСТВО ФИНАНСОВЪ.

Податной инспекторъ. Карамзинъ Г. И.

МИНИСТЕРСТВО ЮСТИЦІИ.

Уѣздный Членъ Лубенскаго Суда. Катериничъ Н. В.

Судебный приставъ Архиповъ П. Л.

Нотаріусы. Добротворскій Н. А. Польманъ В. П.

Повѣренные. Завалишинъ А. А.

Паничъ В. П. Степаненко О. О.

УЧЕБНЫЯ ЗАВЕДЕНІЯ:

Мужская гимназія. Директоръ Орла Л. М.

Женская гимназія. Начальница Лякаяъ Р. А.

Частная женская гимназія. Т. И. Федоренко она же начальница.

1-е 4 хъ классное городское Инспекторъ Угнивенко А. О.

2 е 4-хъ классное Городское Супруненко С. Ф.

Врачи. Краснопольскій Н. Г. Козубовскій Ю. А. Фишеръ Х. И.

Фельдшера. Бакъ И. С. Барскій А. Г. Зинкевичъ Э. М. Клименко Д. М. Савченко В. С.

Ветеринарный врачъ. Михура Г. М.

Повивальныя бабки. Аронсонъ А. М. Сушко М. Н.

Дантисты Бакъ М. Г. Краснеръ М. Г. Смилянскій А. И. Штейнъ Ю. Д.

Торгово-промышленныя фирмы.

Агенты страховыхъ об-въ. Барскій М. А. (Якорь). Гольбергъ Н. (Сѣверное). Кисловскій А. С. (Россійск.). Модель Б. С. (С.-Петербург). Фраткинъ Б. (Россія). Фридъ С. Ф. и Б. Я. (Моск.). Цейтлинъ М. (Русское).

Аптекарскіе товары. Гавриленковой В. И. Александр. ул. Дунаевскій Ш. С. и Медвѣдовскій З. Розенбергъ В. Э. Соколовскій И. Д.

Аптеки. Грундфестъ М. С. Капельсонъ Б. Уѣздное Земство. Завод. Донкеръ О. Я.

Бакалейныя. Бориновскій И. Буклеръ А. М. Дубовицкій М. Котенко Е. М. Милявскаго А. М. Об-во Потребителей. Рабиновичъ С. Х. Семихода А. Ф. Супоницкаго Г. Туровскій. Фраткинъ Л. Хойченко М. Ш.

Банки. **Отдѣленіе Соединеннаго Банка.** Управляющій Вайсловичъ А. С. Бухгалтеръ Гальперинъ К. А.

Городской общественный Управляющій Кисловскій А. С. Бухгалтеръ Мотричъ С. К.

Об-во взаимнаго кредита. Предсѣдатель Фридъ В. Ф. Бухгалтеръ Новогрудскій Л. В.

Библіотека. Городская.

Булочныя и кондитерскія. Барскій М.

Вино. Московченко Ф. М. Рабиновичъ С. В. Фроткинъ Л. Н.

Галантерейные товары. Кацовскій. Крижановскій А. Ривкинъ Г. Славинъ Я.

Гостинницы. «Александровская». «Европейская». «Сѣверная».

Желѣзно-скобяныя. Варановичъ И. Косицкій Г. Смилянскій Д.

Земледѣльческія орудія. Гальперинъ Б. М.

Золотыя и серебр. издѣлія. Евсѣевъ М. Тарощанскій.

Игрушки. Крижановскій М. А.

Four-page entry for the town of Priluki, from the Address Calendar: Poltava Guberniya. *A typical town entry lists type of business or occupation first and then names of individuals within that business, 1914.* 722-A

— 174 —

Складъ керосина и нефти. Маниловъ М. Мировъ И Нобель Вр. Рабиновичъ.

Книжные. Гореликъ А. Х. Капланъ Г. Ясногродскій Д. А.

Кожевные товары. Зискиндъ А. и Р.

Колбасныя. Бернтъ К. Ф. Гофманъ К.

Краски и лаки. Косицкій Г. А. Смолянскій Д. Ш.

Лѣсъ и дрова. Абрунинъ П. Ш. Бѣловъ И. И. Гальперинъ Б. М. Давидовъ З Ш. Маниловъ М. Л. Рохленко и Ко.

Мануфактура. Вольфсонъ и Ко. Золотницкій И. Когановъ А Супоницкій Б. Г. Т-во Мануфактуръ. Шептовицкій А. Шмеркинъ Г.

Мебель. Николаевскій Е.

Музыкальные инструменты. Крыжановскій М.

Мука. Золотницкій Д. Чернявскій А. Эйдельманъ М.

Мѣха: Кисловскій А.

Обои. Зискиндъ А. Кацинскій I.

Обувь. Поляковъ В.

Писче-бумажные. Бриль. Зальцманъ.

Дамское Платье Готовое. Бринъ М. Ш. Сиркинъ И. Н.

Мужское Платье Готовое. Бѣликовъ З. Коноша и Нескинъ. Розовъ А

Посуда. Николаевскій Е. Потребительное Об во. Т во «Идеалъ».

Рыба. Чумаченко Н. Чумаченко С.

Табакъ. Гореликъ Л. Х. Ясногродскій Д. А.

Типографіи. Линковъ Я. М. Мировъ А. Я.

— 175 —

Фотографіи. Вайнштейнъ Я I. Ривкинъ Д. И. Красноиольскій. Лиозинъ П. Т. Николаевскій Л. М. Юнако А.

Хлѣбо-Коммис. Контора. Мееровъ И. I.

Такса извозчиковъ. Конецъ по городу одн. 20 к. » до вокзала 20 к. » отъ вокзала 25 к. » по городу пар. 25 к. » до вокзала 25 к. » отъ вокзала 35 к. Отъ вокзала на Пискуновку 1 р. отъ пассажира Ѣзда по часамъ одн. 35 к. » » » пар. 50 к.

Pages 3 and 4 of the above Priluki town entry in the Address Calendar: Poltava Guberniya 722-B

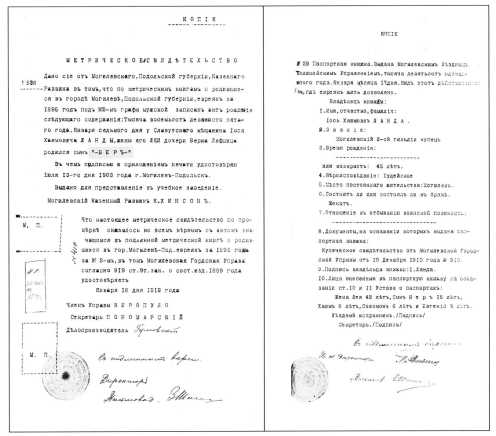

In order to be admitted to a vocational school in Mogilev Podolskiy, Ber Landa (age 15) obtained a certified
copy of his birth certificate, signed by Rabbi K. Khinson. This document, dated 1912, also includes the name
of Ber's mother, Leya (age 42, daughter of Berka Lifshitz), Ber's father, Ios (age 45), and Ber's paternal grandfather, Khaim. Also listed are Ber's brothers, Khaim (age eight), Solomon (age six) and Evgeniy (age three).

723

Two-page property records for the town of Melnitsa Podolskaya.
This document is for Leizor Blitzer, living in house #338 in Melnitsa.

724-A

1879 Melnitsa Podolskaya property records, second page

724-B

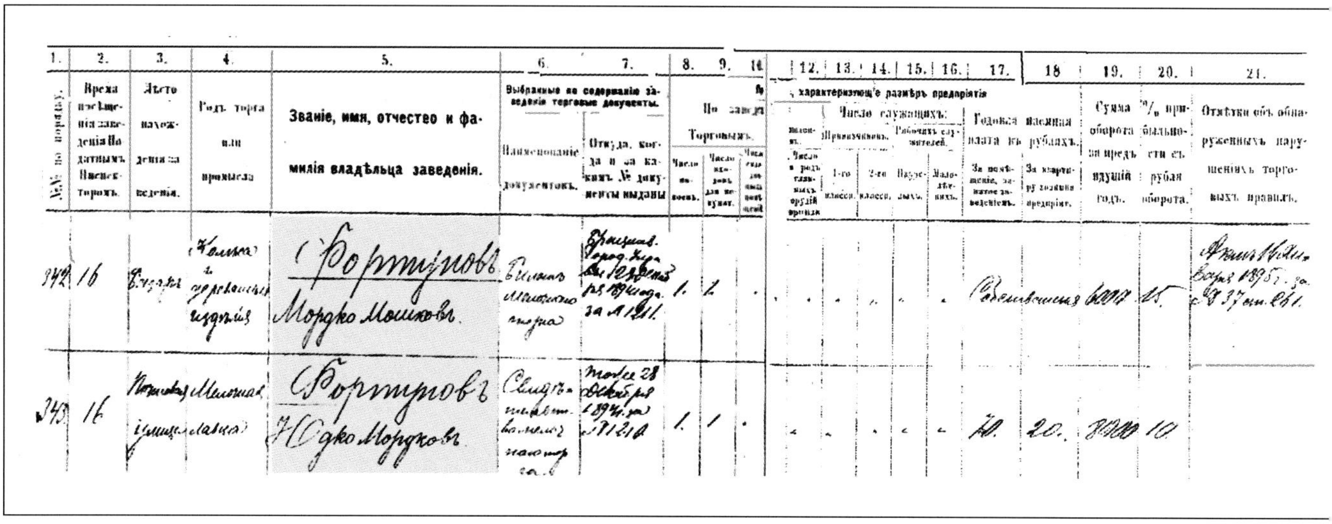

List of shops and small factories in Nemirov. Document #342, dated 1895, relates to Mordko Fortunov, son of Moshko. He has one shop where he sells wooden products and tires. The previous year, he grossed 6,000 rubles with a 50% profit. Document #343 relates to a small shop on Posthova Street rented by Yudko Fortunof, son of Mordko; the rental is 90 rubles per month. The previous year's sales were 8,000 rubles, with a 10% profit.

725

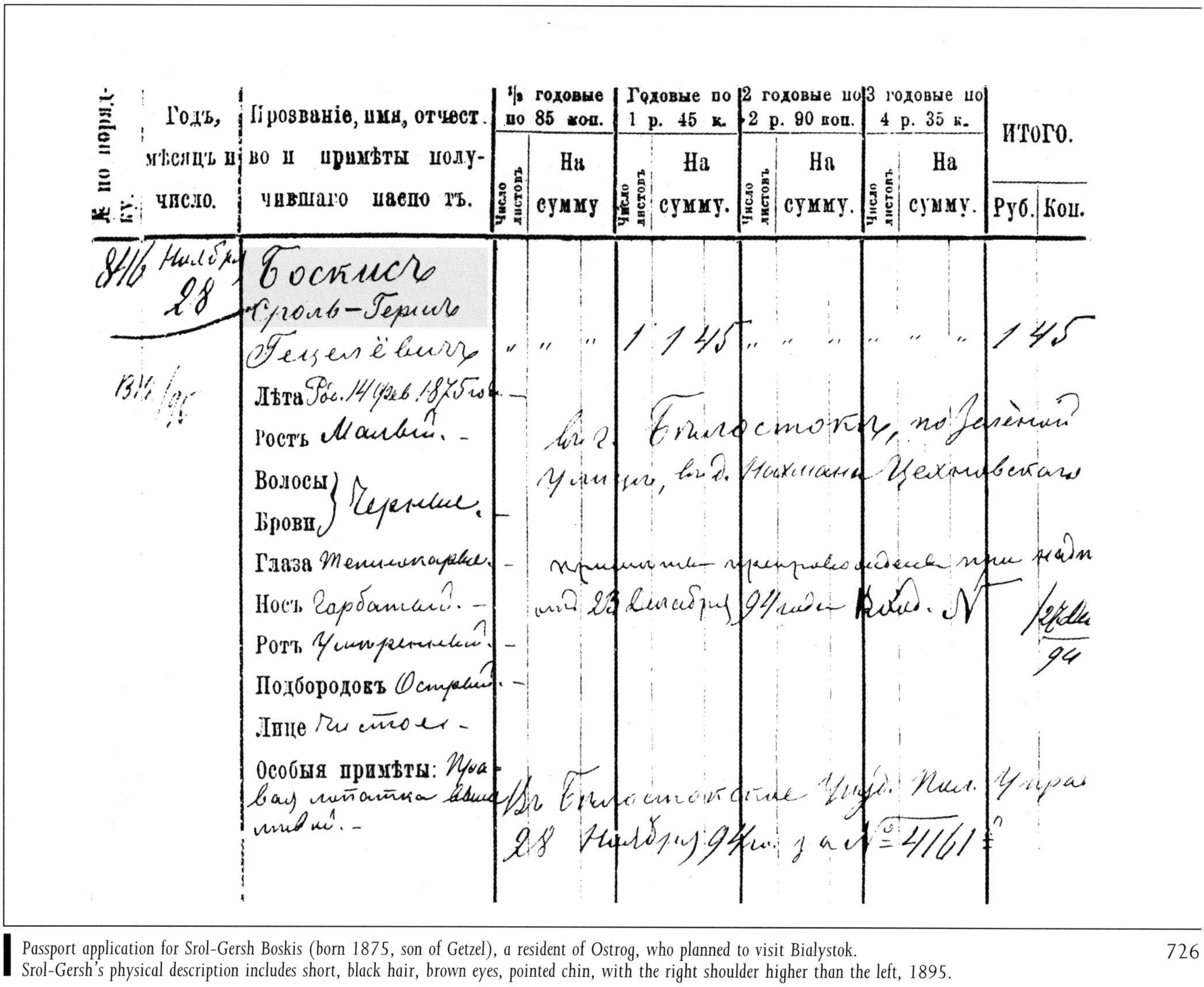

Passport application for Srol-Gersh Boskis (born 1875, son of Getzel), a resident of Ostrog, who planned to visit Bialystok.
Srol-Gersh's physical description includes short, black hair, brown eyes, pointed chin, with the right shoulder higher than the left, 1895.

726

A loan agreement for Hinde Zeiler from Mikulintsy, 1912   727

List of Jews who died in the Lvov Jewish Hospital during the   728
Holocaust. Entries include name, age and cause of death, 1942.

Property list for the town of Ostrog, including entry #1138 for Yankel   729
Litinskiy, who has two wooden buildings (house and shed), 1917

Emigration record for Berisch Schrenzel, age 27, born in Radziwillow   730
and emigrating from Unghene in Bessarabia to Lvov, 1891

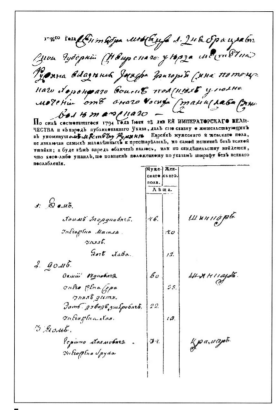

List of inhabitants in Ruzhin (Skvira Uezd), 1795.   731
There are no last names in these records. House #1
consists of Khaim, age 46 (son of Mordko); his wife
Matla, age 40; and their daughter Khava, age 12.
Khaim was a merchant.

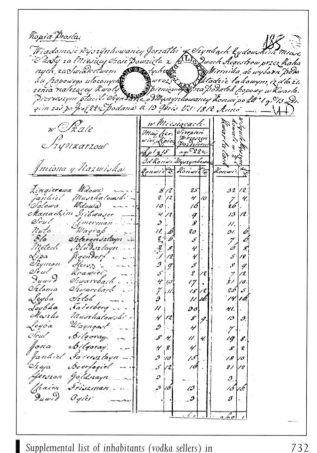

Supplemental list of inhabitants (vodka sellers) in   732
Skala Podolskaya, including #7, Elo Szterensztayn,
1812

Title page of 1938 telephone directory of Lvov,   733
Borislav, Drohobych and surrounding towns

Sample page from 1938 telephone directory (see left),   734
including Dobromil, Dolina and Drohobycz (Drohobych)

List of inhabitants for the Shaya Linskiy family from Novaya Priluka, Berdichev Uezd, Kiev Guberniya, 1851. The discovery of this document in 1995 ultimately reunited two family branches who had been out of touch for more than 70 years: Elizaveta Linskiy Weiner (now living in Vinnitsa, Ukraine) and her first cousin in America, William Lester. A few months after this discovery, Mr. Lester and his son, Dr. Mark Lester, traveled to Vinnitsa to meet their cousins.

735

The document examples on these two pages are in the format of documents from Western Ukraine (Galicia)

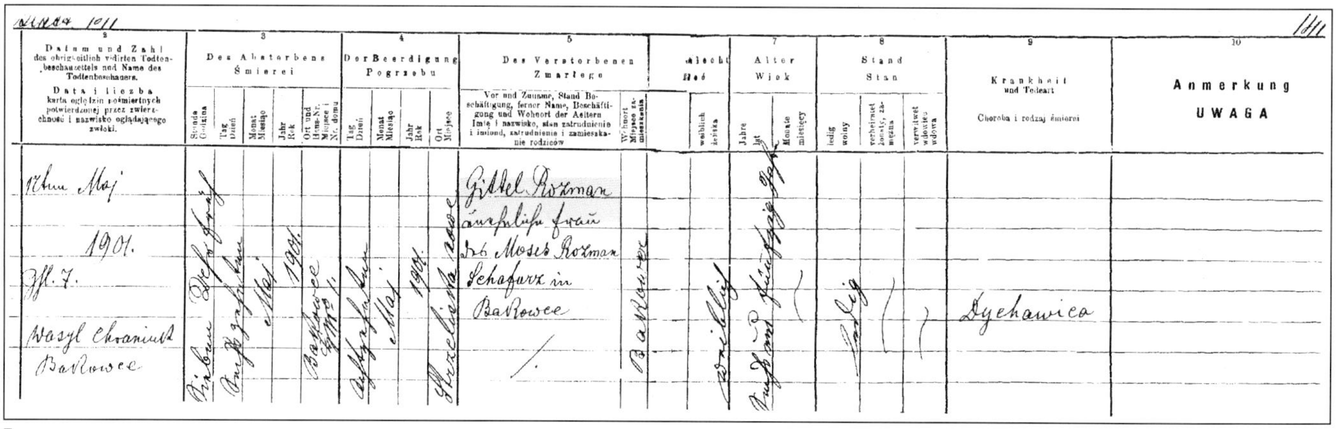

Death record for Gittel Rozman, died in 1901, wife of Moses Rozman, living in Bakovtsy, house #1

736

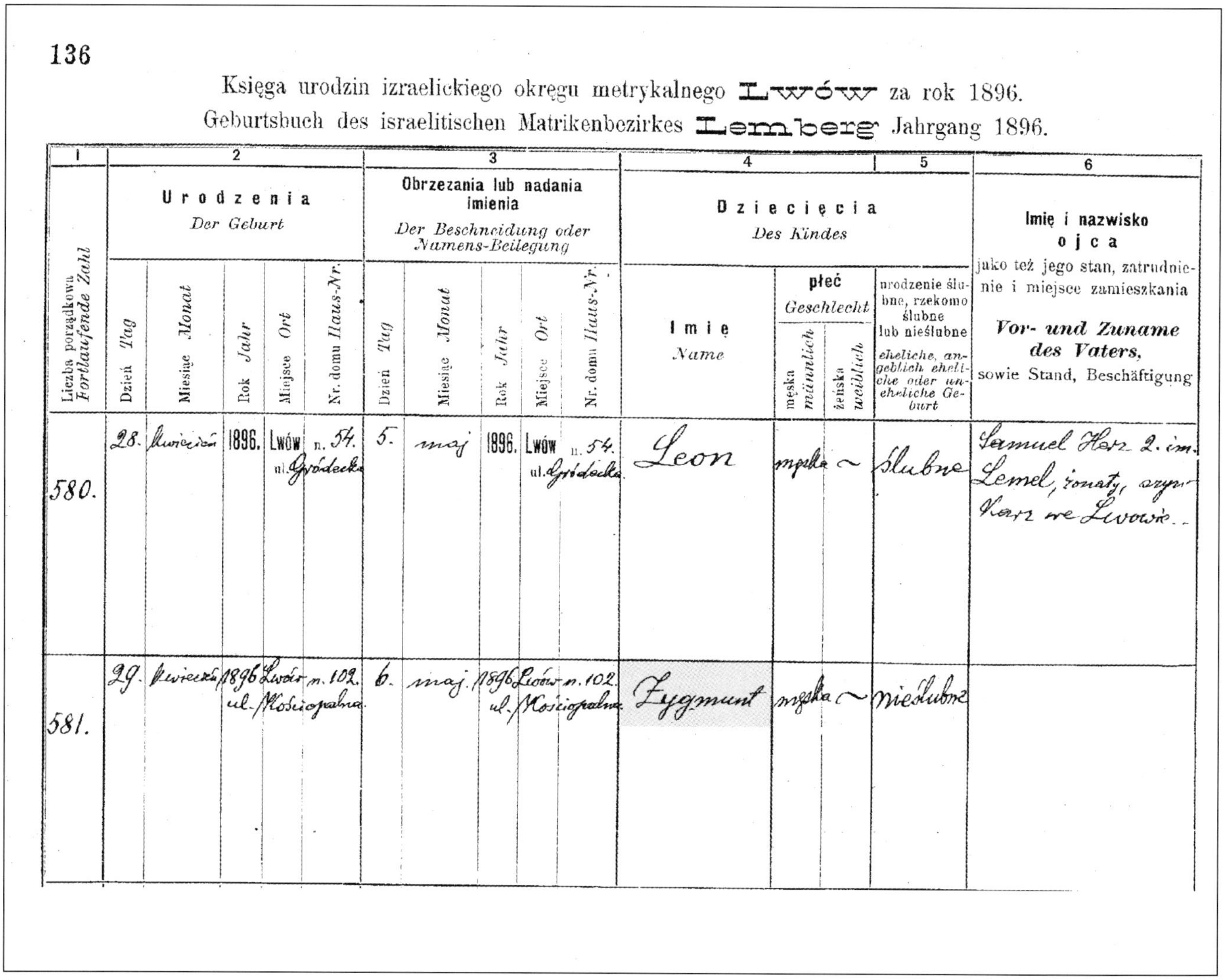

Birth record of Zygmunt Nadel (son of Efraim Nadel) and Freide Streisand (daughter of Hersch and Jütty Streisand), born 1896 in Lvov (first page of document)

738-A

1	2 NARZECZONEGO		Wiek		Stan		3 NARZECZONEJ		Wiek		Stan		4 Zaślubin			5 Własnoręczny podpis		6	7
Liczba porządk.	Imię i nazwisko, miejsce urodzenia, zatrudnienie, miejsce zamieszkania i Nr. domu, niemniej imiona, zatrudnienie i miejsce zamieszkania jego rodziców		Rok	Miesiąc	Wolny	Wdowiec	Imię i nazwisko, miejsce urodzenia, zatrudnienie, niemniej imiona, zatrudnienie, miejsce zamieszkania i Nr. domu jej rodziców		Rok	Miesiąc	Wolna	Wdowa	Dzień	Miesiąc	Rok	Miejsce	funkcjonującego przy zaślubinach rabina (szkolnika)	świadków i ich zatrudnienie z wymienieniem miejsca zamieszkania		UWAGA
2	Leib Blank urodzony i zamieszkały w Czortkowie fryzjer, syn Sary Blank w Czortkowie		1906	23.7	1		Pepi Antler urodzona i zamieszkała w Monasterzyskach, krawczyni córka Salomona Antlera i Chaji Chawy z domu Blech w Monasterzyskach		1909		1		16	styczeń	1938	Monasterzyska	Lipe Meisels rabin w Monasterzyskach	Henryk Fackel i Osias Färber obaj kupcy w Monasterzyskach.		

Marriage record (1938) of Leib Blank, born 1906 in Chortkov (son of Sara Blank) and
Pepi Antler, born 1909 in Monastyriska (daughter of Salomon Antler and Chaya Chana Blech)

737

Księga urodzin izraelickiego okręgu metrykalnego **Lwów** na rok 1896.
Geburtsbuch des israelitischen Matrikenbezirkes **Lemberg** Jahrgang 1896.

136

7 Imię i nazwisko matki, jej stan i zamieszkanie, jako też imię i nazwisko, zatrudnienie i miejsce zamieszkania jej rodziców *Vor- und Zuname der Mutter*, ihr Stand und Wohnort, dann Vor- und Zuname, Beschäftigung und Wohnort ihrer Eltern	8 Własnoręczny podpis z wymienieniem zatrudnienia i miejsca zamieszkania Eigenhändige Unterschrift mit Angabe der Beschäftigung und des Wohnortes kumów lub świadków Sandeka lub Szamesa der Pathen oder Zeugen, des Sandek oder Schames	9 obrzezującego lub obrzezujących des oder der Beschneider	10 akuszerki lub akuszera der Hebamme oder des Geburtshelfers	11 Dzieci nieżywo urodzone Todtgeborene Kinder	12 UWAGA Anmerkung
Chaję Lemel, zamężna we Lwowie, córka nauczyciela Judy Halpern i Dreźli Halpern we Lwowie.	Chaim Juda Halpern, nauczyciel dzieci we Lwowie, sandek, podpisani na karcie meldunkowej	Samuel Bolf,	Regina Halpern, Hladik	~ ~	Rodzice brali ślub w Kleparowie obok Lwowa dnia 20 lipca 1894 roku, wedle okazanej metryki ślubu wystawionej d. 29 lipca 1894 przez M. Weissa, prowadzącego metryki izr. w Zniesieniu (z tamt. Księgi Zaślubin na rok 1894 strona 17. poz. 51)
Freide Streisand (Streisand) wolna, we Lwowie wspólnie z grafikiem Efraimem Nadel zamieszkała, córka rzekomych małżonków spedytora w Przemyślu Herscha Streisand (Streisand) i b.p. Jütty.	Dawid Reich, właściciel realności we Lwowie, sandek, podpisani na karcie meldunkowej	R.F. Bodek,	Julia Hecher,	~ ~ ~	Podpisany Efraim Nadel przyznaje się do ojcostwa i prosi o wpisanie go jako ojca tego dziecka (Zygmunta) Efraim Nadel Salomon Albert świadek Bernard [...] świadek Zgadzam się jako Matka Znak ręczny Freidy Streisand jako położnicy i świadek Salomon Albert [...] #

Second page of document (see facing page, left)

738-B

LIBRARIES IN UKRAINE

The following libraries in Ukraine have many important books and manuscripts that would be of interest to researchers of Jewish family history. There are many other smaller repositories with equally interesting material. The country code for Ukraine is 380. City codes are provided in parentheses.

PLACE/Address	Telephone	PLACE/Address
UNIVERSAL SCIENTIFIC LIBRARY OF ODESSA OBLAST 49/51 Troyitska St. 270045, Odessa	(482) 22-5069	Одеська обласна універсальна наукова бібліотека (ODESKA OBLASNA UNIVERSALNA NAUKOVA BIBLIOTEKA) 270045, Одеса вул. Троїцька, 49/51
ODESSA STATE SCIENTIFIC LIBRARY 13 Pastera St. 270100, Odessa	(482) 23-0252	Одеська державна наукова бібліотека (ODESKA DERZHAVNA NAUKOVA BIBLIOTEKA) 270100, Одеса, вул. Пастера, 13
UNIVERSAL SCIENTIFIC LIBRARY OF THE CHERNIVTSI OBLAST 47 Olhy Kobylyanskoyi St. 274000, Chernivtsi	(3722) 2-2733	Чернівецька обласна універсальна наукова бібліотека (CHERNIVETSKA OBLASNA UNIVERSAL'NA NAUKOVA BIBLIOTEKA) 274000, Чернівці вул. Ольги Кобилянської, 47
SCIENTIFIC LIBRARY OF THE CHERNIVTSI STATE UNIVERSITY AFTER Y. FEDKOVYCH 23 Lesi Ukrayinky St. 274012, Chernivtsi	(3722) 9-8401	Наукова бібліотека Чернівецького державного університету імені Ю. Федьковича (NAUKOVA BIBLIOTEKA CHERNIVETSKOHO DERZHAVNOHO UNIVERSYTETU IMENI Y. FEDKOVYCHA) 274012, Чернівці вул. Лесі Українки, 23
STATE SCIENTIFIC LIBRARY IN KHARKIV AFTER V. KOROLENKO 8 Provul. Korolenka 310003, Kharkiv	(572) 12-6453	Харківська державна наукова бібліотека імені В.Короленка (KHARKIVSKA DERZHAVNA NAUKOVA BIBLIOTEKA IMENI V.KOROLENKA) 310003, Харків пров. Короленка, 8
V. I. VERNADSKIY NATIONAL LIBRARY OF UKRAINE, INSTITUTE OF MANUSCRIPTS 62 Volodymyrska St. 252017, m. Kyiv-17	(44) 244-4418 (44) 224-8256	Національна бібліотека України імені В.І.Вернадського, Інститут рукописів (NATSIONALNA BIBLIOTEKA UKRAYINY IMENI V.I.VERNADSKOGO, INSTYTUT RUKOPYSIV) 252017, м. Київ-17 вул. Володимирська, 62

Source: The above list was provided by Dr. Irina Sergeyeva, chief of the Oriental Department at the Vernadskiy National Library of Ukraine.

THE JEWISH COMMUNITY OF UKRAINE: ITS STATUS AND PERSPECTIVES

by
Josef Zissels

INTRODUCTION

There cannot be a prosperous Jewish community in an unprosperous country.

In May 1989, at the first legal conference of Jewish organizations of the Soviet Union in Riga, Latvia, the concept of "Jewish community" was raised, which even now generates a mass of emotional arguments. To date, this subject has yet to be studied on a serious academic level.

Then, at the dawn of the "Jewish revival," we naively believed that all was within our reach—the concept of a new Jewish community and the realization of this goal, that is, the rehabilitation of Jewish communal life. Just as naively, we believed that the Jewish world, from which we had been cut off for 70 years, would help us to reconstruct Jewish life.

As often happens, following our euphoria came disappointment. The problem lies not in the very fact of disappointment but in the understanding of its cause. If we confront those in whom we are disappointed, then we create an impasse in the path toward cooperation. If we understand that our euphoria was based on pure enthusiasm rather than knowledge, then we can move forward with our development and professional growth.

At that time, the plan proposed by the Jewish world in relation to Eastern European Jewry never received our approval. World Jewry believed that "Soviet" Jews were only a potential for repatriation to other countries and that strengthening their existing communities was not a necessity. As long as all have not yet left the region, the professional structures—Sokhnut, the American Jewish Joint Distribution Committee (the "Joint") and others—would continue to serve the temporarily remaining assimilated Jews.

Ten years have passed. The predictions of almost total repatriation have faded, and we are left with what remains: a large but weak, uncoordinated and unstructured community, burdened by a mass of problems.

THE DEFINITION OF A COMMUNITY

What is a community? In our opinion, it is a structure, consisting of the Jewish population, communal institutions and numerous networks among people, formed with the help of the institutions. In comparing the circumstances of the Jewish population over a 10-year period, the changes provide an example of a rehabilitating community.

An examination of the component parts of the community includes the Jewish population and its infrastructure.

Josef Zissels, president of the Vaad in Ukraine, in his Kiev office, 1998   739

299

Jewish cemetery in Delyatin, 1995

740

DEMOGRAPHY

According to the final Soviet population census, in 1989, 486,000 people in Ukraine identified themselves as Jews. As a rule, these were people whose parents were both Jews and who had the nationality "Jew" written in their Soviet internal passports. We consider this estimate as the "nucleus" of the Jewish population of Ukraine. Demographers suggest a "broadening of the coefficients" of the nucleus by 1.5 to 2.5 times. In such a way, we may conclude that in 1989 the "expanded population" of Jews in Ukraine consisted of more than 1 million people, who, together with non-Jewish family members, enlarged the estimate to 1.2 million–1.3 million people.

In 1995, for every birth, there were more than 10 deaths. Thus, we can estimate that over the past decade, the "natural decline" of the Jewish population was more than 70,000 people.

In mixed marriages among Ukraine's Jews in 1996, men comprised 82 percent and women 74 percent. The median age of Jews in Ukraine is 56 years.

In terms of subethnicities, the Jews of Ukraine are 99 percent Ashkenazi; there are small groups of Karaites (1,230 people in 1994) and Krimchaks (1,000 people) as well as

Bukharan Jews (110 people as of January 1, 1998), Mountain Jews (136 people) and Georgian Jews (56 people).

The religious observance of Jews in Ukraine can be estimated at no more than 3 percent (1 percent go to synagogue almost every day, and 2 percent pray at home, according to data of the Jewish Research Center [of the Institute of Sociology, Russian Academy of Sciences]). About 10 percent (4 to 14 percent, according to the Jewish Research Center) observe traditions in one or another small form. In small cities, as many as 80 percent take part in cultural and other community activities; in big cities, the figure is 30 percent. The religious involvement is on a positive trend. According to the Jewish Research Center, 15 percent are members of organizations, 30 percent are present at activities and 10 percent use services. The research data indicate that only 13 percent of those surveyed did not participate in any form of Jewish activity.

In late 1995 and early 1996, an Israeli sociologist, Nadia Zinger, carried out sociological research entitled "Tendencies of Repatriation from Russia and Ukraine." Commissioned by the Sokhnut (the Jewish Agency), she surveyed 1,500 people in Kiev, Kharkov, Odessa and Lvov.

EMIGRATION AND REPATRIATION

From 1989 to 1998, mass emigration decreased the number of Jews (and their families) in Ukraine by almost half a million people. At the present time, about 700,000 to 800,000 people live in Ukraine who, to one degree or another, may be considered as actual members of the Jewish community or as potential emigrants. The nucleus or core of the Jewish population (1997) is approximately 200,000. The dynamic character of demographics (migration and other cultural processes), together with the absence of demographic specialists in Ukraine, does not allow us to give a more accurate quantitative picture.

The Jews of Ukraine are reacting to the worsening of the country's socioeconomic situation chiefly through emigration and, to a lesser extent, through a transition from the traditional professional activities of the past 60 to 90 years to private business ventures. The basic factors (according to repeated surveys) accounting for the consistently high levels of emigration of Jews from Ukraine are the socioeconomic situation, family reunification, the desire to improve the lives of children (in part due to the effects of Chernobyl), difficulties in professional achievement and changes in the social environment.

Of the nearly 500,000 Jews who have emigrated from Ukraine since 1989, 250,000 have gone to Israel, 120,000 to the United States, 70,000 to Germany and 60,000 to other countries.

The results of Nadia Zinger's research, in relation to the sample numbers of Jews surveyed in Ukraine (and Russia), indicate the following:

- Ukraine: 38 percent intend to emigrate (12 percent are sure and 26 percent are probable).
- Russia: 28 percent intend to emigrate (10 percent are sure and 18 percent are probable).

In Ukraine, according to data from the Jewish Research Center, in late 1993–early 1994, 50 percent of those surveyed intended to emigrate (18 percent sure plus 32 percent probable); 6.5 percent of them were planning to emigrate in 1994. This may mean that the desire to emigrate has substantially decreased. In reality, emigration from Ukraine in 1994 amounted to 58,670; in 1996, 50,612; and in 1997, about 45,000.

Statistics of the Jewish Research Center show that despite the high rate of emigration, more than half of the Jews surveyed believe that the means (funds) being collected in the Jewish world for our community must go, to a greater extent, to the strengthening of the existing community rather than for emigration.

Ms. Zinger's research found that 62 percent of those surveyed did not intend to emigrate from Ukraine (from Russia, 72 percent). Of those in Ukraine, 28 percent were sure that they would not emigrate, while 24 percent thought that they would probably not emigrate. The basic reasons for the lack of desire to emigrate were strong ties to their country of residence and its culture, an unsuitable age, good employment, and apprehensions about the lowering of one's professional and social status after emigration, as so often happens in another country.

A preliminary analysis of the aforesaid indicates that over the next decade, 350,000 to 400,000 people will emigrate (by Jewish channels) from Ukraine. (That means approximately 50 percent of the "enlarged population.") Among those remaining, the "core population" will consist of 100,000 to 120,000.

RE-EMIGRATION

The process of re-emigration, having arisen in recent years and slowly increased, draws attention to itself in the data of the Ministry of Statistics of Ukraine. In the past few years, according to the official data of the Ministry of Statistics of Ukraine, about 6,500 Jews (with their families) have returned to Ukraine (from Israel, the United States, Germany and Russia), a number comprising approximately 5 percent of those who emigrated in the very same period. Some of the re-emigrants are people who received an education and business skills in Israel, the United States, or Europe and wish to employ those skills under the new conditions in Ukraine. Often, such people function as the middlemen for Western and Israeli investors, considering that they are more familiar with the situation in Ukraine, not to mention their knowledge of the language, their understanding of Ukrainian culture and the value of the ties they have maintained.

In this building in Kiev are offices of the Vaad of Ukraine, classes for Torah study, the Holocaust Survivors organization and a Jewish newspaper, 1998.   741

Statue of Sholom Aleikhem in the center of Kiev, 1998   742

Since far from all of the "returnees" officially declare their new status, it is reasonable to assume that the true numbers of re-emigration are two to three times higher than those reported.

According to unofficial Israeli data, over the past few years, 35,000 to 40,000 repatriates returned to the former Soviet countries from Israel.

This phenomenon merits special research, but today we can make a few assertions and assumptions. For example:

- A significant number of Israelis, for a variety of reasons, almost continuously reside in different countries, including countries of destination (personally or in the second generation).
- Despite the unfavorable conditions of life and business in Ukraine, to some extent it appears to be an attractive destination for active people from various countries, including former emigrants.
- Even with a not very significant improvement of the situation in Ukraine, within 15 to 20 years we may encounter a phenomenon of "dynamic equilibrium," in which the annual streams of emigrants and re-emigrants will be approximately equal.
- Along with the obvious factors of re-assimilation and the rehabilitation of Jewish communal life, the eventual

active participation of Israelis and other re-emigrants living in Ukraine can help preserve the Jewish community in Ukraine in terms of both number of people and quality of life.

THE PROBLEMS AND SOCIAL-SERVICE NEEDS OF THE JEWS IN UKRAINE

More than one-third of Ukraine's "enlarged" Jewish community (250,000 to 300,000) consists of pensioners. The average pension of the group is just $20 to $30 per month. Many pensioners are without a family, or their children and other relatives live far away. Some receive financial aid from relatives in Israel, the United States or Germany. The majority of pensioners are not in a position to pay for public services, medical care, transportation, the repair of clothes and shoes, or even to buy a normal ration of food.

It is estimated that 12 to 15 percent of the community (100,000 to 120,000) are in constant need of various forms of aid (products, medicine and money). The most complete list of Jews in Ukraine includes about 60,000 people; that is, only about half of those in need. Some 10,000 to 12,000 elderly and handicapped people are in need of home nursing care and are not in a position to care for themselves.

More than 50,000 victims of the Holocaust (survivors and others) occupy a special place among the socially weak sectors of the Jewish population. These include about 4,000 former prisoners of the ghettos and concentration camps as well as those people who, while fleeing from the advancing German Army, lost their loved ones, their homes and their belongings.

Included among the victims of the Holocaust are those who never started families due to the acute changes in the demographic situation after the war and due to wounds, handicaps or sickness resulting from the war. Today, many of these victims are elderly and sick people living alone. An analogous but smaller group includes victims of the Soviet repressions of the 1920s to 1950s.

Due to our inability to resolve such social problems, either independently or in conjunction with the "Joint," Jewish communities, especially in small cities, often turn to local and foreign Christian organizations for aid.

According to data of the well-known demographer Mark Kupovetsky, about 30,000 Jewish children of school age live in Ukraine at the present time. He predicts that within 20 years, there will be just 10,000.

According to the Center of Jewish Education, only about 10,000 Jewish children, to one or another degree, study within the Jewish education system in Ukraine.

In an effort to briefly characterize the basic problems of the Jewish community of Ukraine, it is necessary to consider the following:

- Insufficient professional staff.
- The almost complete absence of internal financing.
- The absence of serious coordination of the activities of various organizations, including external groups.
- The minimal involvement of youth in community life.

THE INFRASTRUCTURE OF THE COMMUNITY

About 300 Jewish organizations and communities (which, to a considerable extent, exist only nominally) are conditionally united under four structures of an "umbrella" nature: the Vaad, the Union of Jewish Religious Organizations, the Jewish Council of Ukraine and the All-Ukrainian Jewish Congress.

At the present time, Ukraine has about 70 Orthodox and 15 Reform communities. It has 18 foreign Orthodox rabbis (from Israel and the United States), but not a single local rabbi. The more significantly represented and active groups are the Karlin-Stolin Hasidim and Habad. The religious communities have only about 30 synagogues; those without a synagogue use unsuitable facilities or have none whatsoever.

In more than 60 cities in Ukraine, basic infrastructures of social services have been created by local communities with the support of the "Joint." Unfortunately, many do not have separate or suitable locations for work; nor do they have enough professionals, social workers, equipment and volunteers.

It is extremely problematic that the maintenance of equipment and supplies and the support of professionals in communal work rely to a significant degree on foreign organizations. A substantial part of the communal–social infrastructure is managed directly by the "Joint." Many of the directors of Jewish communities and organizations, in one way or another, work for and receive their salaries from foreign Jewish organizations. This practice solves their individual financial problems but creates the problem of dependency of community leaders on external organizations.

The presence and activity of a rabbi create, as a rule, a more balanced situation in the community in both financial and moral matters. In many aspects, a rabbi is closer to the community than the representatives of international and Israeli organizations and, therefore, even if possessing lesser means, "competes" with them. The activities of a rabbi are focused on the strengthening of the community, and he has greater independence; in these ways, his responsibilities and activities differ from those of formal organizations.

In Ukraine, there has not been a sufficient degree of success in involving volunteers in the system of social assistance. Frequently, the volunteers are in need of aid no less than their wards.

There are 16 day schools and about 80 Sunday schools, 11 kindergartens, eight yeshivas (the larger part of them existing only formally), about 150 *ulpan* groups (intensive courses in Hebrew), one university, two colleges and correspondence schools. Within these various educational forums, there are more than 20,000 participants (half of them children and young people) and more than 400 teachers. A significant number of the schools do not have their own buildings, equipment, textbooks and other necessities.

Other elements of the infrastructure of the Jewish community include the Institute of Judaic Studies (20 programs and conferences), the Committee of Preservation of Jewish Heritage, the Jewish press (more than 20 newspapers), the Committee on Repatriation and the Union of Theaters and Ensembles "Kinor."

THE BASIC STAGES OF DEVELOPMENT OF THE COMMUNAL PROCESS

From 1988 to 1992, Jewish social organizations played a significant role in the first stage of the awakening and initial satisfaction of interest of assimilated Jews in Ukraine during the reconstruction of Jewish life.

The period from 1993 to 1996, the second stage of the development of communal life, can be designated as the period of creation and development of professional Jewish structures (schools, charity centers, the press and academic institutions). During this stage, vital aid to the Jewish communities of Ukraine was provided by "outside" factors—intergovernmental and Israeli organizations (primarily the "Joint," the Israeli Embassy, religious organizations and Sokhnut).

Intergovernmental and Israeli organizations shifted from the role of external support networks for the activities of Jewish organizations in Ukraine to the creation of new structures, offering various well-paying positions to many Jewish activists.

At the present time, indigenous social organizations have reduced their roles in the lives of the Jews of Ukraine. This is due primarily to the fact that they do not appear to be in a position to re-adapt to the new stage—the stage of the professionalization of Jewish life, the creation of a professional infrastructure of the Jewish community—and because they could not compete with opportunities from external factors.

The beginning of the third and most recent stage of development of a Jewish communal structure can be traced to 1996, when successful businessmen began to show interest not only in sponsoring community programs but also in actively and personally participating in the governing of communal life. Particularly vivid examples may be found in

Teachers and counselors at a Jewish camp in Klinovka, 1998   743

▌ *Remains of the synagogue in Sokal, 1995*

The administrative expenses of foreign organizations for the management of the above-enumerated programs and projects consist of no less than $3 million to $4 million—15 to 20 percent of the total aid.

Thus, the minimal total need of the Jewish community in Ukraine is estimated at between $80 million and $100 million per year, while actually only about $20 million to $25 million is collected (in the United States and Israel) and spent. In other words, the Jewish community of Ukraine has no more than 25 percent of what it needs.

The same approximate sum ($25 million) is spent annually by Sokhnut for the preparation and transportation of 20,000 Jews to Israel from Ukraine—that is, on services for approximately 2.5 percent of the members of the community. Therefore, for each Jew leaving the community, the Jewish world spends 10 times more than for the Jew who remains in Ukraine and wishes to preserve and develop his or her Jewish identity.

The foreign role in the financing of Jewish life in Ukraine comes to more than 95 percent. Those who act as "inside" sponsors of the Jewish community, most often at the level of city programs, include local businessmen (not necessarily Jews). A small amount of aid, less than 5 percent, is provided by the government, generally through municipal organs.

Local businessmen include citizens of Israel, the United States or Germany, former residents of Ukraine who emigrated previously and then returned to participate in the development of new Ukrainian business. Having become acquainted during emigration with the practice of philanthropy, they (sometimes to a greater extent than local businessmen) are often prepared to participate financially in the support of communal programs. About 150 Israeli–Ukrainian joint ventures support communal Jewish activities in Ukraine.

At the present time, no fewer than 3,000 Jews actively and quite successfully conduct business in Ukraine. Among them, about 30 are considered to be among the 100 most active and well-established businessmen in Ukraine. But only about 10 percent of the active Jewish businessmen in Ukraine occasionally give some assistance to local communities in the form of money, products, building materials, labor and transport. At the same time, these Jewish businessmen annually spend no less than $20 million on non-Jewish charitable activities, supporting a whole series of sports clubs, children's programs, medical programs, and government institutions—often not by their own will but at the order of government functionaries, on whom the existence of private business in Ukraine depends.

An interesting phenomenon, the "privatization of the Jewish community," is being observed in a few cities in Ukraine, where the leaders of the community are businessmen who minimally contribute to the maintenance of community programs. The positive aspects of this phenomenon are to a

Dnepropetrovsk, Odessa, Donetsk and Kiev as well as in the creation of the All-Ukrainian Jewish Congress and the Jewish Foundation of Ukraine.

Thus, at the third stage of development, the communal process is completed by uniting into the Jewish communities all of the human factors deemed necessary—including activists, rabbis, Jewish professionals and businessmen.

THE FINANCIAL ASPECT OF THE ACTIVITIES OF THE COMMUNITY

It is estimated that for the creation, support, and development of social services for the Jewish community of Ukraine, it is necessary to invest no less than $50 million per year. In 1997, only $10 million was placed into programs of social services—that is, just 20 percent of the need. The basic sponsors are: the Claims Conference (Conference on Jewish Material Claims Against Germany), the "Joint," foreign religious organizations (Habad and Yad Israel), European Jewish organizations (the European Jewish Congress and the European Council of Jewish Organizations), the Union of Religious Communities of Ukraine, the Vaad of Ukraine and various local businesses.

At the present time in Ukraine, not more than $5 million per year is spent on Jewish education, while at least $20 million is needed. Sponsors include foreign religious organizations (Habad and Yad Israel), the government of Israel, Sokhnut, the Ministry of Education of Ukraine, the "Joint," the Leon Pinkus Foundation (Israel), Midreshet Jerusalem, the Union of Religious Communities and the Vaad.

Children and youth programs include recreational camps, clubs, circles and game programs, with the participation of 5,000 to 7,000 children and teenagers. About $1 million is spent on these programs, while at least $3 million is needed. The sponsors are Sokhnut and various religious organizations.

Memorial programs, the upkeep of buildings and venues and other expenses absorb about $2 million per year, while the minimal need is for $5 million to $6 million.

744

significant extent counterbalanced by its costs: the monopolization of "power" in the community, the authoritarian system of leadership of the community, the impossibility of selecting another leader and other considerations.

Of 2,000 surviving objects of former Jewish communal properties, no more than 30 have been returned by the government to the Jewish community. The problem of restitution of communal property is not considered by the organs of power in Ukraine in an even preliminary way. At the same time, the process of privatization has already affected some communal buildings in Western Ukraine.

A significant problem related to insufficient financing appears to be the almost complete absence of coordination in activities between different external factors, between regional representatives inside foreign organizations, and between external and internal factors. As a result, the types of communal services available to Jews in Ukraine vary widely between large and small cities and also between different districts within large cities.

Rabbi David Hillel Wilfond, Kiev Congregation Ha-Tikva, conducts Torah study in Kiev, 1998.

745

SUMMARY

Based on the foregoing, our conclusions are as follows:

- The basic differences between the Jewish community of Ukraine and Jewish communities in other countries of the former Soviet Union are both positive and negative.
  Positive:
    - The absence of "Jewish wars."
    - The joint activities of religious and secular organizations.
    - The preparation for *aliya* as part of communal activities.
    - The presence of a developing professional infrastructure.
  Negative:
    - The weak internal sources of financing.
- The Jewish community of Ukraine, despite unfavorable conditions, is creating its own infrastructure and is professionalizing itself.
- International and Israeli organizations have divided among themselves "spheres of influence" within the community and, by means of financing and other mechanisms, try to preserve control over the situation in Ukraine.
- We can try to resolve the problem of self-financing of the Jewish community of Ukraine by initiating, first and foremost, fundraising among local Jewish businessmen, particularly the owners of new enterprises who have returned from emigration to do business in Ukraine.
- Since local communities typically use their financial resources more effectively than do foreign organizations, the concentration in the first period on internal financing on the order of $3 million to $4 million per year could permit the Jewish community of Ukraine to become competitive and on a par with external organizations.
- European Jewish structures can help, most of all, by sharing their experience of self-financing. They can also significantly strengthen the "quiet voice" of new Jewish communities wishing to occupy a niche in the Jewish picture of Europe and the world and protesting against paternalistic, condescending relations. They can help establish direct relations with various foundations.
- The development of direct ties between communities of Ukraine and Jewish communities of Europe, the United States and Canada is an untapped resource. Aid can and must be implemented, not only (and not to such a great extent) through bureaucratic inter-governmental Jewish structures but also by direct ties between communities. This will permit us to increase the effectiveness of every dollar collected in the West for the Jewish communities of Ukraine.
- To a significant extent, the financial problems of the Jewish community can be resolved with the restitution of former Jewish communal property. It follows that the Jewish community should focus its attention on aiding the resolution of the problems in Ukraine—not in the distant future, but right now.

- The coordination of activities between different external and internal economic factors will allow us to use the means at our disposal more effectively.

PROGNOSES

- Within 20 to 30 years, the Jewish community of Ukraine will stabilize at the level of 150,000 to 200,000 people.
- By its activity, the Jewish community of Ukraine will be singled out in Europe in the future.
- Re-emigrants and foreign citizens living and working in Ukraine will become important factors in the activity of the community.
- In the coming years, Israeli governmental and intergovernmental Jewish organizations will continue to remain dominant factors in the financing of the Jewish community of Ukraine.
- At the same time, even with an increase in financing from external factors, the Jewish community of Ukraine will not be able to satisfy its minimal needs, due to the large scale of its socioeconomic problems.
- The local economy will grow slowly but in the next five to ten years will not be able to compete with external factors, due to its insignificant increase and insufficient internal coordination. It could guarantee the minimal needs of the community if the coordination between external and internal factors were to become possible, which appears improbable at this point.

CONCLUSION

Time arranges the priorities of our activities. We must direct our basic means and powers toward the social protection of the community, including education. We do not have the right, in our view, to work toward other goals while people in our community remain unfed and without heat.

At first glance, the picture of our life and the prognoses seem pessimistic. However, in our long history, it is not the first time that, on the verge of despair, we have begun to reconstruct our community.

Josef Zissels was born in 1946 in Tashkent. In 1948, his family moved to Chernovtsy. In 1969, Mr. Zissels graduated from Chernovtsy University with a degree in physics. He then became a teacher. Zissels served in the Soviet Navy in 1969–1970 and has been active in Jewish organizations and causes since 1970. He went to prison twice for a total of six years for the illegal distribution of literature for his work with a commission researching the utilization of psychiatric hospitals for political purposes and for his involvement in the Ukraine–Helsinki organization. Thereafter, his travel was restricted. In Chernovtsy in 1988, Mr. Zissels was the moving force in establishing the first Jewish cultural organization in Ukraine. In 1989, he helped form the Vaad of the Soviet Union, and he became a co-president of this organization (with Mikhail Chlenov from Moscow and Samuel Zilberg from Riga). Since 1991, he has served as president of the Vaad in Ukraine. In 1997, Mr. Zissels established the Jewish Congress in Ukraine, and currently he serves as its vice-president. He is a member of many Jewish organizations throughout the world, including the World Jewish Congress and World Zionist Organization. Mr. Zissels publishes many articles in the Jewish press of Ukraine and the Russian press in Israel. He is married, with three children, and currently lives in Kiev.

Vitali Morozov and Yana Shapiro in front of the Podol District synagogue in Kiev, where they were married in one of the first Jewish weddings since the fall of communism, 1991.

746

The People & the Places

On a summer day, a woman stops work for a few minutes to talk about the people and the places she remembers from her small village in Galicia.

◀ 747
Typical scene along the roadways in Ukraine and Moldova. During times of gasoline rationing, this standby transportion is ever ready, 1993.

748 ▶
Just outside of Vashkovtsy, Ukraine, 1995

◀ 749
A summer day in Kudrintsy, Ukraine, 1995

◀ 750
*A typical scene at the bazaar
in Mogilev Podolskiy, Ukraine, 1993*

751 ▶

*At the bazaar in Mogilev Podolskiy, where Miriam
Weiner inspects a goat, but does not buy it, 1993*

◀ 752
Buying fresh bread in Luboml, Ukraine. Many
small businesses in Ukraine are conducted from
the horse and wagon, 1995.

▲ 753   Shargorod, 1992

▲ 754   The wife of the last Jew in Lubashevka, 1993

▲ 755   Udel Zaidman, Shepetovka, 1994

▲ 756   At the bazaar in Berdichev, 1994

▲ 758   In the local market, Shargorod, 1992

◄ 757   A shoemaker in Starokonstantinov, 1994

▲ 759   Zalik Kroitsman, a watchmaker, in Korsun Shevchenkovskiy, 1994

▲ 761   Interview with the last remaining Jew in Dzygovka, Ukraine, where he describes what he remembers about the Maidenberg family from this town, 1995

▲ 760   Interview with *Anna Frankel, one of the few remaining Jews in Trostyanets, 1995*

762 ▶

Interview with the last remaining Jewish family in Ladyzhin. This woman is describing what she remembers about the Talesnik family from this area, 1995.

◀ 763

In their apartment in Novograd Volynskiy, Faina Goldman (left) and her mother, Paulina Goldman (right), describe their family tree and relationship to Paul Gass of Boston, Massachusetts, whose mother was a Goldman. Mr. Gass later traveled to Ukraine to meet his new relatives, 1993.

▲ 764 *Sharing the highways in Ukraine, traveling south from Kiev to Belaya Tserkov, 1993*

▲ 765 *Typical traffic impediment along the highways of Ukraine and Moldova. This photograph was taken from the inside of the author's car, 1995.*

▲ 766   *In the village of Pechora, the horse and wagon act as a tow truck, 1989.*

▲ 767   *Jewish cemetery in Sadgora, 1994*

A FORMER SHTETL

▲ 768   *At home in Tomashpol, 1992*

▲ 769   *Tomashpol, 1992*

▲ 770   *Tomashpol, 1992*

771 ▶
Miriam Weiner with a Hebrew book, part of an
exhibition in the local museum in Priluki, Ukraine, 1991

◀ 772
A local family in Korolovka, Ukraine,
hold a Torah that was left with them
for safekeeping during World War II.
The Jewish family who left the Torah
never returned for it, 1993.

773 ▶
Bogdan Ivanovich (seated), caretaker in the
Lvov Jewish cemetery, points out names of people
buried in the cemetery to Vitaly Chumak, the
author's colleague and translator in Ukraine,
1994.

774 ▶
In the local museum of Ostrog, Ukraine, director Larisa S. Mazurenko points out the Baskies family documents to Miriam Weiner, 1993.

◀ 775
Vitaly Chumak and Larisa S. Mazurenko hold a Torah, one of dozens housed in the museum, 1993.

▲ 776   Rabbi Shaya Weinberger conducts classes in the Kiev Synagogue, 1990.

▲ 777   In the Gadyach summer camp, Poltava region, 1990

▲ 778   Maksim Peysakhov in Medzhibozh, 1991

▲ 779   The author joins a local resident of Goshcha for a ride on a winter day, 1992.

▲ 780   The Yabluyntsya Pass in the Carpathian Mountains, c. 1990

781
These three women, all named Goldman, were photographed in the synagogue in Novograd Volynskiy, Ukraine. Goldman relatives in the United States sent the author to this town to look for surviving relatives, 1994.

782 ▶
Members of the Jewish community in Novograd Volynskiy, Ukraine, sign a letter of invitation to Paul Gass of Boston, whose relatives come from this town. Mr. Gass later visited the town, met his newly discovered relatives and sponsored the restoration and upkeep of the Jewish cemetery, 1994.

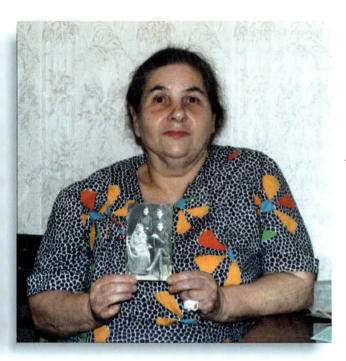

783
Elizaveta Weiner, living in Vinnitsa, Ukraine, holds
a photo of her ancestors who went to America. In Allentown,
Pennsylvania, Dr. Mark Lester found the identical photograph
among his family papers. After discovering Elizaveta (his
father's first cousin), Dr. Lester began traveling to Ukraine on
an annual basis. In addition to visits with his cousins, he
has brought medical equipment to the local hospital, donated
by his clinic in Allentown, 1995.

784
Freida Talesnik, one of the few remaining
Jews in Trostyanets, Ukraine, shares her
memories on video for her newly discovered
cousin in America, Deborah Tall,
1995.

785
The Maidenberg family: Amnon (right), his
wife, Shura, and their son Eduard, an artist, in
their apartment in Kishinev, Moldova, pose for a
photo to be given to their cousin, Michael
Maidenberg of Grand Forks, North Dakota,
1993.

▲ 786 *A Jewish home in Shargorod, 1992*

▲ 787 *Jewish cemetery in Sokolets, 1989*

▲ 788 *Khaim Egorov, a shoe salesman in Mogilev Podolskiy, 1992*

▲ 789　Sholom Aliekhem once lived in this building in Kiev, 1994

▲ 790　Plaque at the Sholom Aleikhem Museum in Pereyaslav-Khmelnitskiy, 1994

▲ 791　Jewish cemetery in Sudilkov, Ukraine, 1994

▲ 792   *Arkadiy Yanover in his shoe shop in Shepetovka, 1994*

▲ 793   *Arkadiy Yanover repairing shoes in Shepetovka, 1994*

▲ 794   *Udel Zaidman at home in Shepetovka, 1994*

▲ 795 Street scene in Kiev, 1989

▲ 796 At work in Shargorod, 1992

▲ 797 Shargorod, 1992

798 ▶
In the local market in Dzygovka, Ukraine, some things have not changed in a century. Here the abacus still functions as the store calculator, although one clerk described it as her "computer," 1992.

◀ 799
People waiting to buy bread in Drogobych, 1998

▲ 800   In *Ataki, Moldova, a Roma (Gypsy) tells the fortune of one of the 20 remaining Jews (left), 1992.*

▲ 801   *In the Kiev Synagogue, 1993*

▲ 802   On the way to Smozhe, a village in Western Ukraine, an area formerly known as Galicia, 1997

The Holocaust

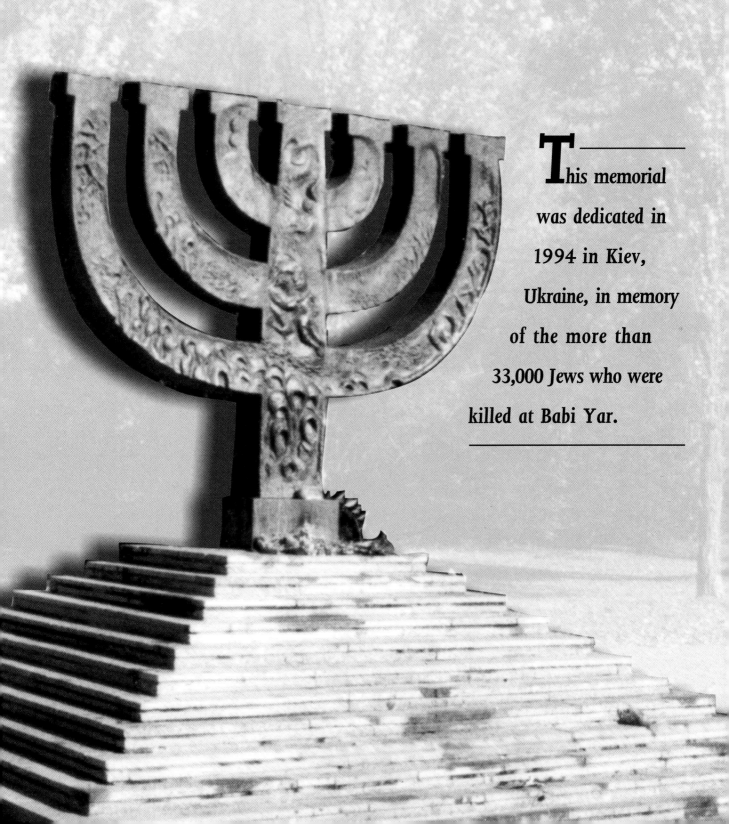

This memorial was dedicated in 1994 in Kiev, Ukraine, in memory of the more than 33,000 Jews who were killed at Babi Yar.

A sea of faces at the dedication of the memorial at Babi Yar, a ravine in Kiev where Sonderkommando 4a of Einsatzgruppe C carried out the mass slaughter of more than 33,000 Jews from Kiev and surrounding towns on September 29–30, 1941. The killings at Babi Yar continued in subsequent months (victims included Jews, Communists and POWs), for an estimated total of 100,000 people.

803

THE HOLOCAUST IN VINNITSA OBLAST

by
Faina A. Vinokurova, *Vice-Director*
STATE ARCHIVE OF VINNITSA OBLAST

History is humanity's memory and hope that violence and cruelty will be prevented in the future. One of the most important obligations of a historian is to propagate knowledge about the Holocaust. The Holocaust was unique; there had never before been such a massive, premeditated and systematic annihilation of a people. The documents testifying to this fact are studied with great interest all over the world.

At the State Archive of Vinnitsa Oblast, there are 275 fonds (14,000 files) concerning the persecution and genocide of the Jewish population of Vinnitsa region from 1941 to 1944.

A significant amount of important information on the Holocaust is concentrated in the Vinnitsa regional, district and town commission fonds, because of the destruction of property and crimes perpetrated against Jews by the German and Romanian occupiers. The historical value of this material is the richness of content and unique information, including witness statements, documents and photographs. There are documented records and statements about the exhumation of graves of people who were executed, the schemes (map plots) of the graves' locations and lists of genocide victims, with numerous photographs, testimonies and eyewitness accounts from those who survived the Holocaust.

In a general statement and questionnaire of Yakov Spivak (in Vinnitsa) is the following testimony: "On April 16, 1941, at the maternity hospital, Jewish women in labor were arrested and carried away to the Pyatnychany forest. On April 17, at the maternity hospital N2, the Fascists packed the new-born Jewish babies into two sacks and threw them from the second floor."

The summary report for Nemirov District states that "on August 7, 1941, the German occupiers and their collaborators first forced the Jewish population of the town to pay 100,000 rubles as a contribution for residence rights. In September 1941, 2,400 Jews (including old men, women and children) were shot at the brickworks near Nemirov. On November 7, 2,580 people were annihilated. In May 1942, the Fascists brought 1,000 Jews from the Romanian zone of occupation and killed them." These notes are followed by signatures of the commission members.

The German and Romanian documents testifying to the practical implementation of the policy of total annihilation of the Jewish population are kept in the fonds of the occupation administration, police departments, Ukrainian local authorities, *Gebietskommissariat* (office of district commissioner), prefectures (chief officers or magistrates) and district and town halls. The orders, declarations and circulatory letters regulated the life of Jews in Vinnitsa Oblast before and after ghetto formation. The information about contributions and fines, forced labor, ghetto formation, confiscation of property, registration of the Jewish population (in order to issue identify cards), statistical data about able-bodied Jews and lists of people for labor duty—all these have great significance for researchers of the Holocaust period.

Faina A. Vinokurova, *vice-director of the State Archive of Vinnitsa Oblast, 1998*

80

Title page of book (26 pages) with alphabetical list of confiscated gold, silver and money from the Jews in Mogilev Podolskiy and surrounding towns, 1942. Note the "C" (Cyrillic "S") stamped in the upper-right corner, which denotes "secret document."

805

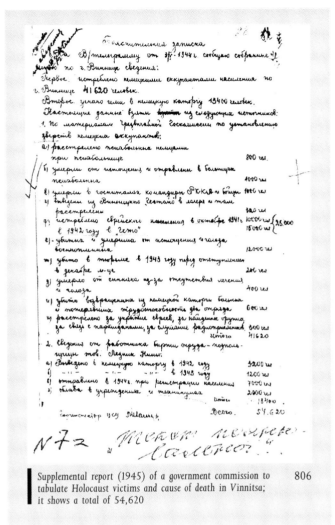

Supplemental report (1945) of a government commission to tabulate Holocaust victims and cause of death in Vinnitsa; it shows a total of 54,620

806

According to the official records of Vinnitsa Oblast, 200,000 Jews from remote areas and districts beyond the borders of the region as well as from Bessarabia and Northern Bukovina were murdered outright or died as a result of starvation or disease in numerous ghettos and concentration camps.

The documents kept in the German and Romanian fonds show the specific character and charateristic features of genocide in the German and Romanian zones of occupation. By the end of July 1941, the Germans occupied all of the territory of Vinnitsa Oblast and artificially dismembered it. Southern and southwest areas from a line drawn through Mogilev Podolskiy, Zhmerinka and Bershad were given to Romania (as the nearest vassal of Nazi Germany). These areas were part of the so-called Transnistria region. The remaining part of Vinnitsa region was ruled by the *Reichkommissariat* of Ukraine.

In the German zone of occupation, all of the Jews were annihilated by the summer of 1943, except for those who escaped to Romanian territory or to partisan detachments and those who were helped by the local population.

The collection of documents from the regional branch of the Security Administration of Ukraine contains interesting information about Adolf Hitler's headquarters, "Wehrwolf," not far from Vinnitsa and the organization of the *Judenfrei* ("Jew-free") zone on the territory of Vinnitsa and its suburbs. These documents consist of correspondence between the Reich Security Service and the *Gebietscommissariat* of Vinnitsa and the "Wehrwolf Guard Service." One of the reports states: "In Strizhavka [a small town not far from the headquarters], there lived 227 Jews. As the construction site is at risk from the Jewish population, it should be 'evacuated.' On January 10, 1942, the Jews were arrested. In order to complete the 'action,' a big hole was dug and after the destruction, it was blown up. On January 11, twelve Jews were arrested, brought to Vinnitsa and then shot. The district became Jew free."

In the Romanian zone of occupation, there were no mass actions against the Jewish population, but there were cases when Romanian military formations joined with the Wehrmacht and Security Service subunits, such as in the small town of Zhabokrich (Kryzhopol District), where they committed a terrible crime: 600 Jews, including women and children, were driven into cellars and shot by machine gun. Several punitive actions were held in Komargorod, Tomashpol and other small towns.

Many documents devoted to the deportation and living conditions of Bessarabian and Bukovinian Jews in ghettos and concentration camps can be found in the fonds of the Romanian occupation administration. Among them are unique documents about the Pechora concentration camp, known as "the dead loop" (Romanian zone of occupation), where more than 35,000 Jews of Vinnitsa Oblast (Bratslav, Tulchin, Shpikov, Ladyzhin and Mogilev Podolskiy) and those deported from Romania, Moldova and Northern Bukovina were prisoners. Every day, 150 to 200 people lost their lives there. More than 12,000 prisoners were tortured or died of starvation and disease in ghettos and concentration camps in Bershad, Obodovka and Shargorod.

As the Romanian authorities also used Jewish labor, different archival documents of an administrative–economic character can be found. In the Romanian administration fonds, there are lists of prisoners (mostly from Mogilev and Yampol Districts), lists of workers sent to Nikolayev region, notes about labor conditions for the workers in the enterprises and ghettos and reports about the confiscation of Jewish property.

Due to the efforts of Wilhelm Filderman, the leader of the Romanian Jewish community, the prisoners of concentration camps and ghettos of Transnistria were sent money and clothes, but unfortunately only in the winter of 1942–1943. Assistance from the American Joint Distribution Committee (the "Joint") was provided until late 1943. Documents are preserved from the Mogilev Podolskiy Prefecture, including postal-order checks and lists of those who received assistance, with their addresses.

There are judicial-inquiry documents about the former head of the Bar police department, Hryhory Andrusev, who took an active part in the murder of 10,000 Jews. (He was found in Romania in 1966 and sentenced to death by a Soviet court.) In addition, we have previously unknown documents about the Zhmerinka Ghetto and its chief, Adolph Gerschman, a Jew from Bukovina. Rumors spread that the prisoners were not killed in the Zhmerinka

Ghetto. Dr. Gerschman was an experienced lawyer and skillfully sued, based upon the German laws and the deficiencies of the Romanian authorities, in the Jewish population's favor. Many Jews from Vinnitsa, Khmelnik, Litin and other small towns survived during the Holocaust because they were in the Zhmerinka Ghetto. However, it was alleged that 275 Jews from Brailov were betrayed by Gerschman and subsequently shot by German authorities. The official documents include a selection of testimonies and recollections of former ghetto prisoners and their rescuers.

I started the document selection in 1989; at present, it numbers 890 documents. Practically all of the ghettos that existed in Vinnitsa Oblast are represented among the documents. Also represented are situations where Jews were saved by local Ukrainians and people of other nationalities, confirmed by the testimonies of the rescuers and the rescued, and the records of the Righteous among the Nations. These are true examples of human generosity and self-sacrifice.

The Dikih family from the village of Kuliga saved the Jewish family of Nakhlis (consisting of eight members)—and sacrificed their lives as a result. A train engineer from Kazatin, Nestor Semko, saved Yosif Braverman, age 13, by transporting

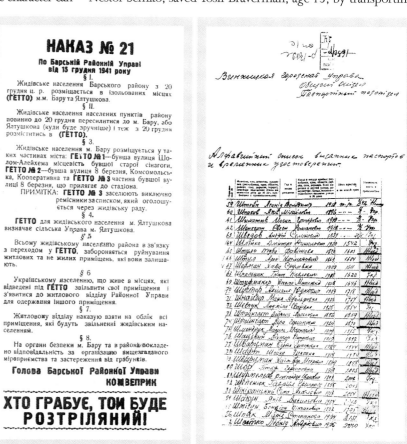

Regulation establishing ghettos in the towns of Bar and Yaltushka, 1941   807

List of passport applicants (note that only Jewish names are underlined), 1942   808

him from the German zone of occupation to the Romanian zone in the locomotive coal box. Yaryna Bombela, a farmer from Oratov, saved her former husband's children from his second marriage (born by a Jewish woman).

A large number of documents is held in the fonds of partisan detachments and the Central Committee of the Communist Party of Ukraine. These documents reveal significant information about the participation of Jews in the anti-Nazi and underground movement in Vinnitsa Oblast. The underground group under the leadership of Ivan Prokopovych-Byaller, the members of the Vinnitsa underground (Maria Irkis, Israel Pekker and Olena Savranskaya) and the participants in the Trostyanets organization were tortured in prison.

Documents about the Jewish partisan detachment that operated in Illintsy in Vinnitsa Oblast may be found here. This list of Jewish heroes of the resistance is lengthy. Six hundred Jewish partisans and members of secret organizations are included in the list.

More than 50 years have passed since the catastrophe of the Holocaust. The Jewish people suffered terrible losses and will need many more years to recover from this damage. According to the 1939 Census of Vinnitsa Oblast, the general population was 2,344,736 people. Jews represented 6 percent of the population, or 141,825 individuals. During the Holocaust, the Nazis murdered 120,000 Jews from Vinnitsa Oblast and 50,000 more who were deported to Vinnitsa from other areas. Jews represented 95 percent of those killed.

At present, the Jewish community of Vinnitsa Oblast is decreasing in number by death and emigration. As of November 1998, only 8,000 Jews remained.

Faina A. Vinokurova with a 1943 map of camps and ghettos in Mogilev District (photo, 1998)

809

Faina A. Vinokurova is a professional historian-archivist. She graduated from the Moscow Historical-Archival Institute in 1973. She is currently vice-director of the State Archive of Vinnitsa Oblast. She has participated in more than a dozen international and local conferences on Jewish history and has lectured at several of them. Ms. Vinokurova is a specialist in the history of the Jews of Podolia and the author of the forthcoming monograph *The Repressed Generation: From the History of Jews in Podolia in the 1920s–1930s.* She is co-editor (with Iosif Maliar) of the first Ukrainian–Israeli selection of testimonies and recollections of Holocaust survivors from Vinnitsa Oblast, *The Catastrophe and the Resistance* (Tel Aviv/Kiev: Ghetto Fighters' House, 1994). The results of her archival research on the Holocaust are represented in document examples to be published by Anthex Publishing in 1999, under the title *The Jews of Vinnitsa Oblast During the Holocaust.*

810 ▶

Kamen Kashirskiy, Ukraine, 1994
Holocaust memorial erected in 1992
in the center of town at the former
ghetto site on Kovel Street where
"3,000 citizens of Jewish nationality
were driven and who became the
victims of the German Fascist
aggressors. Eternal Memory to them!"

◀ 811

Kamen Kashirskiy, Ukraine, 1994
Holocaust memorial erected in 1960 on the
site of the Jewish cemetery "where German
Fascist aggressors and their accomplices shot
2,600 citizens of Jewish nationality. To their
eternal memory."

812 ▶

Kamen Kashirskiy, Ukraine, 1994
Holocaust memorial erected in 1991 in
memory of the "100 citizens of Jewish
nationality who were shot by German
Fascist aggressors at this place"

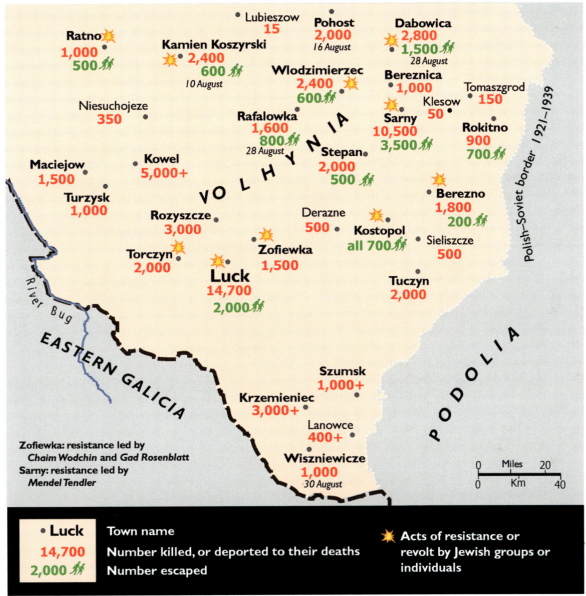

Massacre, Resistance and Escape in Volhynia, August 1942   *Map 7*

VOLHYNIA

In Volhynia, more than 87,000 Jews were murdered in August 1942. As German units came to kill them, as many as 15,000 managed to escape. But fewer than 1,000 of the escapees, who included men, women and children, were able to survive nearly two years of intense hunger, severe winter cold, sickness and repeated German and Ukrainian attacks. Some of the men later joined the small Soviet partisan units that were later parachuted into Volhynia.

Between May and December 1942, more than 140,000 Volhynia Jews were murdered. Some, who had been given refuge in Polish homes, were murdered along with their Polish protectors in the spring of 1943, when, of 300,000 Poles living in Volhynia, 40,000 were killed by Ukrainian "bandits." In many villages, Poles and Jews fought together against the common foe.

The map and text on this page are adapted from *Atlas of the Holocaust*, rev. ed. (New York: William Morrow, 1993) and reprinted here with the permission of the author, Sir Martin Gilbert.

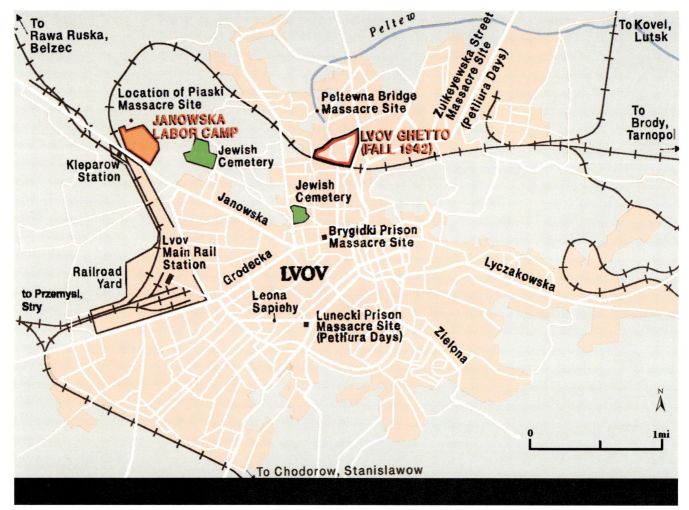

Lvov Environs, 1941–1942   Map 8

LVOV

The city of Lvov in southeastern Poland was occupied by the Soviet Union in 1939, under the terms of the German–Soviet Pact. Lvov was subsequently occupied by Germany after the invasion of the Soviet Union in June 1941.

Encouraged by German forces, Ukrainian Nationalists staged a violent pogrom against the Jews in early July 1941, killing about 4,000 Jews. Another pogrom, known as the Petliura Days, was organized in late July. This pogrom was named for Simon Petliura, who had organized anti-Jewish pogroms in the Ukraine after World War I. For three days, Ukrainian militants went on a rampage through the Jewish districts of Lvov. They took groups of Jews to the Jewish cemetery and to Lunecki Prison and shot them. More than 2,000 Jews were killed and thousands more were injured.

In early November 1941, the Germans established a ghetto in the northern sector of Lvov. Thousands of elderly and sick Jews were killed as they crossed the bridge on Peltewna Street on their way to the ghetto. In March 1942, the Germans began deporting Jews from the ghetto to the Belzec killing center. By August 1942, more than 65,000 Jews had been deported from the Lvov Ghetto and killed. Thousands more were sent for forced labor to the nearby Janowska camp. The ghetto was finally destroyed in early June 1943. The remaining ghetto residents were sent to the Janowska labor camp or deported to Belzec. Thousands of Jews were killed in the ghetto during this liquidation.

The map and text on this page are reproduced with the permission of the United States Holocaust Memorial Museum, from the *Historical Atlas of the Holocaust* (New York: Macmillan Publishing USA and Simon & Schuster Macmillan, 1996).

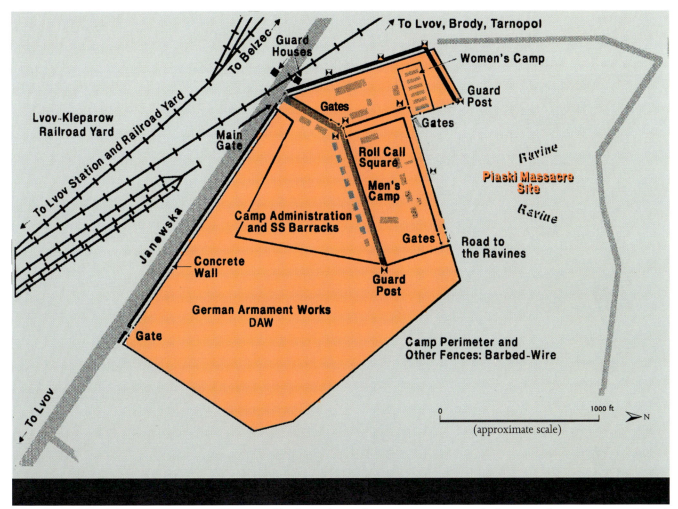

Janowska Labor Camp in Lvov, Fall 1942 (for location of camp, see Map 8, facing page)   *Map 9*

JANOWSKA CAMP

In September 1941, the Germans set up a factory in the northeastern suburbs of Lvov, on Janowska Street. It became part of a network of factories owned and operated by the SS called the German Armament Works (Deutsche Ausrüstungswerke; DAW). Jews were used as forced laborers, primarily in carpentry and metalwork. The Germans established a camp housing them adjacent to the factory in October 1941.

In addition to being a forced-labor camp for Jews, Janowska was a transit camp during the mass deportations of Polish Jews to the killing centers in 1942. Jews underwent a selection process in Janowska similar to that used at Auschwitz-Birkenau and Majdanek. Those classified as fit to work remained at Janowska for forced labor. The majority, rejected as unfit for work, were deported to Belzec and killed or were shot at the Piaski ravine, just north of the camp. In the summer and fall of 1942, thousands of Jews (mainly from the Lvov Ghetto) were deported to Janowska and killed.

The evacuation of the Janowska camp began in November 1943. Prisoners were forced to open the mass graves and burn the bodies, as the Germans attempted to destroy the traces of mass murder (*Aktion 1005*). On November 19, 1943, these prisoners staged an uprising and a mass escape attempt. A few succeeded in escaping, but most were recaptured and killed.

The map and text on this page are reproduced with the permission of the United States Holocaust Memorial Museum, from the *Historical Atlas of the Holocaust* (New York: Macmillan Publishing USA and Simon & Schuster Macmillan, 1996).

◀ 813
Skvira, Ukraine, 1993
Holocaust monument in memory of the
Jews who died there in 1941

814 ▶
Voznesensk, Ukraine, 1993
Holocaust monument in memory
of "more than 20,000 Jews (old
people, women and children) who
were victims of Nazi genocide. We
remember you!"

◀ 815
Voznesensk, Ukraine, 1993
Holocaust monument in memory of
20,000 Jews who died at this site

Einsatzgruppen Massacres (Mobile Killing Units) in Eastern Europe, June 1941–November 1942   Map 10

EINSATZGRUPPEN

Einsatzgruppen (mobile killing units) were German special duty squads, composed primarily of SS and police personnel, assigned to kill Jews as part of the Nazi program to murder the Jews of Europe. The *Einsatzgruppen* also killed Roma (Gypsies), Soviet political commissars, and others whom the Nazis deemed racially or politically unacceptable. *Einsatzgruppen* operated behind the front lines in German-occupied territories in Eastern Europe. During the invasion of the Soviet Union in June 1941, the *Einsatzgruppen* followed the German army as it advanced deep into Soviet territory, and carried out mass-murder operations. The German army was responsible for logistical support for the *Einsatzgruppen*, providing supplies, transportation and housing. At first the *Einsatzgruppen* shot primarily Jewish men. Soon, wherever the *Einsatzgruppen* went they shot all Jewish men, women and children, without regard for age or gender.

The *Einsatzgruppen* following the German army into the Soviet Union were composed of four battalion-sized operational groups. *Einsatzgruppe A* fanned out from East Prussia across Lithuania, Latvia and Estonia toward Leningrad. It massacred Jews in Kovno, Riga and Vilna. *Einsatzgruppe B* started from Warsaw in occupied Poland, and fanned out across Belorussia toward Smolensk. It massacred Jews in Grodno, Minsk, Brest-Litovsk, Slonim, Gomel and Mogilev, among other places. *Einsatzgruppe C* began operations from the western General-gouvernement and fanned out across the Ukraine toward Kharkov and Rostov-on-Don. It committed massacres in Lvov, Tarnopol, Zolochev, Kremenets, Kharkov, Kiev and elsewhere. Of the four units, *Einsatzgruppe D* operated farthest south. It carried out massacres in southern Ukraine and the Crimea, especially in Nikolayev, Kherson, Simferopol, Sevastopol and Feodosiya.

By the spring of 1943, the *Einsatzgruppen* had killed more than a million Jews and tens of thousands of Soviet political commissars, partisans and Roma.

The map and text on this page are reproduced with the permission of the United States Holocaust Memorial Museum, from the *Historical Atlas of the Holocaust* (New York: Macmillan Publishing USA and Simon & Schuster Macmillan, 1996).

▲ 816   Bratslav, Ukraine, 1992
*Holocaust memorial in memory of the
Jewish victims of nazism, 1941–1944*

▲ 817   Gorokhov, Ukraine, 1993
*"At this place, the German Fascist aggressors shot
approximately 2,000 peaceful inhabitants of Jewish
nationality."*

▲ 818   Gorokhov, Ukraine, 1993
*Holocaust monument: "On this place in September 1942, the
German Fascist aggressors shot more than 3,000 Jewish inhabit-
ants of the town of Gorokhov and surrounding villages."*

◀ 819
Stavishe, Ukraine, 1993
Holocaust memorial including brown marble tablets engraved in Hebrew and Russian: "Do not forget. Here are the remains of 1,500 children who never had a chance to grow up." An illustration of an elderly Jew wrapped in a tallis is etched into the marble.

820 ▶
Vladimirets, Ukraine, 1997
Holocaust memorial in memory of the 3,000 Jews who died in this forest in 1942

821 ▶
President William J. Clinton with Rabbi Yakov Bleich at the second Babi Yar memorial in Kiev, 1995

◀ 822
The first Babi Yar monument in Kiev, located a few miles from the actual site of the Babi Yar ravine, 1991

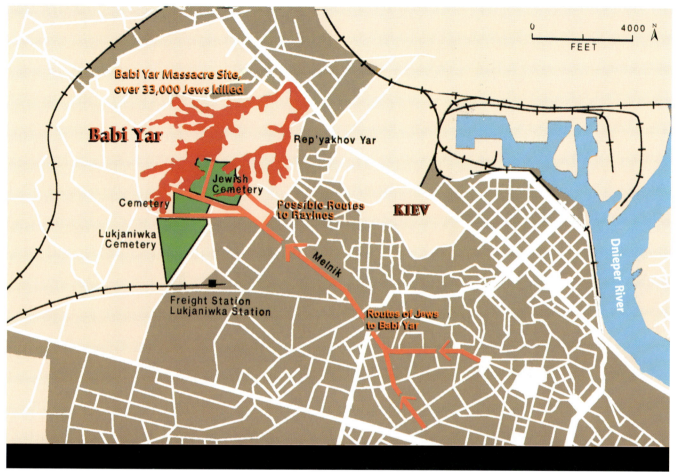

The Babi Yar Massacre in Kiev, September 29–30, 1941

Map 11

BABI YAR

One of the largest massacres perpetrated by members of the *Einsatzgruppen* took place just outside the Ukrainian capital city of Kiev. Tens of thousands of Jews were systematically massacred at Babi Yar, a ravine to the northwest of the city.

German forces entered Kiev in September 1941. During the first days of the occupation, several buildings used by the German army were blown up, apparently by the Soviet security police (the NKVD). The Germans blamed the Jews for the explosion and, ostensibly in retaliation, decided to kill the Jews of Kiev. At that time, there were about 60,000 Jews in the city. Detachments of the *Einsatzgruppen*, together with Ukrainian auxiliary units, were assigned to carry out the massacre.

In late September, the Germans posted notices requiring all Jews to report for resettlement outside the city of Kiev. Failure to report was made a capital offense. Masses of Jews reported and were directed to proceed along Melnik Street toward the Jewish cemetery and Babi Yar. Under guard, the Jews were directed to hand over all their valuables and to disrobe. As the victims moved into the ravine, they were shot in small groups by *Einsatzgruppen* detachments. The massacre continued for two days. It is estimated that over 33,000 Jews were killed in this operation. In the months that followed the massacre, thousands more Jews were shot at Babi Yar. Many non-Jews, including Roma (Gypsies) and Soviet prisoners of war, were also killed at Babi Yar.

In July 1943, as Soviet forces appeared likely to recapture Kiev, the Germans attempted to destroy any trace of the crimes committed at Babi Yar. As part of *Aktion 1005*, which aimed to obliterate the evidence of mass murder all over Europe, the Germans forced prisoners to reopen the mass graves and cremate the bodies. Once this was done, the Germans killed the remaining prisoners. The Soviet army liberated Kiev in November 1943.

The map and text on this page are reproduced with the permission of the United States Holocaust Memorial Museum, from the *Historical Atlas of the Holocaust* (New York: Macmillan Publishing USA and Simon & Schuster Macmillan, 1996).

Holocaust memorial in Pyatidni, Ukraine (near the Polish border), 1995

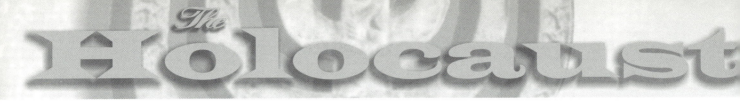

Transnistria is a small strip of land with the Dniester River as its western border (see Map 14). The area shown in Map 14 was part of the larger area shown on Map 13. Between 1941 and 1944, this region was under Romanian administration. It was bordered on the west by the Dniester River, on the north by a line beyond Mogilev Podolskiy, on the east by the Bug River, and on the south by the Black Sea (see Map 13). More than 150,000 Jews were deported to Transnistria from Bessarabia, Bukovina and Ukraine, and more than 120,000 of them perished.

Current Borders of Moldova   *Map 12*

Transnistria, 1941–1944   *Map 13*

Camps and Ghettos in Transnistria, 1941–1944   *Map 14*

CITIES AND TOWNS IN MOLDOVA

PAGES FROM THE PAST AND PRESENT

by
Miriam Weiner

HISTORICAL BACKGROUND

Jews have been living in Moldova (formerly Bessarabia) since the end of the fourteenth century.

The first Jews in Moldova (then Moldavia) were Sephardi. The Ashkenazi came from Poland and Germany in the beginning of the sixteenth century as a result of legislation that restricted their rights. During the sixteenth to eighteenth centuries, Moldavia was under a Turkish regime. Then, as a result of petitions from a few Moldavian princes at the end of the eighteenth century, Russia took control of part of the territory of Moldavia. In 1812, Bessarabia (the entire territory between the Dniester and Prut Rivers, including Moldavia) was annexed by Russia as well.

In 1917, Soviet power was proclaimed in the region, but in 1918, Bessarabia became part of Romania. In 1940, Bessarabia was reclaimed by the Soviet Union. The region was occupied by German troops from 1941 until 1944, when the Soviet Army liberated Bessarabia. From then until 1989, Moldova was part of the Soviet Union. In 1989, with the political changes taking place throughout the Soviet Union, Moldova proclaimed its independence.

Moldova is situated in the southwest part of the former Soviet Union, between Ukraine and Romania. The territory covers approximately 13,500 square miles, with a population of about 5 million people. Moldovans consider themselves to be descendants of Romans and, therefore, the official state language is Romanian.

Today, the general population of Moldova is estimated to include about 35,000 to 40,000 Jews. Approximately 20,000 live in Kishinev.

Many travelers are now visiting Moldova in search of their roots, both in visits to ancestral towns and to conduct research in the Moldovan National Archives. The hospitality of the Moldovan people is well known; and, since it is a small country, it is not difficult to visit almost anywhere in the country and then in the evening return to Kishinev, where there are good hotels and an active Jewish community.

This chapter focuses on seven cities and towns in Moldova where the majority of the Jewish population once lived (see maps on the facing page). There are many Jewish and historic sites remaining in these towns and other smaller towns throughout Moldova. The resources described in Chapter 3 (page 51) are also applicable to the town entries in this chapter.

A Jewish street in Kishinev, pre-Holocaust

824

ATAKI

OTACI (ROM); ATACHI (ALT)

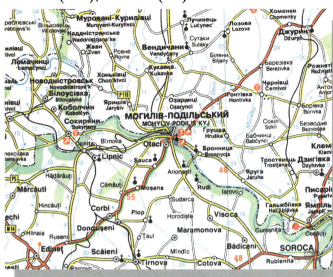

Location

176 km NW of Kishinev
48° 27´/27° 47´

Region

Oknitsa

Jewish Population, Pre-Holocaust

2,781 (79.4% of general population in 1930)

View of Ataki from the Dniester River. The sister city across the river is Mogilev Podolskiy, Ukraine, 1965.

▌ *Former synagogue in Ataki, now a cultural center, 1992* 825

826

Department store formerly owned by a Jewish family in Ataki, c. 1960 827

Jewish cemetery in nearby Volchinets, where the Jews of Ataki were buried. Nearly 1,000 tombstones remain, 1992. 828

Jewish cemetery in nearby Volchinets, 1992 829

Former Jewish district in *Ataki*, 1992   830

Jewish cemetery in nearby *Volchinets*, 1992   831

A former Jewish school destroyed in the 1960s to make way for new houses (photo, c. 1962)   832

BELTSY

BĂLȚI (ROM)

Location

131 km NW of Kishinev
47° 46´/27° 56´

Region

Beltsy

Jewish Population, Pre-Holocaust

14,259 (46% of general population in 1930)

▌ *Only operating synagogue in Beltsy, 1997*

▌ *The center of town, c. 1990*

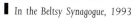
In the Beltsy Synagogue, 1993

835

In the Beltsy Synagogue, 1993

836

Former Jewish cultural center, 1993

837

■ Jewish cemetery, 1993

■ Tombstone of Blima (Roza) Katz, 1925-1959, daughter of Yona (photo, 1993)

■ Tombstone of Rochel Schvartzman, 1875–1900 (photo, 1993)

■ Entrance to Jewish cemetery, 1993

 Jewish children learn in a Hebrew day school, 1993　　　　842

 A Jewish boy recites in Hebrew, 1993　　　　843

 Jewish cemetery with tombstones dating from the late 19th century, 1966　　　　844

357

FALESHTY

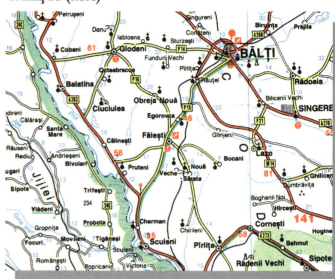

Location

107 km WNW of Kishinev

47° 34´/27° 42´

Region

Faleshty

Jewish Population, Pre-Holocaust

3,258 (51.7% of general population in 1930)

Holocaust memorial in the Jewish cemetery, 1992   845

Enya Rovner, 1910–1975, daughter of Yona (photo, 1992)   846

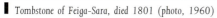

Tombstone of *Feiga-Sara, died 1801 (photo, 1960)*   847

Tsadok, son of Rafael, died 1811 (photo, 1960)   848

Town view, c. 1985   849

■ Jewish cemetery, 1992 850

■ Jewish cemetery, 1992 851

Konstantin A. Andruschak, architect for the city of Faleshty, presents Miriam Weiner with
a book of photographs and architectural drawings of the town in memory of a branch of her family
who once lived in Faleshty, 1992.

852

Entrance to Jewish cemetery, 1992

853

KALARASH

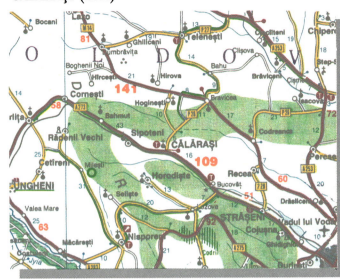

Location

50 km WNW of Kishinev
47° 16′/28° 19′

Region

Kalarash

Jewish Population, Pre-Holocaust

3,662 (76% of general population in 1930)

Jewish cemetery on the hill behind the buildings, 1993   855

Typical street scene, c. 1960   854

Former synagogue, 1993   856

362

Jewish cemetery, 1998

857

View from the window in the mayor's office, 1993

858

KISHINEV

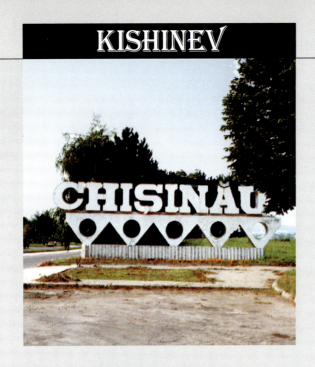

CHIŞINĂU (ROM)

Location

131 km SE of Beltsy
47° 00′/28° 50′

Region

Kishinev

Jewish Population, Pre-Holocaust

41,405 (36% of the general population in 1930)

Town view, c. 1985

Palace Hotel, c. 1920 860

Local pharmacy, c. 1930 861

A former synagogue, 1947 862

Entrance to the only operating synagogue on the left, 1993

863

Interior of the above synagogue, 1993

864

Interior of the above synagogue, 1993

865

Interior of the synagogue on the facing page, 1993

866

Interior of the synagogue on the facing page, 1993

867

▌ Town view, early 1900s

868

Поч. Телегр. Округъ. Кишиневъ.

▌ Post office, c. 1920

869

Jewish cemetery, 1959   870

From left, Chaim, son of Feivish, died 1831. Center tombstone reads "Meir Dov, son of Yitzchak Aisik Ha-Levi, died 1831" (photo, 1959).   871

■ Monument commemorating the 1903 Kishinev Pogrom   872

■ Monument commemorating the 1903 Kishinev Pogrom   873

■ Left, Sara-Rivka, died 1832, daughter of *Asher Shmuel*
Right, Liba, died 1832, daughter of *Yitzchak (photo, 1959)*   874

Left, tombstone of Josef Dvantman, died 1930, son of Mordechai
Right, tombstone of Meyer Feigel, died 1935, son of David (photo, 1959)   875

Jewish cemetery, 1997   876

Holocaust memorial near the entrance of the Kishinev Ghetto (1941–1942). "Martyrs and Victims of the Kishinev Ghetto!   877
We, the Living, Remember You" (in Romanian, Russian, Hebrew and Yiddish), 1998

ORGEYEV

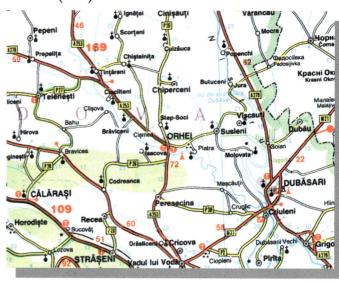

ORHEI (ROM)

Location

45 km N of Kishinev
47° 22′/28° 49′

Region

Orgeyev

Jewish Population, Pre-Holocaust

6,408 (41.9% of general population in 1930)

Jewish cemetery, 1998

Synagogue, 1998   879

Synagogue, 1998   880

Memorial to victims of a Romanian pogrom in 1918–1919.   881
"Fraternal grave of the unknown heroes killed by Romanian
executioners in 1918" (photo, 1998)

Jewish cemetery, 1998   882

Memorial to Holocaust victims, 1998

883

Former Jewish district, 1998

884

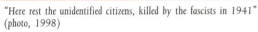
"Here rest the unidentified citizens, killed by the fascists in 1941" 885
(photo, 1998)

Jewish cemetery, 1966 886

Monument to families (Bortnik, Tasnar and Shipman) from the nearby village of Isakova, killed in 1941 by Nazis (photo, 1998) 887

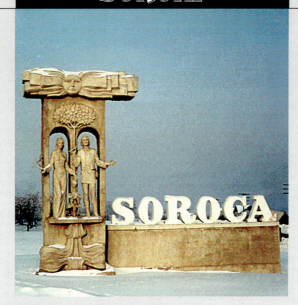

Location

133 km NNW of Kishinev
48° 09´/28° 18´

Region

Soroki

Jewish Population, Pre-Holocaust

5,452 (36.3% of general population in 1930)

SOROCA (ROM)

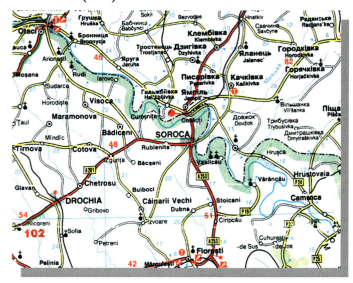

The Dniester River separates Soroki, Moldova, from Ukraine, 1992.   888

Milya Milshtein, 1904–1978, daughter of Nusim (photo, 1995)   889

г. Сороки.

Soroki, c. 1920

890

The old fortress in Soroki, dating from the 16th century, c. 1990

891

Jewish cemetery, 1995

892

Jewish cemetery, after being cleared of brush, 1997

893

▌ Holocaust memorial in the Jewish cemetery, 1995   894

▌ Jewish cemetery, 1995   895

▌ Entrance to the Jewish cemetery, 1995   896

▌ Synagogue in Soroki, 1992   897

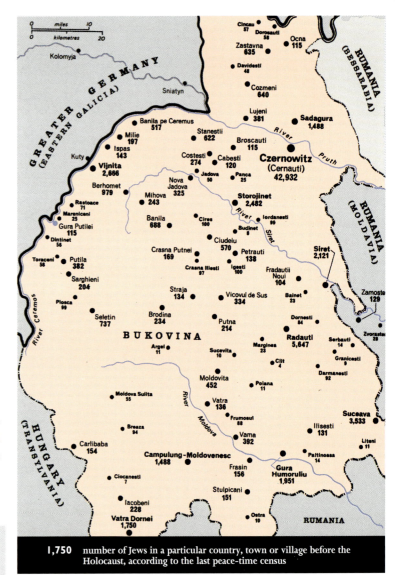

The Jews of Bukovina, like those of Bessarabia, were driven eastward to ghettos in Transnistria. Uprooted from more than 100 communities, they, too, were marched away, interned, and then marched off again. Within a year, more than 120,000 had died.

The maps and text on this page are adapted from *Atlas of the Holocaust*, rev. ed. (New York: William Morrow, 1993) and reprinted here with the permission of the author, Sir Martin Gilbert.

1,750 number of Jews in a particular country, town or village before the Holocaust, according to the last peace-time census

The Jews of Bukovina on the Eve of the War   Map 15

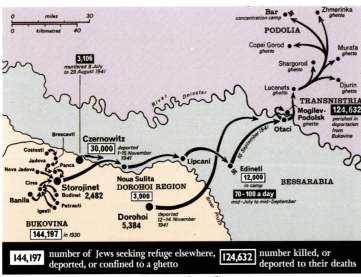

144,197 number of Jews seeking refuge elsewhere, deported, or confined to a ghetto   **124,632** number killed, or deported to their deaths

Deportations and Death Marches from Bukovina, June–November 1941   Map 16

JEWISH GENEALOGICAL RESEARCH IN THE MOLDOVAN NATIONAL ARCHIVES

by
Antonina A. Berzoy

INTRODUCTION

In the nineteenth century, author and historian Vasile Aleksandri stated that "the archives of a country are public property that deserves to be looked after with the utmost care."

Archival documents are what truly reflect past events and form the most precious part of a people's history and memory. The National Archives have the mission of both preserving this treasure of the people of Moldova and placing it at the disposal of researchers.

In Moldova, state institutions began the process of acquiring documents in 1815. The first documents, which lay at the foundation of the archives, are those of the chancellery of the senators, who played the leading role in the councils of Moldova and Wallachia. Also of major importance are the documents of the governor's chancellery. Many other documents contribute as well to the archival fonds of the Republic of Moldova.

Over the years, as a result of additions, revision and careful selection, the holdings of the Moldovan National Archives have continually been enriched. At present, the archives contain approximately 1 million documents of historical importance. They serve as primary sources for the study of all aspects of Moldova's multiethnic past as well as of the history of surrounding countries and their people. These documents, the oldest of which date from the fifteenth century, are included in 2,000 fonds and collections.

These fonds cannot be classified by ethnic or religious origins; therefore, we cannot speak about "Jewish fonds." Historians believe that the appearance of Jews in the territory of the country coincides with the formation of the original Moldavian state in the fourteenth century and that some Jewish names are recorded in the governor's decrees. Unfortunately, these documents are not kept in the National Archives of Moldova. Preserved documents, arranged in chronological order, have been kept in Kishinev (contemporary Chișinău) since 1810. They allow us to see Jews in different capacities: as businessmen, workers, merchants, craftsmen and farmers. It is in the latter capacity that they became an integral part of Moldovan history.

ARCHIVAL HOLDINGS

The holdings of the Moldovan National Archives, by the nature of the institutions that created them and their contents, may be divided into the following fonds: administrative, economic, police, educational, sanitation, welfare, religious and personal categories.

Antonina A. Berzoy, director of the Moldovan National Archives, in her office in Kishinev, with pages from the archives' collection of Yiddish newspapers, 1998

898

The most important of these fonds are those containing information from all the bodies that created the documents: the administrative fonds. We focus on these fonds because of the many different types of documents they contain. These documents mirror various aspects of the social, economic and political life of the people who have lived and who currently live in Moldova.

To those who study the relations of the Moldovan state with other countries, the correspondence, circulars, decrees of the State Council, Foreign Office, Ministry of the Interior and other departments are of considerable interest. In addition, many documents from these fonds deal with the wars of Russia against Iran (1826–1828), Turkey (1877–1878) and Japan (1904–1905) and the Crimean War (1853–1856). Of great importance are the documents concerning World War I. These documents describe Moldovans giving shelter to war refugees; measures taken to combat hunger and epidemics of diseases; hospitals founded; and charity performances put on to help the wounded, sick and orphaned.

Other records contain summary reports, political information, statistics and notes reflecting the mood of the population during those periods.

Agriculture is one of the major themes that may be studied through the documents contained in the Moldovan National Archives. Materials cover the development of agrarian relations, agricultural situations during certain periods, peasants' grievances and continual fight for land, agricultural contracts, and the verdicts of commissions responsible for settling border disputes. These documents are all evidence of the application of agrarian reforms, especially in 1868 on land plots.

Valuable information can also be found in correspondence dealing with Moldovan peasants' grievances against the landowners and tenants, with descriptions of peasants' escapes from one land to another and even of attempted uprisings.

The archives shed some light on industrial development as well as agriculture. References to industrial units and other commercial operations contribute various dates and other valuable information to the documentary basis of Moldova's economic history.

Numerous documents in the archives deal with cultural life. They record such information as the founding of theaters; the opening of printing companies; and the functioning of schools and scientific, cultural, literary, musical and student organizations.

These fonds are formed by a large number of documents, including statutes, verdicts and organizational schemes (plans), which reflect a multitude of occupations and activities. The documents contain data regarding the development of production and technology, contracts, links between firms at home and abroad, and personal files.

The contents of bank fonds contribute information about procedures for opening accounts, and rules for extending credit, dealing with investments and certain exemptions from debt. The collection of accounts of different firms and private

Alphabetical list of births in Kishinev, 1829–1857 (not all years)   899

workshops (which existed until 1944) attracts one's attention by the variety it has to offer. Reports on profits and the number of the employees are in some cases the only written records of these organizations' activities left to us.

Police fonds contain a considerable number of files written during the period 1821 to 1944. The documents in these fonds contain syntheses, political information and memoranda about the people's mood during various periods. The documents dealing with the political situation in the country—such as the preparation for and the outbreak of the Balkan Wars and World War I and the roles that various organizations played in the sociopolitical and spiritual life of the country—are of particular interest.

The documents in these fonds allow one to become acquainted with the procedures for issuing passports, passport control, issuing soldiers' leaves in towns and the administration of prisons. There are also numerous reports and inventories concerned with population censuses, taxation, currency rates, official orders, patents and observations of foreigners.

Educational fonds concern different schools, gymnasiums (high schools) and lyceums (associations providing public lectures). Documents from this category address the development of educational establishments and cultural institutions, the circulation of publications and the organization of cultural activities. Documents in the archives show both the dynamics of the students' lives and the profiles of the schools where they were educated.

The fonds of institutions of higher education are also well worth researchers' attention. Personal documents and official correspondence exist that concern numerous highly qualified specialists known not only within the country but also far beyond its borders. These people played an important part in the development of science and national culture in Moldova.

Religious fonds help us to learn about various aspects of a particular church or synagogue's participation in the people's political, economic, social and cultural life. Many documents have to do with the population and history of localities.

Personal fonds come from people who, by their political, social or cultural activities, have distinguished themselves in various spheres. The Moldovan National Archives have nearly 400 personal fonds. They belong to writers, artists, musicians, scientists and other prominent people. Documents from these fonds are remarkable for their large variety of themes. Researchers can find individuals' biographies as well as learn about different aspects of their activities.

THE RESEARCH PROCESS

Visitors may come to our archives and perform research work themselves, but they must bring their own translators and be prepared to spend days, not hours. It is also possible to arrange for our archivists to conduct the research, however, with payment due at the time of the request (payable in Moldovan currency at the archives).

Another alternative is to hire a professional researcher or firm to do the work. However, the researcher must have a notarized letter of authorization to do research on another person's behalf.

The Moldovan National Archives hope to be able to offer their own research service (by mail) to foreigners in the near future. At this time, we do not have a bank account for foreign currency or any way for foreigners to transfer funds to us in payment for research services; however, we hope that this situation will improve in the near future.

Antonina A. Berzoy was born in 1951 in the village of Kochuleya in Moldova. In 1974, she graduated from the State University in Kishinev with a degree in philology. In 1976, Ms. Berzoy became an archivist in the Research Department of the Moldovan National Archives. In 1988, she was appointed chief of the Research Department. In 1992, she was appointed vice-director, and since July 1, 1995, she has served as director of the archives. Ms. Berzoy is the author of numerous articles about the Moldovan National Archives.

Jewish cemetery in Kishinev; tombstone of Nota Aizik (died 1932), son of Moishe, 1959

900

The following libraries and archives in Moldova have many important documents and manuscripts that would be of interest to researchers of Jewish family history. There are many other smaller repositories with equally interesting material. The addresses in the right-hand column are the same institutions as listed in the left-hand column, but written in the Moldovan language. The country/city code for Moldova/Kishinev is 373/2.

LIBRARIES IN MOLDOVA

PLACE/Address	Telephone	PLACE/Address
NATIONAL LIBRARY OF MOLDOVA 78, 31 August Street 2012 Kishinev Republic of Moldova	22-51-11	**Biblioteca Naţională a Moldovei** Str. 31 August, Nr. 78 Chişinău 2012 Republica Moldova
CENTRAL SCIENTIFIC LIBRARY OF THE MOLDOVAN SCIENTIFIC ACADEMY 1 Stefan Cel Mare Avenue 2001 Kishinev Republic of Moldova	26-42-79	**Biblioteca Centrală Ştiinţifică a Academiei Ştiinţe a Moldovei** Bul. Ştefan cel Mare, Nr. 1 Chişinău 2001 Republica Moldova
SCIENTIFIC LIBRARY OF MOLDOVA STATE UNIVERSITY 60 A. Matievich Street 2009 Kishinev Republic of Moldova	27-07-89 25-12-10	**Biblioteca Naţională Universitarii de stat a Moldovei** Str. A. Matievici, Nr. 60 Chişinău 2009 Republica Moldova
I. MANGER JEWISH LIBRARY 4 Renashteriy Avenue 2005 Kishinev Republic of Moldova	22-15-02	**Biblioteca Evreiască "I. Maier"** Bul. Renasterii, Nr. 4 Chişinău 2005 Republica Moldova

ARCHIVES IN MOLDOVA

PLACE/Address	Telephone	PLACE/Address
Archives of Ancient Acts 82, 31 August Street Kishinev 277012 Republic of Moldova	23-71-53	**Arhiva Actelor Stării Civile** Str. 31 August, Nr. 82 Chişinău 277012 Republica Moldova
Moldovan National Archives 67b Gheorghe Asachi Street Kishinev 277028 Republic of Moldova	73-58-27	**Arhiva Naţională a Republicii Moldovei** Str. Gheorghe Asachi, Nr. 67b Chişinău 277028 Republica Moldova

Source: The above lists were provided by Antonina A. Berzoy, director, Moldovan National Archives.

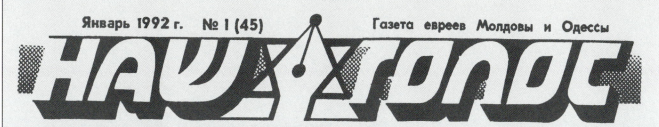

"Our Voice," a local Jewish newspaper published in Kishinev, announcing a regulation (#682, dated December 9, 1991) whereby the government of the Republic of Moldova authorized the development of Jewish national culture and public assistance for local Jews, 1992

901

From left, Aleksander Roman (then director of the Moldovan National Archives), Mitru Gitsiu (then chief of the Department of State Archival Services in Moldova) and Miriam Weiner sign a contract of agreement to publish the archival holdings in Moldova, 1993.

902

Birth of Shimson Cartun in Yedintsy, son of Yankel Cartun (son of Duvid from Dobroveni) and Dvosya Leah (daughter of Moshko), 1857   903

List of inhabitants for the family of Moishe Ancel Bronfman, son of   904-A
Yankel, and his seven children, including their ages and names of spouses
and children, living in Ataki, Moldova (see second page of document, right)

Female family members are listed on the right-hand page   904-B
above and male family members on the left-hand page
(Doc. #168, dated 1848).

Jewish cemetery in Rybnitsa, 1998   905

Petition from the Jews of Ataki to the mayor of Soroki regarding the illegal election of synagogue officers, 1875. The debate continued for   906
the next five years, generating numerous pages of documents and petitions. The court records include the signatures of many members
of the Jewish community in support of their position and resulted in a court decision in 1880 to add more prayer houses, as there was
an insufficient number for the size of the Jewish community.

Visa application of Eidel Mahidman, daughter of Moise, to leave Soroki and visit another country, 1927 — 907

School records of Moise-Elie Bronfman, a student in Yedintsy, born 1921, son of Mihel and Tsirl, 1931 — 908

List of property owners, including Duvid Maghidman, a merchant, living at #63 Regele Carol Street in Soroki, 1941 — 909

List of property owners in Soroki, including Abram Roitberg, a merchant living at 27 Marta Street, 910
House #51; and Zelman Roitberg, a merchant living at 27 Marta Street, House #53, 1941

Membership list in the local Jewish society in Soroki. Line #7 lists Josif-Mehel Meilztein, a 911
merchant, age 65, with two family members; line #13 lists Izic Milztein, a merchant, age 38,
with seven family members, 1921.

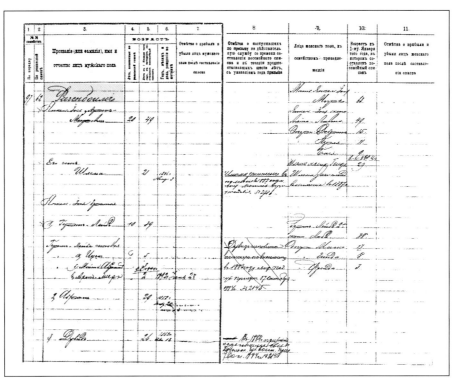

Family list in Shargorod, Ukraine, listing 19 members of Aron-Meyer Faigenboim's family, including ages and relationships, 1888   912

Certificat de examen

(Programa școalelor de minorități)

Certificate of examination, 1922, for Ch. Volco Tucherman, born 1909 in Vertugeni, son of Chelman   913

List of students in the Ataki Cheder, including names, ages, names of fathers and location of school, 1890   914

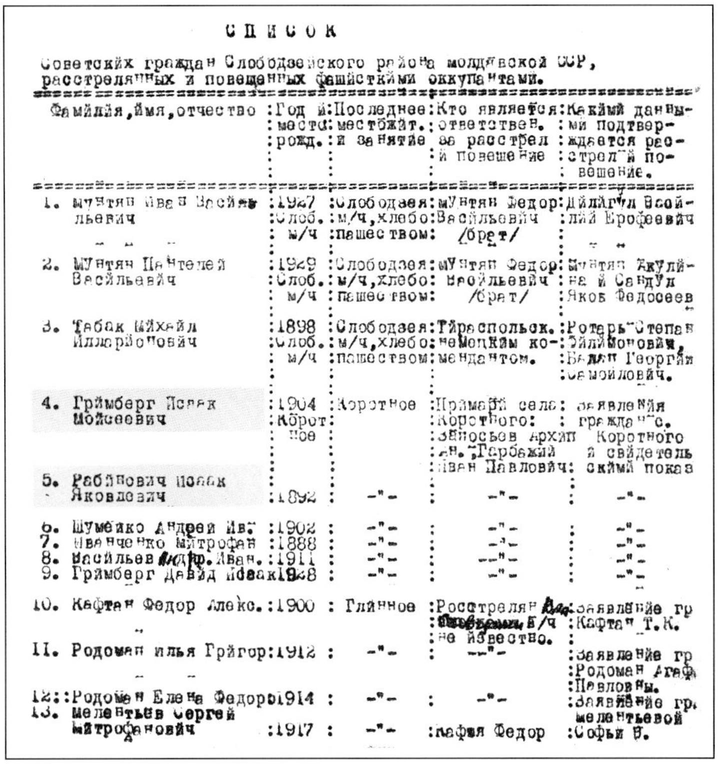

СПИСОК

Советских граждан Слободзейского района Молдавской ССР, расстрелянных и повешенных фашистскими оккупантами.

Фамилия, имя, отчество	Год и место рожд.	Последнее местожит. и занятие	Кто является ответствен. за расстрел и повешение	Какими данными подтверждается расстрел и повешение.
1. Мунтян Иван Васильевич	1927 Слоб. м/ч	Слободзея м/ч, хлебопашеством	Мунтян Федор Васильевич /брат/	Дилигул Василий Ерофеевич
2. Мунтян Пантелей Васильевич	1929 Слоб. м/ч	Слободзея м/ч, хлебопашеством	Мунтян Федор Васильевич /брат/	Мунтян Акулина и Сандул Яков Федосеев
3. Табак Михаил Илларионович	1898 Слоб. м/ч	Слободзея м/ч, хлебопашеством	Тираспольск. немецким комендантом.	Ротарь Степан [illegible], Балан Георгий Самойлович.
4. Гримберг Исаак Моисеевич	1904 Коротное	Коротное	Примарий села Коротного: Запосьев Архип ...Гарбажий Иван Павлович:	заявления граждан с. Коротного и свидетельский показ
5. Рабинович Исаак Яковлевич	1892	-"-	-"-	-"-
6. Шумейко Андрей Ив.	1902	-"-	-"-	-"-
7. Иванченко Митрофан	1888	-"-	-"-	-"-
8. Васильев Андр. Иван.	1911	-"-	-"-	-"-
9. Гримберг Давид Исаак	19[illegible]8	-"-	-"-	-"-
10. Кафтан Федор Алекс.	1900	Глинное	Расстрелян [illegible] б/ч не известно.	заявление гр Кафтан Т.К.
11. Родоман Илья Григор	1912	-"-	-"-	заявление гр Родоман Агаф. Павловны.
12. Родоман Елена Федоровна	1914	-"-	-"-	заявление гр. Мелентьевой Софьи В.
13. Мелентьев Сергей Митрофанович	1917	-"-	Кафтан Федор	

List of Soviet citizens from Slobodziya region who were shot or hanged by the Nazi occupiers (1941–1944), including #4, Isaak Grimberg, son of Moise, born 1904; and #5, Isaak Rabinovich, son of Yakov, born 1892. The last known address and name of the person responsible for the shooting or hanging are also provided. 915

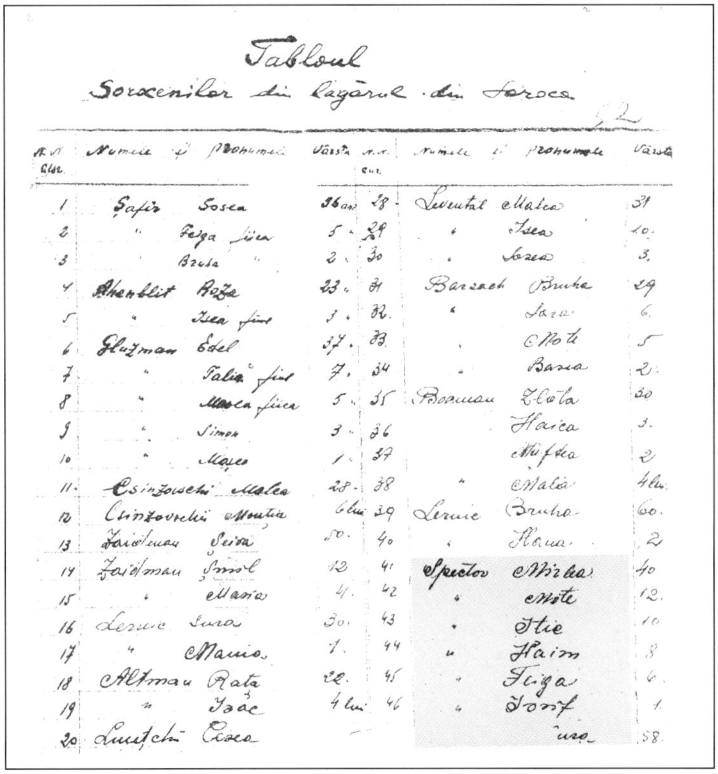

Tabloul

Sorocenilor din lagărul din Soroca

92

Nr. crt.	Numele și pronumele	Vârsta	Nr. crt.	Numele și pronumele	Vârsta
1	Șafir Sosea	36 ani	28	Levental Malca	31
2	" Feiga fiica	5 "	29	" Isea	10
3	Bruha "	2 "	30	" Iosea	3
4	Ahenblit Roza	23 "	31	Barzach Bruha	29
5	" Isea fiu	3 "	32	" Sara	6
6	Gluzman Edel	37 "	33	" Mote	5
7	" Talia fiu	7 "	34	" Basia	2
8	" Masea fiica	5 "	35	Rozman Zlota	30
9	" Simon	3 "	36	Haica	3
10	" Moșe	1 "	37	Miftea	2
11	Csinzowschi Malca	28	38	" Malia	4 luni
12	Csinzovschi Moniția	6 luni	39	Lerner Bruha	60
13	Zaidman Seiva	50	40	" Hana	2
14	Zaidman Șmil	12	41	Spector Mirla	40
15	" Maria	4	42	" Mote	12
16	Lerner Sura	30	43	" Itie	10
17	" Maria	7	44	" Haim	8
18	Altman Rata	22	45	" Feiga	6
19	" Isac	4 luni	46	" Iosif	1
20	Luețchi Cesea			[illegible]ura	58

List of Jews in the Soroki Ghetto in 1941, including the Spector family, entries #41–46: Mirla Spector, age 40; her sons Note, age 12, and Haim, age eight; and her daughters Itie, age 10, and Feiga, age six 916

Notary record #738 for Ikhel Bronfman, son of Gersh-Leib, living in Ataki (Soroki District), referring to   917
an 1894 court decision wherein Leizor Zilberman must pay 65 rubles in damages to Ikhel Bronfman. In
record #739 in 1896, Ikhel Bronfman confirmed that the debt had been paid.

List of Jews in the Kishinev Ghetto, 1941, including Yosif Badas, age 62; his wife,   918
Zlata, age 60; daughter, Manea, age 33; and grandson, Vladimir, age 13

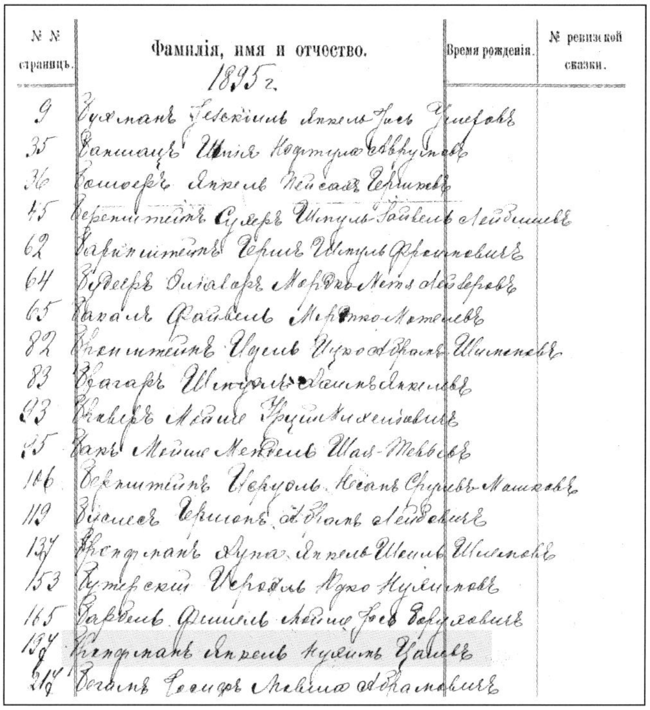

Sample page from alphabetical list of Jewish births in Bessarabia (1889–1896). Entry #197 is for Yankel-Nukhim Bronfman, son of Tsal, born 1895.

919

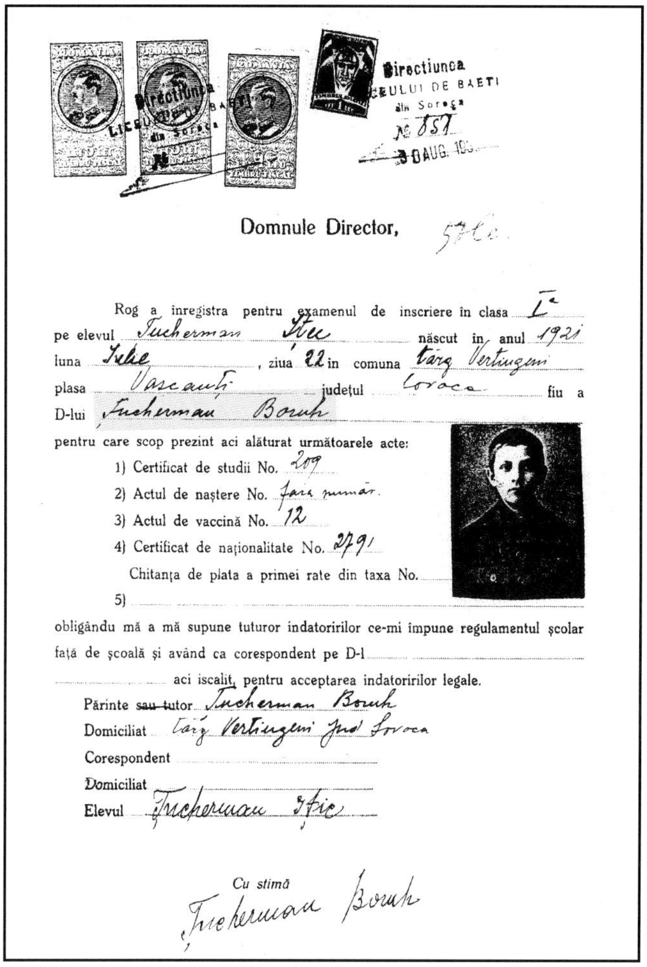

Application letter from Boruh Tucherman, father of Itec Tucherman, born 1921 in Vertugeni. Mr. Tucherman's application to the school director requests an evaluation of his son, as part of the entrance process, 1933.

921

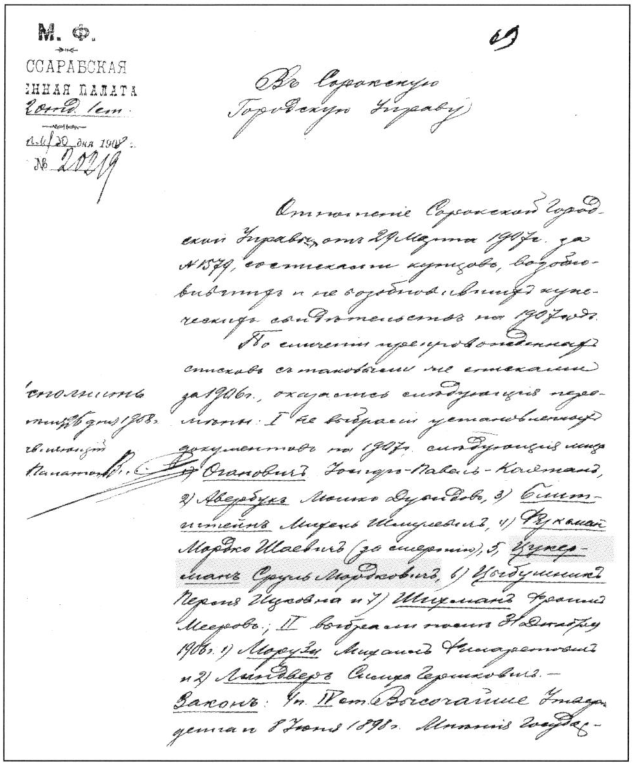

Business-license application (merchant) for Srul Tsukerman, age 60, son of Mordko, living in Soroki, 1907.

920

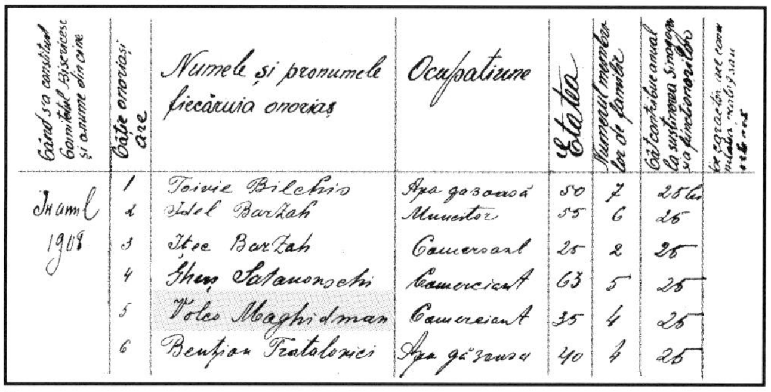

Membership list of Soroki Jewish community, listing Volco Maghidman, a merchant, age 35, four family members, and his contribution of 25 lei to the synagogue, 1939

922

Until 1941, Bessarabia was part of the Russian Empire/Soviet Union. The murder of 49 Jews during the Kishinev Pogrom of 1903 had led to protest demonstrations in London, Paris and New York, and a letter of rebuke from Theodore Roosevelt to the tsar. In 1918, the region became part of Romania but remained strongly anti-Semitic. The city of Kishinev was a focal point of Jewish culture and political life, while Jewish agricultural communities thrived throughout the province.

The maps and text on this page are adapted from *Atlas of the Holocaust*, rev. ed. (New York: William Morrow, 1993), and reprinted here with the permission of the author, Sir Martin Gilbert.

The Jews of Bessarabia on the Eve of the War   **Map 17**

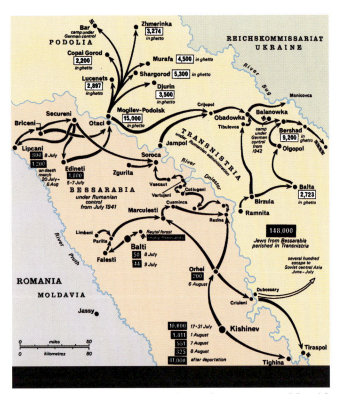

Massacres, Deportations, and Death Marches from Bessarabia, from July 1941   **Map 18**

With the return of Soviet rule to Bessarabia in June 1940, all Jewish institutions were closed, and on June 13, 1941, many of the Jewish leaders, as well as wealthy Jews, were exiled to Siberia, where many died. But with the arrival of the Nazi killing squads in July 1941, the scale of murder, as indicated in Map 18, exceeded anything previously known.

Following the initial killings, internment camps were set up throughout the province. At the camp in Edineti, after the initial slaughter, 70 to 100 people died every day in July and August 1941, most of starvation. Then, in September, the Jews of Bessarabia were forced out of the province in hundreds of death marches, some of which are indicated in Map 18. In all, more than 148,000 Bessarabian Jews perished in the ghettos and camps of Transnistria. During these marches, more than half of the victims died of exposure, disease, hunger, thirst and the savage brutality of the Romanian and German guards, who would often pick out a group of marchers at random, order them aside, and shoot them.

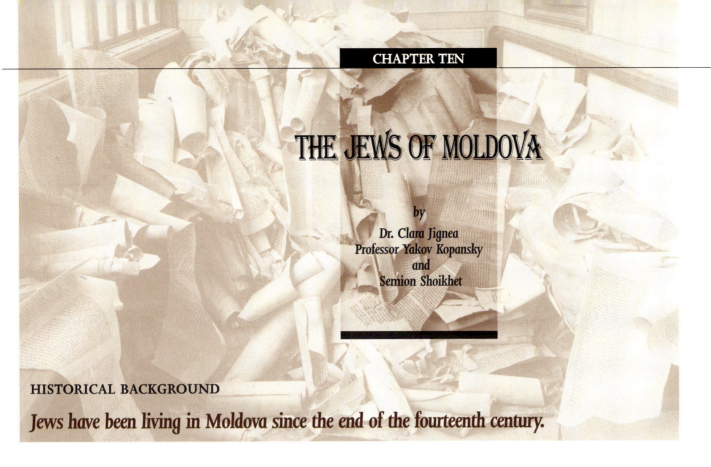

THE JEWS OF MOLDOVA

by

Dr. Clara Jignea
Professor Yakov Kopansky
and
Semion Shoikhet

HISTORICAL BACKGROUND

Jews have been living in Moldova since the end of the fourteenth century.

Jewish names appear in ancient documents of the first princes of the Moldavian principality in the fourteenth and fifteenth centuries. During the nineteenth century, the Jewish population of the territory between the rivers Prut and Dniester (then Bessarabia) increased greatly; by the end of that century, it reached 230,000 people, representing 12 percent of the population of Bessarabia. In many of the towns, Jews made up 50 percent of the population. As merchants, craftsmen, traders, workers, and farmers, the Jews contributed substantially to the economic development of the area. Mutual influence and cooperation with other peoples characterized the spiritual life of the Bessarabian Jews.

The 1930s marked the peak of development of Jewish national life in Moldova. A well-developed cultural infrastructure of the Jewish communities appeared, i.e., the system of religious and political organizations, philanthropic and cultural–educational societies and other institutions. In 1935, 40 towns and shtetls of the area united as the Union of Jewish Communities of Bessarabia.

Among the sad milestones in the history of the Jewish community of Moldova are the Kishinev Pogrom of 1903 and numerous pogroms in 1905. During the years of German occupation, the Jewish population was completely banished from the territory of Bessarabia. More than 100,000 Jews from Bessarabia perished during World War II and the Holocaust.

POPULATION GROWTH

The dynamics of the Jewish population of Bessarabia (contemporary Moldova) can be analyzed with census statistics:

- 1930: 205,000 Jews (7 percent of the population of Bessarabia).
- 1959: 95,200 Jews, primarily families returned from evacuation (3.3 percent of the population).
- 1970: 98,100 Jews (2.7 percent of the population).
- 1979: 80,100 Jews (2 percent of the population).
- 1989: 65,800 Jews (1.5 percent of the population).

Beltsy Synagogue interior, 1997

923

The steady decline in the Jewish population of Moldova has resulted from assimilation, natural decrease and emigration (mostly to Israel). The Jewish population has always been larger than has been reported officially, however, as not all Jews have stated their nationality. Thus, today the Jewish population in Moldova is estimated at between 35,000 and 40,000 people, despite the fact that from 1989 to 1998, more than 44,000 Jews repatriated to Israel.

THE REVIVAL OF JEWISH LIFE

Although the national life of the Jews in Moldova was virtually destroyed during the 1940s, it began to revive in the late 1980s and early 1990s, due to the emerging democratic society. It became possible due to the activities of the local Jewish intelligentsia, support from thousands of Moldovan Jews, assistance from Jews all over the world, the understanding of the government of the Republic of Moldova and help from Israel and international Jewish organizations. Charity services became active in various towns and villages. The following organizations were established: the Society of Jewish Culture, the Association of Former Prisoners of Concentration Camps and Ghettos, the Federation of Jewish Religious Communities, the Organization of Former Refugees, the Organization of Jewish Veterans of World War II, the

women's organization Hava, and the students' organization Hillel. The following Jewish newspapers are published in Moldova: *Nash Golos* ("Our Voice") and *Istoki* ("Roots"). Educational opportunities include courses offered in Hebrew and Yiddish, and activities at the Yiddish Center, the Sunday schools, the Educational University of Jewish Culture in Moldova and the Kishinev Institute of Social and Community Workers. A yeshiva and a women's pedagogical college were also opened.

The following state institutions functioning in educational and cultural fields are making an important impact upon the spiritual revival of the Jewish community:

- The Kishinev Jewish Library (named after I. Manger, which became a major center of Jewish culture).
- Jewish middle schools and kindergartens.
- The Department of Romanian Language and Literature, Yiddish and Hebrew at the Philological Faculty of the State University of Moldova.
- The Department of History and Culture of Jews of Moldova at the Institute of Inter-Ethnic Research at the Academy of Sciences of Moldova.
- The TV program *Af der Yiddisher gas* ("On the Jewish Street").
- The radio program *Yiddish lebn* ("Jewish Life").

▌ In 1903, an infamous pogrom took place in Kishinev. The woman in this photo looks in horror at all that remains of her furnishings.

924

In the Beltsy Synagogue, 1997

925

An important factor in the reawakening of Jewish life and Jewish identity is the moral and financial support from the people and the State of Israel.

ASSOCIATION OF JEWISH ORGANIZATIONS AND COMMUNITIES OF MOLDOVA (AJOCM)

Today, the revived Jewish community life in 12 towns and many other areas of the republic, including the region on the left bank of the Dniester River, is united by the Association of Jewish Organizations and Communities of Moldova (AJOCM). Its board of directors includes representatives from all Moldovan regions and organizations. The AJOCM is legally accepted as a successor of the Union of Jewish Communities of Bessarabia. The AJOCM is busy with many projects, including efforts to increase the number of people actively involved in Jewish national life, a search for local financial sources, the restoration of Jewish properties and other matters. The Association also publicly protests against certain manifestations of anti-Semitism.

The major focuses of the activities of the Association (including its member organizations and communities) are spiritual revival and the development of Jewish societies and social services for those who need it.

The Association of Jewish Organizations and Communities is a member of the Jewish Congress of Europe and the Jewish Board of Europe. The AJOCM collaborates with many organizations and institutions, including:

- The Israel Cultural Center in Kishinev.
- The Jewish Agency (Sokhnut).
- The Conference on Material Claims Against Germany.
- The religious movement Habad-Lubavich.
- The religious–educational organization Agudat Israel of America.
- The World Board of Yiddish Culture.

The development of a national self-consciousness and a return to their roots by the Jews of Moldova are strengthened through education in Hebrew and Yiddish and by the study of Jewish history, religion, traditions and literature. The creativity of Jewish writers and poets, journalists, composers and professional performers, musicians, producers and artists continues to advance. Jewish clubs (by interests), theaters and children's drama schools also exist. Books are being published in history, linguistics and literature. Prestigious international academic forums on Jewish topics also take place in Moldova. In addition, thousands of people fill the largest auditoriums during national holidays and memorial dates in the history of the Jewish people.

SOCIAL-SERVICE NEEDS OF THE JEWS OF MOLDOVA

Social services are especially needed due to the steady decrease in the economic quality of life of the population of Moldova. In December 1998, the average monthly pension of elderly people was $13 or less. Social services for the needy, elderly and handicapped are provided primarily through the system of Hesed organizations created by the initiative and broad financial support of the American Jewish Joint Distribution Committee (the "Joint"), which provides services to approximately 5,000 Jews in Moldova. It is difficult to overestimate the effect of the cultural Hesed programs, which have improved both the spiritual rehabilitation and the communication among elderly Jews. Indeed, the cultural, educational and social programs of the "Joint" have had an especially important role in the revival of Jewish national life in Moldova.

Under the existing circumstances, emigration and *aliya* (emigration to Israel) are motivated both by national feelings and the desire for a better future for the next generation.

Despite the continuous emigration of the Jews from Moldova and the inevitable decrease of the Jewish population, Moldova's Jewish community will survive. Taking this fact into consideration, the AJOCM will begin strategic planning for its further development. However, development depends not only on internal resources but also on the support of world Jewry.

Dr. Clara Jignea is a senior researcher of the Department of Jewish History and Culture of Moldova at the Institute of Inter-Ethnic Research at the Academy of Sciences of Moldova. Dr. Jignea is a specialist in the Jewish history of Bessarabia during the late nineteenth and early twentieth centuries. She is the author of several articles about the Kishinev Pogrom of 1903.

Professor Yakov Kopansky is the director of the Department of Jewish History and Culture of Moldova at the Institute of Inter-Ethnic Research at the Academy of Sciences of Moldova. Professor Kopansky is the author of the book *Joint in Bessarabia: Pages of History* (Kishinev: Liga, 1994); the article "Image of Bessarabian Jewry during the Inter-War Period" (Tel Aviv, 1996, in Hebrew); and a series of other publications on the Jewish history of twentieth-century Moldova. Professor Kopansky is also the chairman of the board of the philanthropic center Hesed Yehuda.

Semion Shoikhet is the chairman of the Association of Jewish Organizations and Communities of the Republic of Moldova and emeritus architect of Moldova. Mr. Shoikhet has designed general construction plans for the cities of Kishinev, Beltsy, Bendery, Dubossary, Kahul, Rybnitsa, Tiraspol and others; many buildings; and various monuments devoted to historical events and famous people, including the memorial plaque dedicated to the victims of the Kishinev Pogrom of 1903 and the memorial complex devoted to those who died in the Kishinev Ghetto.

▋ Tombstone of Shaya Roif (1928–1990), son of Gersh, Vertuzhany Jewish cemetery, 1998   926

Memorial in Vertuzhany, Moldova, in memory of the 20,000 Jews from the region   927
who were murdered during the Holocaust, 1997

Late 19th-century Jewish cemetery in Orgeyev, 1966   928

Rabbi Zalman Abelsky, in his office at the Kishinev Synagogue, 1998

929

TOWN CLIPS

The following section both expands upon and supplements Chapter 3 and Chapter 8 by providing a further glimpse of what was and what is, through a collection of striking photographs in towns throughout Ukraine and Moldova.

Synagogue in Belz, early 20th century   930

Jewish cemetery, 1995   931

Eliezer (died 1881), son of   932
Josef (photo, 1995)

Jewish cemetery, 1998   933

Jewish cemetery, 1994   934

Artist's view, 1916   935

Artist's view, 1925   936

Town square, 1997   937

Berezhany in the distance, 1997   938

939-B

939-A

The war memorial in Berezno. The plaque states: "In this place, August 25, 1942, Fascist German occupiers shot 3,680 Soviet citizens." There is no specific mention of Jews, 1998.

A former synagogue in Berezno, c. 1936

940

404

House in Boguslav, 1993　　941

Shafra Gershberg, a journalist, visits the Boguslav Jewish cemetery, 1994.　　942

Hinda Erdel at home in Boguslav, 1994　　943

Jewish cemetery, 1994   944

Jewish cemetery, 1993   945

Jewish cemetery, 1994   946

Former synagogue in Bolekhov, dating from the early 20th century, currently used as a club, 1993   947

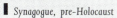
Synagogue, pre-Holocaust   948

Jewish cemetery, 1993   949

Jewish cemetery, 1993   950

Jewish cemetery, 1995   952

Jewish cemetery, 1995   951

Jewish cemetery, 1995   953

Former synagogue, dating from the late 19th century, 1993   954

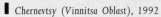
Chernevtsy (Vinnitsa Oblast), 1992   955

Chernevtsy (Vinnitsa Oblast), 1992   956

Jewish resident of Chernevtsy, 1992   957

Jewish cemetery, 1992   958

Jewish (Karaite) cemetery, 1993   959

Jewish (Karaite) cemetery, 1993   960

View of Galich, 1911   961

Jewish cemetery, 1998   962

Holocaust memorial to the Jews of Gorodenka   963
who were killed on April 13, 1942 (photo, 1998)

Synagogue, 1998   964

Jewish cemetery, 1993   965

Synagogue in Gorokhov, c. 1920 (see photo below, at right in background)   966

Town view of Gorokhov, with the synagogue visible on the right side of the photo (tallest building), c. 1920   967

Former synagogue, now a museum, 1995   970

Synagogue in Gusyatin, Ukraine, pre-Holocaust   968

Synagogue in Gusyatin, c. 1914   969

Museum (former synagogue) interior, 1995   971

More than 2,000 Jews from Korets, Ukraine, were led down this road through the forest (see photo 973 below) to mass graves, where they were shot in May 1942 (photo, 1994).

972

Highway leading to Holocaust memorial, 1994

973

Jewish cemetery, 1994

974

Holocaust memorial in the forest near Korets, Ukraine

975

PLACE-NAME VARIANTS IN EASTERN GALICIA
(refers only to localities included in archival inventories)

Polish	Russian	Ukrainian
Biały Kamień	Belyy Kamen	Bilyj Kamin
Bóbrka	Boberka	Bibrka
Bohorodczany	Bogorodchany	Bohorodchany
Bolechów	Bolekhov	Bolekhiv
Bołszowce	Bolshovtsy	Bilshovtsy
Borszczów	Borshchev	Borshchiv
Borysław	Borislav	Boryslav
Brody	Brody	Brody
Brzeżany	Berezhany	Berezhany
Buczacz	Buchach	Buchach
Budzanów	Budanov	Budzaniv
Bukaczowce	Bukachevtsy	Bukachivtsi
Bursztyn	Burshtyn	Burshtyn
Chocimierz	Khotmir	Khotmir
Chodorów	Khodorov	Khodoriv
Chorostków	Khorostkov	Khorostkiv
Czerwonogród	Chervonograd	Chervonograd
Czortków	Chortkov	Chortkiv
Czortowiec	Chortovets	Chortovets
Dobromil	Dobromil	Dobromyl'
Dolina	Dolina	Dolyna
Drohobycz	Drogobych	Drohobych
Dunajow	Dunayev	Dunaiv
Gliniany	Gliniany	Hliniany
Gołogóry	Gologory	Holohory
Gródek Jagielloński	Gorodok	Horodok
Grzymałów	Grimaylov	Hrymaliv
Gwoździec	Gvozdets	Hvizdets
Halicz	Galich	Halych
Horodenka	Gorodenka	Horodenka
Husiatyn	Gusyatin	Husiatyn
Jagielnica	Yagelnitsa	Yagolnitsa
Janów Trembowelski	Ivanovka	Ivanivka
Jaryczów Nowy	Novyy Yarychev	Yarychiv Novyj
Jaworów	Yavorov	Iavoriv
Jezierna	Ozernaya	Ozerna
Jezierzany	Ozeryany	Ozeryany
Jezupol	Zhovten	Yezupil
Kalusc	Kalush	Kalush
Kamionka Strumiłowa	Kamenka Bugskaya	Kamianka Buzka
Kołomyja	Kolomyya	Kolomyia
Komarno	Komarno	Komarno
Kopyczyńce	Kopychintsy	Kopychyntsi
Kosów	Kosov	Kosiv
Kosowa	Kozova	Kozova
Kozłów	Kozlov	Kozliv
Krakowiec	Krakovets	Krakovets
Kropiwnik Stary	Kropevnik	Kropiwnik Stary

PLACE-NAME VARIANTS IN EASTERN GALICIA
(refers only to localities included in archival inventories)

Polish	Russian	Ukrainian
Krzywcze	Verkhneye Krivche	Kryvche
Kudryńce	Kudrintsy	Kudryntsi
Lwów	Lvov	Lviv
Łysiec	Lisets	Lysets
Marjampol	Marinopol	Marinopil
Mielnica	Melnitsa Podolskaya	Melnitsa
Mikołajów	Nikolayev	Mikolaiv
Mikulińce	Mikulintsy	Mikulyntsi
Monasterzyska	Monastyriska	Monastyryska
Mościska	Mostiska	Mostyska
Mosty Wielkie	Velikiye Mosty	Mosty Velyki
Mraźnica	Mrazhnitsa	Mraznitsya
Nadwórna	Nadvornaya	Nadvirna
Narajów	Narayev	Naraiv
Nawarja	Navarya	Navariya
Obertyn	Obertin	Obertyn
Okopy	Okopy	Okopy
Olchowiec	Olkhovets	Olkhovets
Olesko	Olesko	Olesko
Podhajce	Podgatysy	Pidhajtsi
Podkamień	Podkamen	Pidkamin
Podwołoczyska	Podvolochisk	Pidvolochyska
Pomorzany	Pomoryany	Pomoryany
Probużna	Probezhnaya	Probizhna
Przemyślany	Peremyshlyany	Peremyshlyany
Radziechów	Radekhov	Radekhiv
Rawa Ruska	Rava Russkaya	Rava Ruska
Rohatyn	Rogatin	Rohatyn
Rozdół	Rozdol	Rozdil
Rudki	Rudki	Rudky
Sądowa Wisznia	Sudovaya Vishnya	Sudova Vyshnya
Sambor	Sambor	Sambir
Sasów	Sasov	Sasiv
Satanov	Satanov	Sataniv
Schodnica	Skhodnitsa	Skhidnitsya
Skała Podolska	Skala Podolskaya	Skala Podolskaya
Skałat	Skalat	Skalat
Skole	Skole	Skole
Śniatyn	Snyatyn	Snyatyn
Sokal	Sokal	Sokal
Sokołówka	Sokolovka	Sokolivka
Sołotwina	Solotvina	Solotvina
Stanisławów	Ivano-Frankovsk	Ivano Frankivsk
Stara Sól	Staraya Sol	Stara Sil
Stare Miasto	Stare Miasto	Starye Misto
Stary Sambor	Staryi Sambor	Staryj Sambir
Stojanów	Stoyanov	Stoyaniv
Stratyn	Stratyn	Stratyn
Stryj	Stryy	Stryi

PLACE-NAME VARIANTS IN EASTERN GALICIA
(refers only to localities included in archival inventories)

Polish	Russian	Ukrainian
Suchostaw	Sukhostav	Sukhostav
Świrz	Svirzh	Svirzh
Szczerzec	Shchirets	Shchyrets
Tarnopol	Ternopol	Ternopil
Tartaków	Tartakov	Tartakiv
Touste	Tolstoye	Tovste
Trembowla	Terebovlya	Terebovlya
Turka	Turka	Turka
Uhnów	Ugnev	Uhniv
Ułaszkowce	Ulashkovtsy	Ulashkivtsi
Winniki	Vinniki	Wynnyky
Witków Nowy	Novyy Vitkov	Noviy Vytkiv
Żabie	Verkhovina	Verkhovina
Zabłotów	Zabolotov	Zabolotiv
Założce	Zalozhtsy	Zaliztski
Zawałów	Zavalov	Zavaliv
Zbaraż	Zbarazh	Zbarazh
Zborów	Zborov	Zboriv
Zimna Woda	Zimna Voda	Zymna Voda
Złoczów	Zolochev	Zolochiv
Zniesienie	Znesinniya	Znesinnya
Żółkiew	Nesterov	Zhovkva
Żurawno	Zhuravno	Zhuravno
Żydaczów	Zhidachov	Zhydachiv

Note: Because German was one of the administrative languages of the Austro-Hungarian Empire, a few localities in the above list, principally large cities, were also known by German versions of the place names—for example, Lwów (Lemberg) and Stanisławów (Stanislau).

▌ The sanitorium (resort) at Truskavets in Western Ukraine, c. 1937   1186

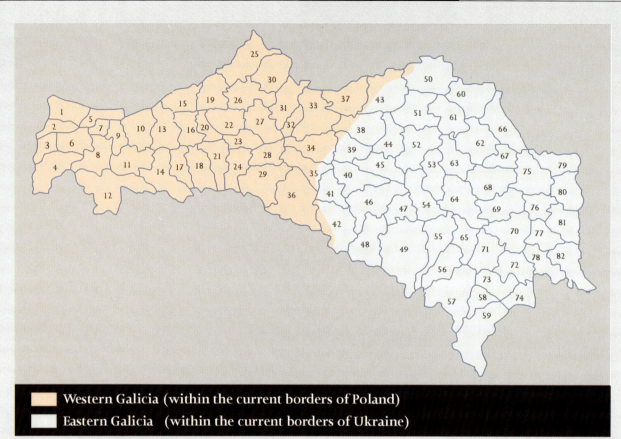

■ **Western Galicia** (within the current borders of Poland)
□ **Eastern Galicia** (within the current borders of Ukraine)

Galicia: Administrative Districts, 1906–1914   **Map 19**

MAP KEY					
Biała	3	Kolbuszowa	26	Rudki	45
Bóbrka	53	Kolomyja	73	Rzeszów	27
Bochnia	10	Kosów	59	Sambor	40
Bohorodczany	56	Kraków	5	Sanok	29
Borszczów	82	Krosno	24	Skałat	80
Brody	66	Lańcut	31	Skole	48
Brzesko	13	Limanowa	11	Śniatyn	74
Brzeżany	68	Lisko	36	Sokal	50
Brzozów	28	Lwów	52	Stanislawów	65
Buczacz	70	Mielec	19	Stary Sambor	41
Chrzanów	1	Mościska	39	Stryj	47
Cieszanów	37	Myślenice	8	Stryżów	23
Czortków	77	Nadwórna	57	Tarnobrzeg	25
Dąbrowa	15	Nisko	30	Tarnopol	75
Dobromil	35	Nowy Sącz	14	Tarnów	16
Dolina	49	Nowy Targ	12	Tłumacz	71
Drohobycz	46	Oświęcim	2	Trembowla	76
Gorlice	18	Peczeniżyn	58	Turka	42
Gródek Jagielloński	44	Pilzno	20	Wadowice	6
Grybów	17	Podgórze	7	Wieliczka	9
Horodenka	72	Podhayce	69	Zaleszczyki	78
Husiatyn	81	Przemyśl	34	Zbaraż	79
Jarosław	33	Przemyślany	63	Zborów	67
Jasło	21	Przeworsk	32	Złoczów	62
Jaworów	38	Radziechów	60	Żołkiew	51
Kalusz	55	Rawa Ruska	43	Żydaczów	54
Kamionka Strumiłowa	61	Rohatyn	64	Żywiec	4
		Ropczyce	22		

Source: Lenius, Brian J. *Genealogical Gazetteer of Galicia,* 3rd ed. Anola, Manitoba: B. Lenius, 1998.

Throughout Eastern Galicia, Ukrainian peasants frequently set upon the Jews, murdering hundreds before the German killing squads arrived. But it was the German squads whose work was on the larger scale, including the first "five figure" massacre of Jews by *Einsatzgruppe D* in Kishinev between July 17 and 31, 1941 [see Map 18, page 394]. On August 27 and 28, there was a second "five figure" massacre of Jews who had earlier been deported to Kamenets Podolsk from Hungary.

The map and text on this page are adapted from *Atlas of the Holocaust*, rev. ed. (New York: William Morrow, 1993) and reprinted here with the permission of the author, Sir Martin Gilbert.

Eastern Galician Killings, Summer 1941   Map 20

Український   The Ukrainian Alphabet

Printed	Cursive	English
А а	*Аа*	a
Б б	*Бб*	b
В в	*Вв*	v
Г г	*Гг*	g
Ґ ґ	*Ґґ*	h
Д д	*Дд*	d
Е е	*Ее*	e
Є є	*Єє*	ye
Ж ж	*Жж*	zh
З з	*Зз*	z
И и	*Ии*	y
І і	*Іі*	i
Ї ї	*Її*	yi
Й й	*Йй*	y
К к	*Кк*	k
Л л	*Лл*	l
М м	*Мм*	m
Н н	*Нн*	n
О о	*Оо*	o
П п	*Пп*	p
Р р	*Рр*	r
С с	*Сс*	s
Т т	*Тт*	t
У у	*Уу*	u
Ф ф	*Фф*	f
Х х	*Хх*	kh

Printed	Cursive	English	Printed	Cursive	English
Ц ц	*Цц*	ts	Ю ю	*Юю*	yu
Ч ч	*Чч*	ch	Я я	*Яя*	ya
Ш ш	*Шш*	sh	Ь ь	*Ьь*	'
Щ щ	*Щщ*	shch	–	–	–

Ukrainian is one of several Slavic languages that use a form of the Cyrillic alphabet (others include Belarussian, Bulgarian, Macedonian, Serbian, and Russian). The alphabet shown here is that used in standard modern Ukrainian. Under Soviet influence there was a tendency to replace the г, which sounds like a hard *g* as in English "go," with г, which sounds somewhat like *h* in English; but г should be included in any chart of the alphabet, as one certainly may see it in records. Ukrainian words are almost always pronounced just as they are spelled.

Even a superficial glance at the Cyrillic alphabet reveals that it is not totally foreign. When St. Cyril (traditionally regarded as the author of this alphabet) undertook devising a way to write Slavic sounds, he borrowed extensively from the Greek alphabet, and also modified some characters to represent distinctively Slavic phonemes. A few sounds were so foreign to Greek that he borrowed characters from other sources, e. g., ש and צ from Hebrew to make ш and ц, representing the *sh* and *ts* sounds.

Besides the printed and cursive forms, italic letters appear in documents. Even after one becomes familiar with the normal printed forms, a few italic forms can be puzzling, e. g., *m, д, г*, but the answer is simple: some italic forms are derived from their cursive equivalents. So *m* = т, *д* = д (∂ and *g* are both forms of д one may encounter), *г* = г, and so on.

The basic sounds of Ukrainian vowels are comparable to those of other European languages. They roughly approximate the following English sounds: a = *a* as in "father," е = *e* as in "let," и = *i* as in "sit," о = the *o* in English "more," and у = *u* as in "rude." The vowels я, є, і, and ю have the same sounds as а, е, и, and у (though і sounds more like the *i* in English "machine"), but are considered "soft" versions of them. These soft vowels, except for і, are preceded with a slight *y* sound; when і is preceded by that *y* sound, it is spelled ї —the name for "Ukraine," Україна, is pronounced roughly "oo-krah-yee´-nah." This is why one often sees я transcribed as *ya*, є as *ye*, ї as *yi*, and so on; the vowels are written differently to reflect the hard or soft quality of their pronunciation (or of the consonants preceding them). The combination "yo" is spelled йо if it does not follow a consonant, or ьо if it does (e. g., його vs. нього).

The table at left shows approximate English equivalents of the sounds represented by Ukrainian consonants, but more must be said. The letter ж (often rendered in English as "zh") sounds like *s* in English "pleasure." The ц sounds like *ts* in English "cats," the ч sounds like the *ch* in "church," the ш like the *sh* in "sheet," and щ is *sh* and *ch* run together, as in the word щастя ("fortune, fate"), pronounced "shchástya." The х can be misleading because it is not pronounced like English *x*, but rather like guttural *ch* in German "Bach" or Scottish "loch." The ь indicates that the preceding consonant is palatalized; an apostrophe ' indicates that the preceding consonant is not palatalized (e. g., об'ява, "revelation, announcement"). Palatalization affects the pronunciation of consonants, but this feature is best studied by imitating native speakers. Note that й is a consonantal *y* in English "yacht," not like the vowel sound in "very."

Source: Hoffman, William F., and George W. Helon. *First Names of the Polish Commonwealth: Origins and Meanings.* Chicago: The Polish Genealogical Society of America, 1998.

Русский

The Russian Alphabet

Printed	Cursive	English
А а	*А а*	a
Б б	*Б б*	b
В в	*В в*	v
Г г	*Г г*	g
Д д	*D g*	d
Е е	*Е е*	ye
Ё ё	*Ё ё*	yo
Ж ж	*Ж ж*	zh
З з	*З з*	z
И и	*И и*	i
Й й	*Й й*	y
К к	*К к*	k
Л л	*Л л*	l
М м	*М м*	m
Н н	*Н н*	n
О о	*О о*	o
П п	*П п*	p
Р р	*Р р*	r
С с	*С с*	s
Т т	*Т т*	t
У у	*У у*	u
Ф ф	*Ф ф*	f
Х х	*Х х*	kh
Ц ц	*Ц ц*	ts
Ч ч	*Ч ч*	ch

Printed	Cursive	English	Printed	Cursive	English
Ш ш	*Ш ш*	sh	- ь	*- ь*	—
Щ щ	*Щ щ*	shch	Э э	*Э э*	e
- ъ	*- ъ*	—	Ю ю	*Ю ю*	yu
- ы	*- ы*	—	Я я	*Я я*	ya

Russian is one of several Slavic languages that use a form of the Cyrillic alphabet (others include Belarussian, Bulgarian, Macedonian, Serbian, and Ukrainian). There are minor variations in the forms of Cyrillic used in the Slavic languages; the alphabet shown here is that used in modern Russian. Pre-1917 Russian documents also used the characters i and v, equivalent to modern и; the character ѣ, equivalent to modern е; and ѳ, equivalent to modern ф.

Even a superficial glance at the Cyrillic alphabet reveals that it is not totally foreign. When St. Cyril (traditionally regarded as the author of this alphabet) undertook devising a way to write Slavic sounds, he borrowed extensively from the Greek alphabet, and also modified some characters to represent distinctively Slavic phonemes. A few sounds were so foreign to Greek that he borrowed characters from other sources, e. g., ש and צ from Hebrew to make ш and ц, representing the *sh* and *ts* sounds.

Besides the printed and cursive forms, italic letters appear in documents. A few italic forms can be puzzling, e. g., *г, д, т*, but the answer is simple: some italic forms are derived from their cursive equivalents. So *т* = т, *д* = д (*д* and *g* are both acceptable cursive forms of д), *г* = г, and so on. Alternate cursive forms of т or *m* include *ϯ* and what looks like an *i* with a line over it, rather than a dot.

Russian vowels are roughly similar to those of other European languages: a = *a* as in "father," э = *e* as in "let," и = *i* as in "machine," o = a sound somewhere between the *o*'s in "October," and y = *u* as in "rude" — but а, э, ы, о and y follow what are termed "hard" consonants, while the forms я, е, и, ё and ю follow consonants that are "softened" or palatalized. The basic distinction is illustrated by the word нет ("no"), pronounced "nyet" because the *e* vowel follows a palatalized *n* — a word pronounced like English "net," with a hard *n*, would be spelled нэт. This is why one often sees я transcribed as *ya*, ё as *yo*, and so on; the vowels are written differently to reflect the hard or soft quality of the consonants they follow. Standard Russian pronunciation gives full value only to vowels in accented syllables, and the farther the vowel is from the stress the less distinctly it is pronounced: молоко ("milk"), accented on the last syllable, is not pronounced like "mo-lo-ko'" but more like "muh-lah-ko'."

The table at left shows approximate English equivalents of the sounds represented by Russian consonants, but more must be said. The letter г does generally sound like the English *g* in "go," but at the end of words it can sound like *k*, and in the declensional suffixes -oro, -ero, and archaic -яго and -aro it sounds like English *v*. The letter ж (often rendered in English as "zh") sounds like *s* in English "pleasure." The ч sounds like the *ch* in "church," the х is pronounced like *ch* in German "Bach" or Scottish "loch," the ш sounds like the *sh* in "sheet," and щ is *sh* and *ch* run together, as in the name "Khrushchev."

Of the letters with no English equivalents given, ъ signifies that the preceding consonant is not softened or palatalized, ь shows that it is softened or palatalized, and ы represents a unique sound somewhat like the *y* in "very."

Source: Shea, Jonathan D., and William F. Hoffman. *Following the Paper Trail: A Multilingual Translation Guide.* Teaneck, NJ: Avotaynu, Inc., 1994.

𝕯𝖊𝖚𝖙𝖘𝖈𝖍   The German Alphabet

Roman	Fraktur	Cursive
A a	𝕬 𝖆	
B b	𝕭 𝖇	
C c	𝕮 𝖈	
D d	𝕯 𝖉	
E e	𝕰 𝖊	
F f	𝕱 𝖋	
G g	𝕲 𝖌	
H h	𝕳 𝖍	
I i	𝕴 𝖎	
J j	𝕵 𝖏	
K k	𝕶 𝖐	
L, l	𝕷 𝖑	
M m	𝕸 𝖒	
N n	𝕹 𝖓	
O o	𝕺 𝖔	
P p	𝕻 𝖕	
Q q	𝕼 𝖖	
R r	𝕽 𝖗	
S s	𝕾 ſ 𝖘	
T t	𝕿 𝖙	
U u	𝖀 𝖚	
V v	𝖁 𝖛	
W w	𝖂 𝖜	
X x	𝖃 𝖝	
Y y	𝖄 𝖞	
Z z	𝖅 𝖟	

Roman	Fraktur	Cursive
Ä ä		
Ö ö		
Ü ü		
ß		
ch		
sch		
ck		
tz		

The rather intimidating typeface known in German as *Fraktur* was generally used in Germany until before World War II, but has since been replaced in common usage by the alphabet familiar to us. Even in the modern Roman-based alphabet there are a few modified letters used for special sounds in German, and these are listed on the right-hand side of the chart: *ä* (a-umlaut), *ö* (o-umlaut), *ü* (u-umlaut) and *ß* (eszet). The other letter combinations (*ch, sch, ck,* and *tz*) are shown because their printed or cursive forms can be hard to recognize; but they are not regarded as separate characters and do not affect alphabetical order. Note also the alternate forms of lower-case s in *Fraktur* and cursive: ſ and the usual forms, ß and ƃ are used at the end of words or at dividing spots in compound words. We've all seen similar usage in older English-language documents such as the Declaration of Independence, where the letters that look like uncrossed *f*'s are actually *s*'s.

German cursive script can be as intimidating as the printed *Fraktur*. Consider *Gesundheit*, a familiar expression to most Americans—it looks like a series of angular scrawls, but it's "Gesundheit," what you say when someone sneezes! Any combination of *n (e)*, *ɾ (c)*, *m (m)*, *u (n)*, *ü (u)*, *ʋ (v)*, and *w (w)* can be frustrating to decipher, especially if the penmanship is sloppy. The best approach is to identify the easier letters, such as *b*, *ᴅ*, *ɑ*, and *v*; distinguish *ſ (s)* and *f (h)* by their extending above and below the other letters; then start counting up-and-down strokes and trying to match them with problem letters. Hints: *ü (u)* should always have that little curve over it, and *ʋ (v)* and *w (w)* end with tailing curves that are usually discernable. Your odds improve if you have a limited list of candidate words to choose from; if you've inferred that the word in question might refer to a parent, *Mutter* can suddenly go from "M—r" to *Mutter,* "mother." So a good dictionary can help a lot with deciphering written words.

Source: Shea, Jonathan D., and William F. Hoffman. *Following the Paper Trail: A Multilingual Translation Guide.* Teaneck, NJ: Avotaynu, Inc., 1994.

Român

The Romanian Alphabet

Printed	Cursive
A a	*A a*
Ă ă	*Ă ă*
Â â	*Â â*
B b	*B b*
C c	*C c*
D d	*D d*
E e	*E e*
F f	*F f*
G g	*G g*
H h	*H h*
I i	*I i*
Î î	*Î î*
J j	*J j*
K k	*K k*
L l	*L l*
M m	*M m*
N n	*N n*
O o	*O o*
P p	*P p*
Q q	*Q q*
R r	*R r*
S s	*S s*
Ş ş	*Ş ş*
T t	*T t*
Ţ ţ	*Ţ ţ*
U u	*U u*
V v	*V v*

Printed	Cursive	Printed	Cursive
W w	*W w*	Y y	*Y y*
X x	*X x*	Z z	*Z z*

Romanian uses the Roman alphabet, modified for the phonetic needs of the language. The Romanian language has undergone a series of spelling reforms, the most recent in 1992, so older documents may well contain orthographic renditions which conflict with a current dictionary, as is evident in many of the documents you will find. The letters *k*, *q*, *w*, *x*, and *y* can be considered part of the alphabet, but appear only in foreign words and certain surnames. The alphabet as shown at the left is given in a form to acquaint readers with the various letters one sees, but generally *ă, â, ê, ş* and *ţ* are not considered separate letters in their own right. Some letters not normally seen at the beginning of words are shown here in upper- as well as lower-case forms because documents often capitalize entire words for emphasis and one might see upper-case forms of those letters in that context. In addition to the cedilla under *ş* and *ţ,* Romanian uses two other diacritical marks, a caret over the vowels *â* and *î* and a breve over the vowel *ă.* In older documents other possibilities may be seen; for instance, *đ* and *ĕ* appear in some records.

Many people have the notion that Romanian is a Slavic language, perhaps because Romania is located in southeastern Europe and was long a Communist state. In fact Romanian is a Romance language, specifically, a representative of the eastern Romanic branch of the Romance language family; it exhibits the most complicated grammar of any of the Romance literary languages. As the only survivor of the Latin language as spoken in the Eastern Roman Empire whose evolution was not as influenced by medieval Latin as its western cousins, Romanian conserves more of the features of the Romance mother language.

The evolution of Romanian was influenced by the Slavic and other languages spoken by its immediate neighbors. Thus one finds Serbian, Turkish, Hungarian, Albanian, and Greek influences in the language; but a significant chunk of its core vocabulary remains of Latin origin.

The vowels *e, o* and *u* resemble the sounds in the English words "t<u>e</u>n," "h<u>o</u>me," and "m<u>oo</u>n"; *a* and *i* without diacriticals are similar to English "f<u>a</u>ther" and "d<u>ee</u>p." The other vowel sounds are more complicated and may vary depending on the position in which they're found. The *ă* represents a central mid vowel close to the English sound in "d<u>e</u>ntal," and *â* and *î* are also central vowels somewhat like the sound in "b<u>o</u>ttom."

Many Romanian consonants require no special remarks, but several deserve attention. Usually *c* is pronounced as in English "<u>c</u>ool" but *ce* is pronounced as in English "<u>ch</u>ain" and *ci* as in "<u>ch</u>eek." To conserve the *k*-sound with these consonants an -*h*- is inserted, so that *che* sounds like the sound in "<u>k</u>ept" and *chi* like that of "<u>k</u>ey" (much as in Italian). The *g* behaves the same way; normally it is pronounced as in "gold" but *ge* and *gi* are pronounced much like the *je* sounds in "jet" and "jeep," respectively, while *ghe* and *ghi* resemble the sounds in "gay" and "geese." The letter *j* is pronounced like the *si* in English "colli<u>si</u>on," and the *r* is trilled as in Spanish. The *ş* is like the *sh* in "<u>sh</u>ip" and *ţ* is rendered as the *ts* sound heard in the English word "ca<u>ts</u>."

Source: Shea, Jonathan D., and William F. Hoffman. *Following the Paper Trail: A Multilingual Translation Guide.* Teaneck, NJ: Avotaynu, Inc., 1994.

עברית

The Hebrew Language — *by Zachary M. Baker*

Printed	Cursive	Rashi	English
א	ነc	ħ	'/silent
ב	ב	ב	b/v
ג	८	ג	g
ד	ʒ	ד	d
ה	ה	ה	h
ו	ו	ו	v/u/o
ז	ﬧ	ז	z
ח	n	ח	ḥ
ט	6	ט	t
י	י	י	y/i
כ	כ	כ	k/kh
ך	₽	ך	final k
ל	ß	ל	l
מ	אr	מ	m
ם	p	ם	final m
נ	J	נ	n
ן	ן	ן	final n
ס	o	ס	s
ע	ð	ע	'/silent
פ	⑨	פ	p/f
ף	₽	ף	final p
צ	₃	צ	ts
ץ	₽	ץ	final ts
ק	p	ק	k
ר	ﬧ	ר	r
ש	e	ש	sh/s
ת	♪	ת	t/s

Hebrew is a Semitic language, closely related to ancient Phoenician and Aramaic, and to classical and modern Arabic. The basic Hebrew alphabet consists of 22 consonants, five of which (כ, מ, נ, פ, צ) possess additional forms used only at the end of words; each is shown in the chart at left as a separate character, in the column immediately below the standard form. There is no distinction between upper- and lower-case forms in Hebrew.

Vowel signs and other diacritical marks ("points" or "dots") are sometimes used above, below, within, and between Hebrew letters. The chart on the next page illustrates their use, using the consonant ה [h] to demonstrate their positioning. Generally the vowels appear below the consonant they follow in pronunciation, as with הַ [ha], but notice the exception הֹ, [ho], with the point above the consonant. "Pointed" texts are largely limited to poems, children's literature, liturgy, and Hebrew Bible editions; otherwise, Hebrew is customarily written or printed without vowel signs. Thus, the pronunciations and meanings of Hebrew words can often be inferred only by context. An authoritative Hebrew-English dictionary, such as those cited below, is an essential tool for reading Hebrew.

Like other languages employing the Hebrew alphabet (such as Yiddish, Ladino, and Judeo-Arabic), Hebrew is written from right to left. Most written documents in Hebrew employ cursive script; printed texts most frequently use "square" letters, though a rounded typeface commonly referred to as "Rashi script" is also found in some religious publications and early Hebrew imprints.

Hebrew words are most often formed on the basis of three-letter consonantal roots. For example, the common stem זמן [zeman] = "time," "date," generates such words as להזמין [le-hazmin] = "to invite," הזמנה [hazmanah] = "invitation," and הזדמנות [hizdamnut] = "chance," "occasion." Hebrew possesses two genders: masculine and feminine. In nouns, the feminine form is frequently signaled by the presence of ה and ת at the end of words.

Over the millennia, Hebrew has evolved from the now-archaic language of the Bible, to Aramaic-tinged rabbinic Hebrew, and most recently, to the revived spoken and written vernacular of the modern State of Israel. Standard Israeli Hebrew follows Sephardic norms of pronunciation; in Eastern Europe, by contrast, the Ashkenazic pronunciation was used. The accompanying alphabet table relies on the Library of Congress standard for the transliteration of Israeli Hebrew, but also includes Ashkenazic pronunciations where these differ from Sephardic. The most striking differences between the two are:

(1) In Sephardic Hebrew most words are stressed on the last syllable, while in Ashkenazic Hebrew they are

stressed on the preceding syllable, e.g.: שבת *[shabat]* (Sephardic) vs. *[shabos]* (Ashkenazic) = "Sabbath."

(2) Ashkenazic Hebrew distinguishes between ת *[t]* and ת *[s]*; in Sephardic Hebrew both forms of the letter are pronounced *[t]*, as the previous example indicates.

(3) Ashkenazic Hebrew distinguishes between the vowels ָ *[o]* and ַ *[a]*, while in Sephardic Hebrew both vowels usually are pronounced *[a]*, e. g.: אָמֵן *[omein]* (Ashkenazic) vs. *[amen]* (Sephardic) = "Amen."

Four Hebrew letters — shown here in their "pointed" (or "dotted") forms — can represent different consonants in both Ashkenazic and Sephardic Hebrew: בּ *[b]* vs. ב *[v]*, כּ *[k]* vs. כ *[kh]*, פּ *[p]* vs. פ *[ff]*, and שׁ *[sh]* vs. שׂ *[s]*. The letters ח *[h]* and כ *[kh]* are pronounced alike (as in Scottish "loch"), though the Library of Congress transliteration system represents them differently. Similarly, ט and ת are both pronounced *[t]*, and ס and שׂ are both pronounced *[s]*.

Two letters can function as either consonants or vowels: ו *[v/o/u]* and י *[y/i/ei]*. There are two variant spelling systems in Hebrew, one of which makes special use of ו and י: "defective" (without vowels) and "plene" (where selected vowels are indicated by the insertion of the letters ו and י), e. g.: ספור ("defective" spelling) vs. סיפור ("plene" spelling), *[sipur]* = "story."

The letter ה is pronounced *[h]*, except at the end of words, when it is silent. The letter א can either be silent or act in lieu of vowels. The letter ע functions similarly to א, though some Hebrew speakers pronounce it with a guttural inflection, and it is usually transliterated by an inverted apostrophe *[']*. The letter ר *[r]* is pronounced with the soft palate.

Traditional Hebrew texts use letters to represent numbers, including dates. Abbreviations are also frequently encountered in written and printed Hebrew. This example illustrates both concepts: תרס״ד לפ״ק = [5]664 "according to the shortened reckoning" (of the year), or 1903/04 C.E. (תרס״ד adds up to 664, omitting the letter ה׳ [= 5,000], indicating the millennium — see the accompanying chart. לפ״ק is short for לפרט קטן *[li-ferat katan]* = "according to the shortened reckoning").

Honorifics are also represented in abbreviated forms, of which perhaps the most common is ר׳, short for "rabbi" or "master." Abbreviations and honorifics are

included in authoritative dictionaries; separate lists have also been published.

In pre-World War II Hebrew-language documents and publications, especially those from Europe, personal names of non-Hebrew derivation are often spelled according to their phonetic Yiddish renderings, for example בלומע ראָזען *[Blume Rozen]*, rather than בלומה רוזן — the accepted Israeli Hebrew spelling.

Sources:

Alcalay, Reuben. *The Complete Hebrew-English Dictionary.* Tel-Aviv: Massadah, 1963 [and subsequently].

Baltsan, Hayim. *Webster's New World Hebrew Dictionary.* New York: Prentice Hall, 1992.

Hebraica Cataloging: A Guide to ALA/LC Romanization and Descriptive Cataloging. Prepared by Paul Maher. Washington, D.C.: Cataloging Distribution Service, Library of Congress, 1987.

The Numerical Values of Hebrew Letters

Letter	Value	Letter	Value
א	1	ף / פ	80
ב	2	ץ / צ	90
ג	3	ק	100
ד	4	ר	200
ה	5	ש	300
ו	6	ת	400
ז	7	תק	500
ח	8	תר	600
ט	9	תש	700
י	10	תת	800
ך / כ	20	תתק	900
ל	30	א׳	1,000
ם / מ	40	ב׳	2,000
ן / נ	50	ג׳	3,000
ס	60	ד׳	4,000
ע	70	ה׳	5,000

A shortcut formula for figuring out the civil calendar (C.E.) equivalent of a Hebrew year, according to the "shortened reckoning": add 1240 to the Hebrew year, e. g., תרס״ד *= 664 + 1240 = 1904 C.E. Note: the Hebrew year begins in the autumn of the previous civil calendar year, so 5664 actually began in the autumn of 1903.*

Vowel points, using the consonant ה *[h] to illustrate their positioning*	הַ	*ha*	הִ	*hi*
	הָ	*ha/ho*	הֻ	*hu*
	הֵ	*he*	הְ	*hə/h*
	הֶ	*he/hei*	הֹ	*ho*

Source: The text and alphabets for the Yiddish and Hebrew pages were prepared by Zachary M. Baker, head librarian of YIVO Institute for Jewish Research; the font was adapted with the assistance of Jeffrey Salant, director of Yiddish Language Programs at YIVO Institute of Jewish Research; and the page layout was done by William F. Hoffman, linguist and desktop publishing specialist.

ייִדיש

The Yiddish Language — *by Zachary M. Baker*

Printed	Cursive	English
א	lc	silent
בּ	ב	b
בֿ	ב̄	v
ג	ﻉ	g
ד	ﻭ	d
ה	ה	h
ו	ן	u
ז	ﻝ	z
ח	ת	kh
ט	ﻉ	t
י	،	y/i
כּ	ﻭ	k
כ	ﻭ	kh
ך	ﻕ	final kh
ל	ﻝ	l

Printed	Cursive	English
מ	א	m
ם	ﻕ	final m
נ	ﻝ	n
ן	ן	final n
ס	ﻭ	s
ע	ﻭ	e
פּ	ﻭ	p
פֿ	ﻭ̄	f
ף	ﻝ	final f
צ	ﻝ	ts
ץ	ﻉ	final ts
ק	ﻭ	k
ר	ﻝ	r
ש	ﻉ	sh
שׂ	ﻉ̇	s

Printed	Cursive	English
תּ	ﻭ	t
ת	ﻭ	s

Variants & Combinations

Printed	Cursive	English
אַ	lc	a
אָ	lc̣	o
וּ	·ן	u
וו	ןן	v
וי	·ן	oy
יִ	،	i
יי	،،	ey
ײַ	،،	ay
זש	ﻉﻝ	zh
דזש	ﻉﻝﻭ	dzh
טש	ﻉﻉ	ch

Yiddish, the vernacular of Ashkenazic Jews, uses the Hebrew alphabet in a form adapted to reflect its diverse components. Like other languages employing that alphabet (such as Ladino, Judeo-Arabic, and of course Hebrew), Yiddish is written from right to left. The basic Hebrew alphabet has 22 letters, plus forms of five letters that are used only at the end of words. There is no distinction between upper- and lower-case forms of letters in Yiddish. Most Yiddish written documents employ cursive script, as opposed to the "square" letters found in printed texts.

The underlying structure of Yiddish and most of its vocabulary is Germanic (deriving from Middle High German); Yiddish also contains Romance elements, a substantial Hebrew/Aramaic component, and an extensive Slavic vocabulary. The three principal dialect regions of Yiddish in Eastern Europe are Central ("Polish" and "Galician"), Northeastern ("Lithuanian"), and Southeastern ("Ukrainian"). Standard Yiddish, the basis for the transliterations shown in the accompanying alphabet ta-

ble, largely reflects Northeastern Yiddish pronunciations.

Yiddish employs a spelling system that, in Uriel Weinreich's words, "is based on an integration of two underlying patterns." Words deriving from the non-Hebrew/Aramaic components of the language are rendered phonetically, "in a system with excellent overall correspondence between sounds and letters.... Another part of the vocabulary, of Hebrew-Aramaic derivation, on the whole retains the traditional spelling used in those languages." Because Standard Yiddish Orthography was codified as recently as 1936 (by the YIVO Institute for Jewish Research, in cooperation with the Central Yiddish School Organization in Poland), variant spelling systems will inevitably be encountered in Yiddish texts.

Standard Yiddish Orthography distinguishes between different letters through the use of diacritical marks. Since non-standard Yiddish spelling usually omits diacritics, no distinction is made there between the letters בּ [b] and בֿ [v]; יי [ey], ײַ [ay], and יִי [yi]; כּ [k] and כ [kh]; פּ [p] and

פ *[f]*; שׁ *[sh]* and שׂ *[s]*; תּ *[t]* and ת *[s]*. In non-standard Yiddish, therefore, the pronunciation of some letters and letter combinations can be inferred only by context.

In standard Yiddish, the silent א is normally employed only at the beginning of a word (e. g., אין *[in]* = "in"), while in non-standard Yiddish, the silent א will be encountered in other positions as well (e.g., [non-standard] וואו *[vu]* = "where," vs. [standard] וווּ). In non-standard Yiddish, ב *[b]* may sometimes be written בּ; also, ע *[e]* may be inserted before a final ל *[l]* (e.g., [non-standard] זעקעל *[zekel]* vs. [standard] זעקל *[zekl]* = "pouch") or ן *[n]* (e. g., [non-standard] האָבען *[hoben]* vs. [standard] האָבן *[hobn]* = "to have"), and פ used in place of either פּ *[p]* or פֿ *[f]*.

Since Hebrew/Aramaic words in standard Yiddish use traditional, consonantal spellings (i. e., with vowels omitted), their pronunciations can be arrived at only by consulting an authoritative dictionary such as Weinreich's (cited below). Ashkenazic Hebrew — as opposed to Sephardic, or Israeli — serves as the basis for the pronunciation of Yiddish words (including names) deriving from Hebrew and Aramaic, e. g.: אמת *[emes]*, not *[emet]* = "truth"; אָדם *[odem]*, not *[adam]* = "Adam." The Hebrew/Aramaic component of Yiddish employs six letters that are not encountered elsewhere in Yiddish: בֿ *[v]*, ח *[kh]*, כּ *[k]*, שׂ *[s]*, תּ *[t]*, ת *[s]*.

(**Note:** In Soviet Yiddish orthography, beginning in the 1920s, these six letters were eliminated and words of Hebrew/Aramaic origin spelled phonetically, e. g.: עמעס *[emes]* = "truth," rather than אמת. Final Hebrew letters were often eliminated in Soviet Yiddish as well, e.g.: לעבנ *[lebn]* = "life," rather than לעבן.)

Yiddish has five basic vowels, pronunced much like those in other European languages. Some letters and letter combinations representing vowels and diphthongs vary in pronunciation, depending on dialect. Examples include: זאָגן *[zogn]* (NE Yiddish) vs. *[zugn]* (C and SE Yiddish) = "to say"; פּוטער *[puter]* (NE Yiddish) vs. *[piter]* (C and SE Yiddish) = "butter"; ברויט *[broyt]* (C and SE Yiddish) vs. *[breyt]* (NE Yiddish) = "bread"; פלייש *[fleysh]* (NE and SE Yiddish) vs. *[flaysh]* (C Yiddish) = "meat."

Yiddish consonants are for the most part similar to those used in English, with the notable exceptions of ח and כ *[kh]*, pronounced as in Scottish "loch," and ר *[r]*, produced with the tip of the tongue or the soft palate.

Yiddish is an inflected language, possessing nominative, accusative, dative, and genitive cases. As with German, Polish, and Russian, three genders are employed in Yiddish: masculine (דער מאַן *[der man]* = "the man"), feminine (די פֿרוי *[di froy]* = "the woman"), and neuter

Sources:

Hebraica Cataloging: A Guide to ALA/LC Romanization and Descriptive Cataloging. Prepared by Paul Maher. Washington, D. C.: Cataloging Distribution Service, Library of Congress, 1987.

Weinreich, Max. *History of the Yiddish Language.* Translated by Shlomo Noble, with the assistance of Joshua A. Fishman. Chicago: University of Chicago Press, 1980.

Weinreich, Uriel. *Modern English-Yiddish, Yiddish-English Dictionary.* New York: McGraw-Hill, 1968 [reprinted by Schocken].

Source: The text and alphabets for the Yiddish and Hebrew pages were prepared by Zachary M. Baker, head librarian of YIVO Institute for Jewish Research; the font was adapted with the assistance of Jeffrey Salant, director of Yiddish Language Programs at YIVO Institute of Jewish Research; and the page layout was done by William F. Hoffman, linguist and desktop publishing specialist.

Magyar

The Hungarian Alphabet

Printed	Cursive
A a	*A a*
Á á	*Á á*
B b	*B b*
C c	*C c*
Cs cs	*Cs cs*
D d	*D d*
E e	*E e*
É é	*É é*
F f	*F f*
G g	*G g*
Gy gy	*Gy gy*
H h	*H h*
I i	*I i*
Í í	*Í í*
J j	*J j*
K k	*K k*
L l	*L l*
Ly ly	*Ly ly*
M m	*M m*
N n	*N n*
O o	*O o*
Ó ó	*Ó ó*
Ö ö	*Ö ö*
Ő ő	*Ő ő*
P, p	*P p*

Printed	Cursive	Printed	Cursive
R r	*R r*	Ú ú	*Ú ú*
S s	*S s*	Ü ü	*Ü ü*
Sz sz	*Sz sz*	Ű ű	*Ű ű*
T t	*T t*	V v	*V v*
Ty ty	*Ty ty*	Z z	*Z z*
U u	*U u*	Zs zs	*Zs zs*

The Hungarian language uses the Roman alphabet, but with a number of modifications. Specifically, it features the consonant combinations *cs, gy, ly, ny, sz, ty*, and *zs* (*cz* is seen only in names and has become otherwise obsolete) and the short/long vowel pairs *a/á, e/é, i/í, o/ó, ö/ő, u/ú*, and *ü/ű*. It also lacks the letters *q, w*, and *x*, except in foreign words. The consonant and vowel combinations may look intimidating, but in fact most of the sounds represented by these letters have approximate equivalents in English. Alphabetical order in Hungarian dictionaries and lists of names can present a few difficulties; each short/long pair is treated as the same vowel for listing purposes, but *ö/ő* follows *o/ó* and *ü/ű* follows *u/ú*, so that *több* follows *továbadd* and *tüdő* follows *túró*. A good rule of thumb is to check above and below the place in a list where a word would appear by English alphabetical order.

Hungarian comes from an entirely different family from the Indo-European languages (Italian, German, Russian, and so on), but its vowel sounds are like those of most European languages. The *á* sounds like the *a* in "car," the *é* like the *a* in "gate," the *í* like the *i* in "machine," the *ó* like that in "tore," and the *ú* like the *oo* in "moon." The short sounds *a, e, i, o, u* are just that, shorter versions of the long vowels; the *a* and *o* are most unlike their English counterparts, more like the sounds in "hut" and "horn" respectively. The *ö/ő* pair is a short/long version of the sound in German "Goethe," almost like saying "fir" but not quite pronouncing the *-r*. The *ü/ű* pair is a short/long version of German *ü* or French *u*, much like saying "ee" with rounded lips. As in German, the *ö/ő* and *ü/ű* have sometimes been spelled *oe* and *ue*, a fact that may be significant in searching old records for specific words or names.

The pronunciation of most Hungarian consonants is comparable to that of their English counterparts, but a few require attention. The *c* is pronounced like *ts* as in "gets," the *g* is always hard as in "go," and a *j* sounds like English *y* as in "yes." The consonant pairs are initially tricky; *cs* is pronounced like English *ch* in "cheek," *ly* is pronounced like *y* in "yes," *sz* is pronounced like *s* in English "sing" (but Hungarian *s* is pronounced like English *sh* in "short": "Budapest" is pronounced "Budapesht"), and *zs* is pronounced like the *s* in "pleasure." The *gy, ny*, and *ty* pairs are palatalized sounds, like a combination of *d + y, n + y*, and *t + y* respectively; something similar is heard in "would you," "can you," and "let you" in British or very precise American pronunciation.

Hungarian words are always stressed on the first syllable, and the stress has no effect on the quality or length of vowels.

Source: Shea, Jonathan D., and William F. Hoffman. *Following the Paper Trail: A Multilingual Translation Guide.* Teaneck, NJ: Avotaynu, Inc., 1994.

Polski

The Polish Alphabet

Printed	Cursive
A a	*A a*
Ą ą	*Ą ą*
B b	*B b*
C c	*C c*
Ć ć	*Ć ć*
D d	*D d*
E e	*E e*
Ę ę	*Ę ę*
F f	*F f*
G g	*G g*
H h	*H h*
I i	*I i*
J j	*J j*
K k	*K k*
L l	*L l*
Ł ł	*Ł ł*
M m	*M m*
N n	*N n*
Ń ń	*Ń ń*
O o	*O o*
Ó ó	*Ó ó*
P p	*P p*
R r	*R r*
S s	*S s*
Ś ś	*Ś ś*
T t	*T t*

Printed	Cursive	Printed	Cursive
U u	*U u*	Z z	*Z z*
W w	*W w*	Ź ź	*Ź ź*
Y y	*Y y*	Ż ż	*Ż ż*

Polish is one of the Slavic languages that use the Roman alphabet, not the Cyrillic, largely because writing came to the Poles by way of Roman Catholic rather than Greek Orthodox clergy. The letters *q, v,* and *x* are not used in Polish, and the distinctly Polish characters *ą, ć, ę, ł, ń, ó, ś, ź* and *ż* are considered separate letters of the alphabet, each following its unmodified counterpart (*ą* after *a, ć* after *c,* and so on). The *ą, ę, ń,* and *y* never appear initially and thus are seldom capitalized; but since documents sometimes highlight words by spelling them out in upper-case letters, it seems best to show all upper-case forms, even those rarely seen.

The basic vowels of Polish are much as in the Romance languages: *a* is like the *a* in "father," *e* like that in "let," *i* like that in "machine," *o* somewhat like that in "hot," *u* like the *oo* in "book," and *y* like the short *i* sound in "hit." The vowel *ó* is pronounced exactly the same as Polish *u,* and some words are spelled either way (*Jakób* vs. *Jakub,* for example). The nasal vowel *ą* sounds like English "own" with the *n*-sound never quite finished, but before *b* or *p* it sounds more like *om* in "home." The nasal *ę* is generally pronounced like *en* in "men," again without quite finishing the *n*-sound; before *b* or *p* it sounds more like *em* in "memory," and in some positions it loses its nasal quality. But generally pronouncing *ą* like *on (om)* and *ę* like *en (em)* will approximate the correct sound. Polish does not distinguish between long and short vowels.

The *i* is special because it often follows consonants as a sign of softening; thus Poles pronounce *ne* as somewhat like "neh," but *nie* more like "nyeh." The consonants *ć, ń, ś,* and *ź* are spelled that way only when they precede other consonants; before vowels they're spelled *ci, ni, si,* and *zi.* In either case they are pronounced, respectively, more or less like soft *ch* (as in "cheese"), *ni* (as in "onion"), *sh* (as in "sheep") and the sound of the *s* in "pleasure." In a word like *cicho* (quiet, quietly) the *i* not only softens the *c* to a *ch*-sound, it also supplies the first syllable's vowel.

Many consonants are pronounced much as in English, but the *l* is more like that in "leaf" than that in "hill," and the *r* is lightly trilled, as in Italian. Polish *h* and *ch* are pronounced the same, a little harsher than an initial *h* in English but not quite so guttural as *ch* in German "Ba*ch*." Polish *w* sounds like English *v* and Polish *ł* is pronounced like English *w* (all of which explains how "Lech Wałęsa" can come out sounding like "Lekh Vawensa"). The *c* is pronounced like a combined *ts* (e. g., English "knigh*ts*"), the *g* is always as in "gone" (never as in "gym"), and the *j* is always pronounced like *y* in "yield." The *s* is pronounced as it is in English "soon," and *z* is pronounced as in "zebra" (but remember the softened pronunciation of *ci, ni, si,* and *zi*).

The *cz, rz, sz* combinations are similar to *ć, ż,* and *ś,* respectively, but are articulated differently; *ż* is pronounced the same as *rz.* The combination *dż* or *dzi* sounds like an English *j* in "jail." In Polish the accent almost always falls on the next-to-last syllable of any given word. Mastering certain sound combinations can be difficult for non-Poles, but once you do master them you'll find Polish words are pronounced exactly as they're spelled!

Source: Shea, Jonathan D., and William F. Hoffman. *Following the Paper Trail: A Multilingual Translation Guide.* Teaneck, NJ: Avotaynu, Inc., 1994.

GENERAL GLOSSARY

Bet Din (Y)   Rabbinical court
Bet Midrash (H)   House of study
Bimah (H)   Platform in the synagogue from which the Torah is read during services
Chevra Kadisha (H/Y)   Burial society
CIS   Commonwealth of Independent States
Council of the Four Lands   *See* Vaad Arba Aratzot
Delo (R)   Archival notation for a file within an opis
Evreiskii (R)   Jewish
Fond (pl. *fondy* or *fonds*) (R)   Archival notation for a collection or record group (of documents or material)
Gmina (P)   Local administrative district
Gorod (R)   Town
Guberniya (R)   Province (established in 1775) in the Russian Empire and in the
                                                           Kingdom of Poland (prior to World War I)
Hasid (pl. *Hasidim*) (H/Y)   Follower of disciples of Pietist movement founded by Israel Ba'al Shem
                                                           Tov in the second half of the eighteenth century
Haskalah (H/Y)   Jewish Enlightenment, a movement that sought to spread modern European
                                                           culture among Jews from the late eighteenth to the late nineteenth centuries
Landsmanshaftn (H/Y)   Organization of Jews from the same town or region
Kahal (H/Y)   Jewish community council
Kehillah (H/Y)   Jewish community
Metricheskii Knigi (R)   Registers of births, deaths and marriages (commonly known as metrical books)
Miasto (pl. *Miasta*) (P)   Town
Misnaged (pl. *Misnagdim*) (H)   Opponent of Hasidism
Nova, Nove, Novy (R)   New
Oblast (R)   Soviet and current term for district (province)
Opis (R)   Archival notation for an inventory or subdivision of a collection (within a fond)
Pale (L)   District separated from the surrounding country by definite boundaries or
                                                           distinguished by a different legal and administrative system
Patronymic   Name derived from that of the father
Pinkas (pl. *Pinkassim*) (H/Y)   Jewish register book
Plac (P)   Square (as in town square or plaza)
Posemeinyi Spisok (R)   Family register (an archival document)
Raion (R)   Region
Revizskie Skazki (R)   Poll-tax census
Rynok (P/R)   Market (square)
Shtetl (pl. *Shtetlach*) (H/Y)   Small town
Shtibel (pl. *Shtiblekh*) (H/Y)   Small prayer house, generally Hasidic
Starosta (P)   Provincial administration
Stary, Stara, Stare (P)   Old
Tsaddik (pl. *Tsaddikim*) (H/Y)   Pious, righteous man; often refers to a Hasidic charismatic leader;
                                                           also known as *rebbe* or leader
Uezd (R)   District
Ulitsa (ul.) (P/R)   Street
Urząd Stanu Cywilnego (P)   Registrar's office (in Poland) of local vital records (within the last 100 years)
Vaad Arba Aratzot (H/Y)   Council of the Four Lands (Jewish National Council)
Volost (R)   Township
Yizkor Book   Memorial book published by Holocaust survivors from a particular town
                                                           or region
ZAGS (R)   Otdel Zapisi Aktov Grazhdanskogo Sostoyaniya (ZAGS), an office where vital
                                                           records are registered, usually located in the local town hall or mayor's office

---

LEGEND: (G) German   (L) Latin   (P) Polish
                          (H) Hebrew   (R) Russian   (Y) Yiddish

HOLOCAUST GLOSSARY

American Jewish Joint Distribution Committee (JDC or "Joint")
An organization founded in 1914 by American Jews to provide financial and material aid to Jews overseas. During World War II, the "Joint" sought to aid Jews across German-occupied Europe. After the war, it provided aid to Jewish displaced persons, detainees on Cyprus, and emigrants to Israel.

Bessarabia
Territory in eastern Romania located between the Prut and Dniester Rivers (present-day Moldova). It was occupied by the Soviet Union in 1940.

Bukovina
Territory in northeastern Romania, along the Carpathian Mountains. The Soviet Union occupied the northern part of Bukovina in 1940.

Concentration Camps (Konzentrationslager; KL)
Places of incarceration in which people were detained without regard to due process and the legal norms of arrest and detention. The extensive German camp system also included labor camps, transit camps, prisoner-of-war camps and extermination camps.

Einsatzgruppen (sing. Einsatzgruppe)
Mobile killing units; German "special-duty squads," composed mainly of SS and police personnel, assigned to kill Jews in Eastern Europe following the German invasion of the Soviet Union in June 1941.

Extermination Camps
The six killing centers—Chełmno, Bełżec, Sobibór, Treblinka, Auschwitz-Birkenau and Majdanek—established by the Germans in occupied Poland.

General Gouvernement (general government)
A territory in central and southern Poland established after the defeat of Poland in September 1939; it had a German civilian administration.

Ghetto
An enclosed district of a city where the Germans forced the Jewish population to live under conditions of severe crowding and deprivation. Ghettos were established in Poland, the Baltic states, the Soviet Union, the Protectorate of Bohemia and Moravia, and Hungary.

Greater Germany
A term referring to Germany and its annexed territories. It came into common German usage after the incorporation of Austria in 1938.

Judenfrei ("Jew-Free")
A Nazi euphemism used to describe areas from which all Jews had been deported or killed.

Judenrat
A Jewish Council, established on German orders in the Jewish communities of occupied Europe.

Reichskommissariat Ukraine
A territory established after the German invasion of the Soviet Union in June 1941. It encompassed part of eastern Poland and most of Ukraine, as far east as the area around the cities of Kiev and Dnepropetrovsk, and had a German civilian administration.

Sonderkommando
A prisoner forced-labor detachment assigned to work in the killing area of an extermination camp.

Transcarpathian Ukraine
A region in eastern Czechoslovakia annexed by Hungary according to the first Vienna Award of November 1938. It became part of the Soviet Union after World War II.

Transnistria
A territory transferred to Romanian rule after the invasion of the Soviet Union in 1941, located between the Bug and Dniester Rivers in Western Ukraine.

Source: *Historical Atlas of the Holocaust* by the United States Holocaust Memorial Museum. Copyright 1996 by Yechiam Halevy. New York: Macmillan Publishing USA, a Simon & Schuster Company.

ARCHIVES

Central State Cinephotofono Archive of Ukraine, Kiev ▏ Chapter 2/41-A,41-B; Chapter 3/107,109,111,113,143, 179,234, 282, 284,288–289,292,395,408,410,501,594,655; Chapter 11/992; Chapter 12/1036; Appendix 1/1044,1060–1061, 1076,1078,1090,1130,1135

Central State Historical Archive of Ukraine, Kiev ▏ Introduction/13; Chapter 2/41-A,41-B; Chapter 4/Title photo,696,704–705,708, 722-A,722-B

Central State Historical Archive of Ukraine, Lvov ▏ Introduction/20; Chapter 1/26–28; Chapter 2/42-A, 42-B; Chapter 4/687,690-A,690-B,693,695,716,718–721,724-A,724-B,728,730,732–734,738-A,738-B; Chapter 12/1031–1032; Appendix 2/1185

Kamenets-Podolskiy City-State Archives, Ukraine ▏ Introduction/10,14–15; Chapter 4/709; Chapter 12/1028

Moldovan National Archives, Kishinev, Moldova ▏ Introduction/19; Chapter 1/23; Chapter 8/826–827,832,860–862,870–871,874–875; Chapter 9/899–900,903–904,906–922; Chapter 10/Title page,924

State Archive of Chernigov Oblast, branch archive in Nezhin ▏ Chapter 4/691

State Archive of Chernigov Oblast, branch archive in Priluki ▏ Chapter 4/706,714,717

State Archive of Kiev Oblast ▏ Chapter 4/735

State Archive of Kirovograd Oblast, Kirovograd, Ukraine ▏

State Archive of Odessa Oblast, Odessa, Ukraine ▏ Introduction/12; Chapter 3/436,438,441,443–444,446; Chapter 4/707

State Archive of Ternopol Oblast, Tarnopol, Ukraine ▏ Introduction/9; Chapter 4/694,727

State Archive of Vinnitsa Oblast, Vinnitsa, Ukraine ▏ Chapter 3/51,409; Chapter 4/703,723,725,731; Chapter 7/805–808; Chapter 12/1027

State Archive of Volynsk Oblast, Lutsk, Ukraine ▏ Introduction/17; Chapter 3/302,514; Chapter 11/940; Appendix 1/1079–1080,1093,1103

State Archive of Zhitomir Oblast, Zhitomir, Ukraine ▏ Chapter 1/25; Chapter 4/715

Urząd Stanu Cywilnego Warszawa-Şródmieşcie, Warsaw, Poland ▏ Chapter 4/736–737; Chapter 12/1039

GOVERNMENT OFFICES

Aeroflot Soviet Airlines, Kishinev, Moldova ▏ Chapter 8/859

Mayor's Office, City of Faleshty, Moldova ▏ Chapter 8/849

Mayor's Office, City of Kalarash, Moldova ▏ Chapter 8/854

Mayor's Office, City of Novaya Ushitsa, Ukraine ▏ Chapter 2/40

Odessa Address Bureau ▏ Chapter 2/29

ZAGS Office, Khmelnitskiy, Ukraine ▏ Chapter 2/33

ZAGS Office, Novaya Ushitsa, Ukraine ▏ Chapter 2/34

ZAGS Office, Priluki, Ukraine ▏ Introduction/11; Chapter 4/713

ZAGS Office, Rovno, Ukraine ▏ Chapter 2/32

ZAGS Office, Shargorod, Ukraine ▏ Chapter 12/1033

ZAGS Office, Soroki, Moldova ▏ Chapter 2/36; Chapter 8/891

ZAGS Office, Zhitomir, Ukraine ▏ Chapter 2/35

INSTITUTIONS

American Jewish Joint Distribution Committee ▏ Chapter 8/824

Instytut Sztuki Polskiej Akademii Nauk, Warsaw, Poland ▏ Chapter 3/77–78,168,173,188,301,314,316–317,330,339,375, 466,541,552,620–622; Chapter 11/930,948,969,986,1020; Appendix 1/1057,1067–1069,1077,1099,1104–1105

Jewish Historical Institute, Warsaw, Poland ▏ Chapter 3/58–59,68,70,83,124,128,132,299,315,342,345,374,464,649,652 Chapter 11/934,945–947, 949–950,954,959–960,965,968,997,999,1021,1026; Appendix 1/1074–1075,1086,1094,1129, 1134,1136–1137

Ostrog Regional Museum, Ostrog, Ukraine ▏ Chapter 2/45; Chapter 4/726,729

Vernadskiy National Library of Ukraine ▏ Chapter 2/44-A,44-B,44-C

YIVO Institute for Jewish Research, New York ▏ Chapter 3/557; Chapter 8/868; Chapter 12/1037

PHOTOGRAPHERS

Eleonora Bergman | Chapter 3/340,343-A,344; Chapter 11/932
Brock Bierman | Chapter 8/872–873,876,893
Debra Braverman | Chapter 3/380,383,571,576,580,582,584,586–587
Vitaly Chumak | Introduction/title photo,21; Chapter 2/47; Chapter 3/62–63,67,69,71, 73–74,96,99–103,120–121,141, 144–147,149,151,186,197,200–204,206–211,217–218,220–223,228–232,244–246,248,250–252,264–272,283,290–291, 303–304,306–312,392,452,454–455,458–459,479–484,486,489–490,517,519,521,523–524,550,566,613–616,623–625, 629–633,635–637,656–664,666–676; Chapter 4/692,702; Chapter 5/744; Chapter 6/title photo,751,774,799,802; Chapter 7/title photo,814–815,820; Chapter 8/833,842,852,857,877–885,887; Chapter 9/902,905; Chapter 10/923,925; Chapter 11/931,939A–939B 962–964,989,998,1004–1012; Appendix 1/1054–1055,1058–1059,1062,1110– 1112,1115,1121–1126,1143–1144,1146–1148,1156; Appendix 2/1170,1175–1177,1182; Appendix 7/1187–1194
Maurice R. Commanday | Chapter 3/285–287
I. Dovgobroda | Chapter 3/412
Natasha B. Elkin | Chapter 6/771,798; Chapter 4/712A
I. Y. Franko | Chapter 3/366
Marjorie Goldberg | Chapter 3/261–262,367,370
Jerzy Grabarczyk | Chapter 3/128,132,158; Chapter 11/934,945,947,949–950,959–960,965,997,999; Appendix 1/1094, 1129,1134,1136–1137
David Goberman | Chapter 8/844,847–848,886,928
Jan Jagielski | Chapter 3/91,105-B,106,115–117,119,129,133–136,138,155,159,162,167,175,189,193,213,219,300,328– 329,350–351,467,473,476–477,485,487,529,535; Chapter 5/740; Chapter 11/933,944,946,951–953,970–971,977– 982,990,991-A,991-B,1022; Appendix 1/1128,1131–1133; Appendix 7/1195
Mariola Jeziak | Acknowledgements/5
Alter Kacyzna | Chapter 3/328,331,333
M. Kipnis | Chapter 3/174
I. V. Kibziy | Chapter 8/834
Arnold Kramer | Foreword/2
V. Krimchaka | Chapter 3/198
S. Kryachka | Chapter 3/97
Olga Marushak | Appendix 2/1167
Max Mermelstein | Chapter 3/559–560,564–565,568
B. Mindelya | Chapter 3/243,435,439–440,442,445,447,583
Feliks Pecherskiy | Chapter 3/634
Dmitry Peysakhov | Table of Contents/title photo,1; Chapter 3/75,105-A,114,118,122,258–259,378,434,488,578,609; Chapter 6/753–759,766–770,776–778,786–797,800–801; Chapter 7/803,816,821–822; Chapter 11/941–943,955– 958,1013,1016
V. Pilipyuka | Chapter 3/362
V. Polyakov | Chapter 3/279
Ruth Rosenbloom | Appendix 1/1089
Jacquelyn Sanders | Chapter 3/433,520,522,525
Dmitry G. Savetsky | Chapter 3/184
Mark Shraberman | Chapter 3/352; Chapter 4/710
Janusz Smaza | Chapter 3/299
David Snyder | Chapter 3/83; Chapter 11/954
Benjamin Solomowitz | Appendix 1/1084,1102
K. Starobuvan | Chapter 6/780
Galina Tikhonovska | Chapter 6/779,798; Appendix 2/1166
Miriam Weiner | Acknowledgments/3–4; Introduction/8,18; Chapter 2/37; Chapter 3/52,54–56,66,72,76,80–82,84,86– 87,89,92–93,95,105-C,110,125,130–131,137,148,150,154,157,160–161,164,169,171–172,176–178,180–183,185,190–191, 194–196,214,216,224,237–242,247,249,254,256,260,263,273–276,281,293–294,318, 321–323,325-A,325-B,335–338, 343-B,346–349,360–361,363,368–369,371–372,376,378–379,381–382,384,387,389–391,393–394,398,400–407,411, 414–432,448–449,456-A,456-B,457,460–463,465,468–471,474–475,478,492–494,499,501–513, 526,528,531,533–534, 536–540,542–549, 551,554–556,558,562,572,574–575,579,581,585,588–593,595,597–601,606–608,611–612,617–618, 638,640–641,643–648,650–651,654,679–684; Chapter 4/686,688–689,697–701,712-B; Chapter 5/739,741–742,745– 746; Chapter 6/747–750,752, 760–765,772–773,775,781–785; Chapter 7/804,809–813,817–819, 823; Chapter 8/825, 828–831,835–841,843,845–846,850–851,853,855–856,858,863–867,888–889,892,894–897; Chapter 9/title photo, 898; Chapter 10/926–927, 929; Chapter 11/937–938,972–975,984–985,987–988,993–996,1000–1003,1014–1015, 1017– 1019,1024–1025; Chapter 12/1030; Appendix 1/1050,1054,1063–1065,1070–1073,1085,1087–1088,1092,1095–1098, 1100–1101,1106–1109,1113, 1115,1117–1120,1127,1139–1142,1145,1150–1154,1157–1159; Appendix 2/1160–1165,1168– 1169,1171–1174,1178–1181,1183–1184; Appendix 7/1197–1199
Michał Witwicki | Chapter 3/58,70
Josef Zissels | Chapter 5/743

Boris Feldblyum Collection | **Chapter 3**/60
Jeffrey K. Cymbler Collection | **Chapter 3**/163,298,355
Luboml Exhibition Project | **Chapter 3**/313,319–320,324
Max Mermelstein Collection | **Chapter 3**/561,563,567,569
Mikola Dzei Collection, Luboml, Ukraine | **Chapter 3**/324
Miriam Weiner Collection | **Introduction**/6–7; **Chapter 1**/title photo,22,24; **Chapter 2**/title photo; **Chapter 3**/title photo,
  49–50,53,57,61,64–65,79,85,88, 90,94, 98, 104,108,112,123,126–127,139–140,142,152–153,156,165–166,170,187,192,
  199,205,212,215,225–227,233,235–236,253,255,257,277–278,280,295–297,305,332,334,341,353–354,356–359,364–
  365,385–386,388,396–397,399,413,437,450–451,453,472,491,495–498,500,515–516,527,530,532,570,573,577,596,
  602–605,619,626–628,639,642,653, 665,677–678,685; **Chapter 5**/title photo; **Chapter 8**/title photo, 869,890; **Chapter
  11**/title photo,935–936,961,966–967,976,983,1023,1034–1035; **Appendix 1**/1038–1043,1045–1049,1051–1053,1056,
  1081–1082,1091,1116,1138,1149,1155; **Appendix 3**/1186; **Appendix 7**/1196
Michael Salzberg Collection | **Chapter 2**/43-A,43-B
Ostrog Jewish Community | **Chapter 2**/38-39
Rabbi Moishe Leib Kolesnik | **Chapter 2**/46,48; **Appendix 1**/1083
Shepetovka Jewish Community | **Chapter 3**/553
Sidney Braverman Collection | **Chapter 3**/326,377
Stefan Pankevicz Archives, Korolovka, Ukraine | **Chapter 2**/31
Stephen Mednick Collection | **Introduction**/16
Sudilkov Sick Support Society | **Chapter 3**/610
Tomas Wiśniewski Collection | **Chapter 3**/342
William Gross Collection | **Chapter 3**/68,124,649,652; **Appendix 1**/1086
Zinaida Sandler Collection | **Chapter 4**/711

Our Voice, The Jewish Newspaper of Moldova and Odessa, Kishinev, Moldova | **Chapter 9**/901
Memory Book of Ukraine, Chernigov Oblast, Vol. 5 (Kiev: Ukrainian Encyclopedia, M.P. Bazhana, 1996) | **Chapter 2**/30
The Vanished World, by Raphael Abramovitch (New York: Forward Association, 1947) | **Chapter 3**/174,328,331,333,518;
  Chapter 8/824

COPYRIGHT OF PHOTOGRAPHS
All photographs are owned and/or copyrighted by the named photographer or institution.

MAP CREDITS

Maps 2, 4	*Encylopedia Judaica* and Keter Publishing House Jerusalem Ltd., Cecil Roth, ed. (Jerusalem: Keter Publishing House Ltd., 1971–1972).
Map 3	*Atlas of Russian History,* by Sir Martin Gilbert (New York: Oxford University Press, 1993).
Maps 7, 15, 16, 17, 18, 20	*Atlas of the Holocaust,* rev. ed., by Sir Martin Gilbert (New York: William Morrow, 1993).
Maps 8, 9, 10, 11	*Historical Atlas of the Holocaust* by the United States Holocaust Memorial Museum. Copyright 1996 by Yechiam Halevy (New York: Macmillan Publishing USA, a Simon & Schuster Company).
Maps 13, 14	*Pinkas Hakehilot, Rumania, Vol. 1, Encyclopedia of Jewish Communities* (Jerusalem: Yad Vashem, 1969).
Map 19	*Genealogical Gazetteer of Galicia,* 3rd ed., by Brian J. Lenius (Anola, Manitoba: B. Lenius, 1998).

MAP GRAPHICS

Adaptation of maps	Dorcas Gelabert and Stephen Freeman
Maps 1, 5, 6, 12	Stephen Freeman
Maps 3, 13–14	Dorcas Gelabert and Stephen Freeman

Tombstone of Shlomo Maidenberg, died December 23, 1939, son of Meier, buried in the Dzygovka Jewish cemetery, 1997 — 1187

Dzygovka Jewish cemetery, 1997 — 1188

Tombstone of Benzion Milir, son of Shlomo, 1881–1871, buried in the Dzygovka Jewish cemetery, 1997 — 1189

Holocaust memorial in the Krivoye Ozero Jewish cemetery, 1998   1190

Jewish cemetery in Krivoye Ozero, 1998   1191

The Polisar family from New York look for family tombstones in the Krivoye Ozero Jewish cemetery, 1998.   1192

Jewish cemetery in Krivoye Ozero, 1998   1193

 *Savran Jewish cemetery, 1997* 1194

Viennese coffeehouse in Stryj, 1920 1196

Memorial to the Jews of Khmelnitskiy (formerly Proskurov) 1195
who were killed in the 1919 pogrom (photo, 1995)

 Holocaust memorial in Turiysk, 1994: "Here are buried the Jews of 1197
Turiysk and nearby towns, who were shot by the German Fascist occupiers
and their accomplices on September 10, 1942. To their eternal memory."

1198

"To the eternal memory of the first Jews who perished for the sanctification of God's name under the cruelty of the German Nazi Murderers, July 7, 1941, in our city of Zborov," presented by the Zeiger family of the United States

▲ 1199   *Holocaust memorial in Zborov, Ukraine, 1998*